Strategic Application Deployment with Argo CD
Mastering Automation for Kubernetes Infrastructure

Nova Trex

© 2024 by Wang Press. All rights reserved.

No part of this publication may be reproduced, distributed, or transmitted in any form or by any means, including photocopying, recording, or other electronic or mechanical methods, without the prior written permission of the publisher, except in the case of brief quotations embodied in critical reviews and certain other noncommercial uses permitted by copyright law.

Published by Wang Press

For permissions and other inquiries, write to:
P.O. Box 3132, Framingham, MA 01701, USA

Contents

1 Introduction to Continuous Delivery and Argo CD — 9
- 1.1 Understanding Continuous Delivery 10
- 1.2 Challenges in Traditional Software Deployment 15
- 1.3 Introduction to Argo CD 18
- 1.4 How Argo CD Fits into the CD Ecosystem 22
- 1.5 Advantages of Using Argo CD for Continuous Delivery . 27
- 1.6 Real-world Use Cases of Argo CD 32
- 1.7 Setting the Stage for Learning Argo CD 37

2 Getting Started with Kubernetes — 43
- 2.1 Kubernetes Basics and Fundamental Concepts 44
- 2.2 Setting Up a Local Kubernetes Environment 47
- 2.3 Working with Kubernetes Objects 51
- 2.4 Understanding Kubernetes Networking 54
- 2.5 Managing Kubernetes with kubectl 58
- 2.6 Deploying Your First Application on Kubernetes 62
- 2.7 Exploring Kubernetes Logging and Monitoring 66

3 Understanding Argo CD Architecture — 71

3.1	Core Components of Argo CD	71
3.2	Exploring Application Repositories	75
3.3	The Role of GitOps in Argo CD	79
3.4	Argo CD's Application Controller	83
3.5	Config Management in Argo CD	88
3.6	Networking and Security within Argo CD	94
3.7	Understanding Argo CD User Interface	100

4 Setting Up Argo CD for Continuous Delivery — 105

4.1	Prerequisites for Argo CD Installation	105
4.2	Installing Argo CD on Kubernetes	109
4.3	Configuring Access and Authentication	112
4.4	Connecting Argo CD to Application Repositories	117
4.5	Configuring Applications in Argo CD	121
4.6	Using Argo CD CLI and User Interface	126
4.7	Verifying the Setup	131

5 Automating Kubernetes Deployments with Argo CD — 137

5.1	Understanding GitOps Workflows with Argo CD	138
5.2	Defining and Synchronizing Applications	142
5.3	Automated Rollbacks and Rollouts	147
5.4	Handling Multi-environment Deployments	152
5.5	Using Argo CD Hooks for Automation	157
5.6	Monitoring Deployment Health and Logs	162
5.7	Case Studies: Successful Automation with Argo CD . .	167

6 Managing Application Lifecycles with Argo CD — 173

6.1	Overview of Application Lifecycles	173
6.2	Deploying Applications with Argo CD	177

- 6.3 Updating and Modifying Applications 180
- 6.4 Implementing Blue-Green and Canary Deployments . . 184
- 6.5 Versioning and Rollback Practices 189
- 6.6 Cleaning Up and Archiving Applications 193
- 6.7 Monitoring and Maintaining Application Health 197

7 Integrating Argo CD with CI/CD Pipelines 203
- 7.1 Understanding CI/CD Pipelines 203
- 7.2 Role of Argo CD in CI/CD 208
- 7.3 Integrating Argo CD with Jenkins 214
- 7.4 Using Argo CD with GitLab CI/CD 219
- 7.5 Leveraging Argo Workflows with Argo CD 224
- 7.6 Triggering Deployments from CI Pipelines 229
- 7.7 Managing Secrets and Configurations 234

8 Best Practices for Scaling Argo CD Implementations 241
- 8.1 Scaling Argo CD Deployments 242
- 8.2 Optimizing Performance and Resource Usage 246
- 8.3 Managing Multiple Clusters with Argo CD 250
- 8.4 Role-based Access Control for Large Teams 255
- 8.5 Architectural Patterns for High Availability 260
- 8.6 Automating Scaling Strategies 264
- 8.7 Monitoring and Observability at Scale 270

9 Security and Compliance in Argo CD Deployments 277
- 9.1 Securing Argo CD Installations 277
- 9.2 Implementing Role-Based Access Control 281
- 9.3 Handling Secrets and Sensitive Data 285
- 9.4 Ensuring Compliance with Standards 289

9.5 Monitoring and Auditing Argo CD Activities 293

9.6 Network Security and Argo CD 297

9.7 Integrating Security Tools in CI/CD Pipelines 301

10 Troubleshooting and Monitoring Argo CD Deployments **307**

10.1 Identifying Common Issues in Argo CD 308

10.2 Debugging Failed Deployments 312

10.3 Effective Log Management 316

10.4 Monitoring Deployment Health 321

10.5 Using Argo CD's Built-in Tools 325

10.6 Proactive Alerts and Notifications 330

10.7 Case Studies: Overcoming Deployment Challenges . . . 334

Introduction

In the dynamic and continuously changing landscape of software development, the concept of continuous delivery (CD) has steadily gained repute as a crucial mechanism, reshaping how development teams approach software deployment processes. CD sets its objectives on the automation of the release workflow, ensuring accelerated and secure deployment of software into production ecosystems. As the adoption of microservices architectures and containerization becomes more widespread, Kubernetes has emerged as the leading platform to orchestrate containerized applications, accommodating dynamic, scalable environments. Against this backdrop, Argo CD has gained significant traction, as it provides powerful tools for GitOps-based continuous delivery tailored for Kubernetes infrastructure.

Argo CD presents itself as a declarative, GitOps-centric continuous delivery tool specifically constructed for Kubernetes environments. Its unique feature is the ability to directly manage and synchronize application deployments from version control repositories. This ensures that the deployed applications consistently reflect configurations as described in source control, reinforcing operational consistency and reliability. With Git serving as the single source of truth, Argo CD dramatically reduces the operational risks and inconsistencies often associated with manual deployments. In an era where software delivery pipelines grow increasingly complex, a tool like Argo CD becomes indispensable by providing robust automation solutions aligned with modern DevOps principles of traceability, security, and agility.

This book, "Strategic Application Deployment with Argo CD: Mastering Automation for Kubernetes Infrastructure," furnishes a thorough exploration of Argo CD's architecture, operational paradigms, and industry best practices. The book is aimed at delivering a deep, both theoretical and practical, understanding of setting up, maintaining, and scaling Argo CD environments, as well as integrating them into existing CI/CD frameworks effectively. Readers will acquire invaluable insights on managing application lifecycles within scalable architectures.

At the core of Argo CD's operation is Kubernetes, whose extensive orchestration capabilities provide the backbone of this powerful tool. A solid foundational knowledge of Kubernetes is necessary to fully grasp the deployment and management mechanics within this robust ecosystem. This book addresses every nuance, from configuring Argo CD in complex multi-cluster environments to mastering its advanced features such as automated rollbacks and progressive rollouts, all set within a thoughtful context that underscores each component's contribution to the broader system architecture.

With security and compliance becoming increasingly critical in software production cycles, detailed strategies for enhancing the security posture of Argo CD deployments and ensuring compliance standards are met are explored in depth. Alongside the focus on usability, each chapter integrates practical guidelines for troubleshooting potential issues and monitoring system health, equipping readers to maintain high availability and robust performance of their deployments.

As you explore the contents of this book, you will develop the expertise to proactively orchestrate Kubernetes deployments using Argo CD. Gain insights into scalable architectures and seamless integration into existing CI/CD pipelines. Both professionals in the industry and academic scholars will find this book an essential resource for mastering the intricacies of continuous delivery at scale. Through rigorous exposition and precise technical guidance, readers will be empowered to leverage Argo CD's capabilities to their fullest in both professional and personal pursuit of excellence.

Chapter 1

Introduction to Continuous Delivery and Argo CD

Continuous delivery is a foundational practice in modern software development, enabling teams to deliver product updates safely, quickly, and sustainably by automating the entire software release process. This chapter examines the challenges associated with traditional deployment methods and presents Argo CD as an effective solution within the continuous delivery ecosystem. Emphasizing its role in implementing the GitOps model, Argo CD offers distinct advantages such as enhanced consistency, traceability, and flexibility. Through real-world use cases, the reader will grasp the practical benefits of adopting Argo CD, setting the stage for a deeper exploration of its capabilities and applications.

1.1 Understanding Continuous Delivery

Continuous delivery (CD) stands as a pivotal practice in the ecosystem of modern software development, offering a streamlined approach to the software release process. It facilitates the rapid and reliable release of software by automating and optimizing numerous stages within the deployment pipeline. At its core, continuous delivery aims to ensure that software can be reliably released at any time by maintaining software in a deployable state throughout its lifecycle.

The principles underpinning continuous delivery emphasize the importance of automating the release process, fostering collaboration among developers and other stakeholders, and adopting small, incremental changes. These practices collectively serve to reduce the risks associated with software releases while emphasizing the importance of immediate feedback and continuous improvement. In this section, we will explore the principles and benefits of continuous delivery to understand its transformative impact on software engineering.

Principles of Continuous Delivery

Continuous delivery embodies several key principles, each contributing to a holistic improvement in the software development lifecycle:

- *Automated Build and Deployment:* Automation lies at the heart of continuous delivery. It is critical to have a standardized and automated build and deployment process that ensures consistency and reliability across environments. Tools such as Jenkins, GitLab, and Travis CI are commonly used in automating these processes, significantly reducing the time and error potential compared to manual deployments.

- *Version Control of Artefacts:* Every change made to the codebase is stored in a version control system like Git. This system provides an audit trail of changes and facilitates rollback if necessary. Ensuring that artefacts are version controlled means that the software and its environment configurations can be replicated with exactitude at any point in the future.

- *Continuous Integration (CI):* Although distinct from continuous delivery, CI is a foundational principle where developers frequently integrate code changes into a shared repository. Automated tests are executed to validate the integrations, ensuring that errors are quickly detected.

- *Environment Consistency and Infrastructure as Code (IaC):* Utilizing tools like Docker, Kubernetes, and Terraform, developers can define infrastructure specifications as code, ensuring that environments are consistent across development, testing, and production stages. This consistency mitigates common deployment issues related to environment discrepancies.

- *Feedback Loops:* Continuous delivery relies on effective feedback mechanisms that provide rapid insights into software integrity and performance. Automated testing, monitoring, and notifications are essential components of these feedback loops.

- *Incremental Updates:* Smaller, incremental updates are shipped more frequently rather than large, monolithic releases. This practice reduces risk, facilitates easier problem tracing, and can vastly improve response times to market demands.

Benefits of Continuous Delivery

The implementation of continuous delivery offers a multitude of benefits, both technically and strategically, that enhance overall software quality and align development with business objectives.

- *Reduced Deployment Risks:* By automating deployment pipelines and making environment changes incremental, CD reduces the uncertainty and potential errors associated with deployment. This targeted reduction of complexities allows for smoother releases.

- *Enhanced Product Quality:* Automated tests contribute significantly to product quality by providing frequent, reliable validation of new code. These tests can detect defects early in the development cycle, preventing flaws from reaching production environments.

- *Improved Time-to-Market:* A rigorous CD pipeline accelerates delivery speed, allowing businesses to ship new features more quickly and maintain competitive advantage. This capability fosters agility and aligns with dynamic market demands.

- *Better Collaboration:* Continuous delivery encourages cross-functional teams to work together, from developers to operations and QA. Collaborative workflows reduce silos and promote shared ownership of the software delivery process.

- *Scalability and Flexibility:* The automated and adaptable nature of CD pipelines supports scalability within organizations. As teams grow, or projects evolve, CD practice can flexibly accommodate these changes without necessitating significant procedural overhauls.

- *Business and Customer Alignment:* Continuous delivery aligns with business strategies by fostering transparent, predictable, and frequent deliveries that can readily incorporate customer feedback or market changes.

Coding Example: Setting Up a Continuous Delivery Pipeline

To illustrate the implementation of a continuous delivery pipeline, consider the following example using a tool such as Jenkins for an application stored in a Git repository. The pipeline automates the stages of fetching, building, testing, and deploying the software to a staging environment.

```
pipeline {
    agent any

    // Environment configuration
    environment {
        JAVA_HOME = "/opt/java/openjdk"
        PATH = "${env.JAVA_HOME}/bin:${env.PATH}"
    }

    // Defining the stages
    stages {
        stage('Fetch Code') {
            steps {
                git 'https://github.com/your-repo/project.git'
            }
        }

        stage('Build') {
            steps {
                sh 'mvn clean package'
            }
```

```
        }
        stage('Test') {
            steps {
                sh 'mvn test'
            }
        }
        stage('Deploy to Staging') {
            steps {
                sh 'scp target/project.war user@staging-server:/deployments'
            }
        }
    }
    // Post actions
    post {
        always {
            archiveArtifacts artifacts: '**/target/*.war', fingerprint: true
        }
        success {
            echo 'Deployment was successful!'
        }
        failure {
            echo 'Deployment failed.'
        }
    }
}
```

In this Jenkins pipeline, the following steps are undertaken:

- *Fetch Code:* The 'git' directive pulls the latest code from a designated repository.

- *Build Stage:* Utilizes Maven to clean and compile the project, creating an executable WAR file.

- *Test Stage:* Executes the test cases included within the project, validating the new code's functionality.

- *Deploy to Staging:* Copies the WAR file to a staging server, signifying a deployment practice before moving to production.

- *Post Actions:* Archives the build artefacts, setting fingerprinting for traceability, and sends notifications based on success or failure.

Survey of Industry Adoption

Continuous delivery has seen widespread adoption across industries owing to its numerous benefits and alignment with modern agile practices. Tech giants and innovative startups often pioneer CD practices to facilitate rapid innovation and robust product deployment. As an illustration, companies like Amazon, Netflix, and Google employ hyper-efficient CD pipelines to deliver thousands of deploys per day, continuously refining their offerings while maintaining superior service uptime.

A relevant case study involves a large financial firm transitioning from traditional release methods to continuous delivery, leading to a significant reduction in downtime and an improvement in customer satisfaction. By adopting CD, this firm could better address security compliance requirements with automated testing and deployment processes and more rapidly integrate customer feedback into their software products.

In practice, successful continuous delivery requires a culture shift within organizations. Teams need to embrace collaborative approaches, and management needs to invest in both training and necessary automation tools. The journey to a fully realized CD ecosystem involves gradual improvements and refinement, focusing on maintaining high quality and reliability standards throughout the development lifecycle.

Conclusion on Continuous Delivery

The adoption and practice of continuous delivery represent a transformative shift in software development methodologies. By automating the process and ensuring continuous integration and deployment, organizations can significantly enhance their efficiency, quality, and responsiveness to changing user needs. Continuous delivery not only strengthens the technical framework of software releases but also aligns more closely with business strategies and customer centricity within modern enterprises.

1.2 Challenges in Traditional Software Deployment

Traditional software deployment processes have long been fraught with a multitude of challenges that hinder efficiency, reliability, and timeliness. Such challenges are rooted in manual processes, limited automation, siloed teams, and a distinct lack of immediate feedback mechanisms. In this section, we will delve into the intricacies and inherent limitations of traditional deployment methods, highlighting specific areas where they fall short and how these obstacles impact software development and delivery.

Manual Processes and Errors

One of the central challenges of traditional deployments is the reliance on manual processes. These processes are inherently error-prone and time-consuming. Each time software is to be deployed, a sequence of manual steps must be executed, often including code compilation, resource configuration, environment setup, and several rounds of testing. This dependency on human intervention opens up substantial room for errors, such as incorrect configurations, missed steps, or miscommunication among team members.

Manual deployments also suffer from a lack of consistency. Human errors can introduce discrepancies between environments, making it difficult to ensure that the production environment matches the earlier testing or staging environments. These inconsistencies often lead to unexpected behavior when applications are moved into production.

```
# Manual steps to deploy
echo "Stopping current application instance"
ssh user@server 'sudo systemctl stop app-service'

echo "Transferring new build to server"
scp /local/build/app.war user@server:/opt/deployments/

echo "Updating configuration files"
ssh user@server 'cp /opt/deployments/configs/config.yml /etc/app/config.yml'

echo "Starting new application instance"
ssh user@server 'sudo systemctl start app-service'
```

Without automation, each step, as seen in the example above, is performed manually for each release, adding to the time and complexity of deployment operations.

Siloed Teams and Communication Gaps

Traditional deployment approaches are often executed by small, isolated teams where development, testing, and operations function within their respective silos. This segregation leads to a lack of cooperation and communication, significantly hindering the overall deployment process. Developers, tasked with writing the code, may not engage closely with testers or operations staff responsible for deployment and maintenance. This separation results in silo mentality, where each team is unaware or uninterested in other parts of the process beyond its own scope.

The lack of a unified workflow intensifies potential for delays and mistakes. Developers may push code that is deemed complete within their context but not aligned with operation requirements. Operations may, in turn, face unexpected challenges when code fails to deploy as intended due to missing test validations or lack of documentation. Bridging these gaps requires cultural changes within organizations, driving towards interdisciplinary collaboration and integrated processes.

Lack of Immediate Feedback

Immediate feedback is a cornerstone of efficient software delivery; however, traditional deployment methods often suffer from belated feedback loops. Testing in these environments ranges from being sparse and isolated to almost non-existent until code reaches a staging phase late in the development cycle. This approach results in delayed discoveries of significant issues, which increases the cost and complexity of corrections.

In such traditional setups, workflows tend not to support sophisticated monitoring tools that provide real-time feedback and metrics upon deployment. As a result, rapid insights into performance degradation, user issues, or application anomalies are unavailable. Engineers may end up troubleshooting blind or needing to sift through disparate logs to identify root causes, contributing to longer resolution times.

```
# Illustrative delayed feedback scenario
Deploying release -> Staging tests fail after one week -> Roll back
-> Developers investigate the issue -> Code refactoring
```

Early feedback, automated and seamlessly integrated into the deployment pipeline, is essential for identifying and resolving issues efficiently, thereby addressing customer needs with agility.

Complex Environment Management

Managing the various environments in which software operates presents a further challenge. Each environment – be it development, testing, staging, or production – requires specific configurations and resources. Traditional deployments lack the easily reproducible setups that modern practices like Infrastructure as Code (IaC) provide.

The manual setup of environments often leads to "environment drift," where discrepancies between configurations in different environments arise over time. Such drift results in scenarios where software functions optimally in one setup but fails in another, due to inconsistencies in dependency versions, library paths, or system variables.

The absence of comprehensive tooling exacerbates these configuration drift issues. Conventional methods do not capitalize on containerization or orchestration technologies like Docker or Kubernetes, which provide standardized environments and make applications transferable and consistent across different environments.

Monolithic Deployments

Conventional software systems often embody a monolithic architecture, where all modules and components are intertwined and need to be deployed together. Such monolithic systems present significant hindrances due to their complexity and dependency on a full system update every time a change is made, regardless of its magnitude.

Handling and maintaining these systems becomes a monumental task. A minor modification to a component potentially requires a full retesting and redeployment of the entire application. This setup is not only resource-intensive but also risks introducing new bugs and errors across seemingly unrelated parts due to the tight coupling of components within the monolith.

Moving toward microservices, where applications are logically divided into independently deployable services, addresses many of these challenges but requires a paradigm shift both in architecture and deployment strategies.

Security and Compliance Challenges

Traditional deployment practices often struggle with maintaining stringent security and compliance standards, an essential aspect in today's regulatory environments. The lack of automated provisioning implies that configuration changes, password updates, or security patch installations may be inconsistent across environments, leaving security vulnerabilities exposed.

Moreover, tracking and auditing user activities, changes, and deployments in a landscape devoid of synchronized documentation and automated processes is problematic. For regulated industries, the absence of traceable records and automated checks is a critical shortfall, hindering compliance with standards and exposing the organization to potential legal and financial risks.

Conclusion on Traditional Software Deployment Challenges

Traditional deployment methods present a wide array of challenges that undermine efficient and effective software delivery. The reliance on manual processes introduces errors, slows deployments, and suffers from inconsistency. The deployment practices often lack the collaboration and automation essential for rapid feedback and improved quality assurance.

Modern continuous deployment approaches address these challenges by emphasizing automated processes, integrated collaboration, real-time feedback, and environment consistency. Embracing these modern practices equips organizations to respond to market dynamics effectively, providing reliable and frequent updates to their software with reduced risk and improved quality.

1.3 Introduction to Argo CD

Argo CD is a declarative, GitOps continuous delivery tool specifically tailored for Kubernetes native applications. Its design facilitates efficient, automated deployment processes by using Git repositories as the single source of truth for application state. As such, it offers a profound improvement to traditional Kubernetes deployment methods, aligning closely with DevOps practices to provide enhanced productivity, traceability, and synchronization across environments.

Argo CD operates under the umbrella of the Cloud Native Computing Foundation (CNCF), underscoring its relevance within the modern cloud-native ecosystem. At its core, Argo CD is driven by the principles of GitOps, a framework that tightly couples a Git-based workflow with Kubernetes operations to foster a more reliable and reproducible infrastructure.

Core Concepts of Argo CD

Understanding Argo CD starts with its foundational elements, which underscore its functionalities and benefits:

- *Declarative Setup:* Argo CD embraces the GitOps philosophy, where infrastructure and application definitions are stored declaratively in Git repositories. This ensures that the desired state is reflected accurately and consistently across environments and can be reproduced or audited easily.

- *Automatic Synchronization:* Argo CD continuously monitors the Git repository for any changes in the application's state. When these changes are detected, it automatically synchronizes the live state with the desired state defined in the repository, reducing manual intervention.

- *Environment Consistency:* By using Git as the source of truth, Argo CD ensures consistent deployment strategies across different environments, minimizing "drift" between them. This consistency is achieved by explicitly defining infrastructure and application dependencies.

- *User Interface and CLI:* Argo CD provides a comprehensive web-based interface and command-line interface (CLI) for managing application deployments, viewing logs, and evaluating application statuses, facilitating ease of use and accessibility for DevOps teams.

- *Policy Management:* With role-based access control (RBAC) enabled, Argo CD allows precise governance over who can do what within the GitOps framework, enhancing security and compliance.

Practical Implementation with Argo CD

Implementing an Argo CD deployment begins with setting up the Argo CD application, followed by configuring repositories and deploying applications. The steps involved in setting this up highlight the streamlined process Argo CD offers:

1. *Installing Argo CD:* Installation typically involves deploying Argo CD to a Kubernetes cluster. This can be executed using the default YAML manifests provided by the Argo CD project.

   ```
   kubectl create namespace argocd
   kubectl apply -n argocd -f https://raw.githubusercontent.com/argoproj/argo-
       cd/stable/manifests/install.yaml
   ```

2. *Accessing Argo CD UI:* After installation, access to the Argo CD UI is possible via port forwarding or by integrating a Service with an external IP or LoadBalancer for broader accessibility.

   ```
   kubectl port-forward svc/argocd-server -n argocd 8080:443
   ```

3. *Configuring a Git Repository:* Users define application manifests within a Git repository. Argo CD will systematically monitor this repository, synchronizing the defined states to the Kubernetes cluster.

4. *Creating an Application:* Argo CD requires the creation of an Application resource comprising the source (Git repo), destination (cluster and namespace), path, project, and confirmed synchronization parameters.

   ```
   apiVersion: argoproj.io/v1alpha1
   kind: Application
   metadata:
     name: example-app
     namespace: argocd
   spec:
     project: default
     source:
       repoURL: 'https://github.com/company/example'
       targetRevision: HEAD
       path: app
     destination:
       server: 'https://k8s-cluster.local'
       namespace: default
     syncPolicy:
       automated:
   ```

```
prune: true
selfHeal: true
```

5. *Synchronization and Validation:* Once an application is created, Argo CD orchestrates the deployment in a Kubernetes cluster. It maintains ongoing synchronization with the Git repository, reverting any unauthorized changes made directly to the cluster.

Advantages of Argo CD

Argo CD's design and architecture provide numerous advantages, putting a spotlight on its ability to enhance DevOps workflows and Kubernetes application management. These include:

- *Improved Deployment Speed and Reliability:* Automatic synchronization ensures that deployments occur with minimal delays and human intervention, while reliability is enhanced by maintaining consistent states defined in Git.

- *Enhanced Auditability and Traceability:* By leveraging Git as a centralized source of truth for application states, Argo CD avails discernible audit trails of changes, which simplify debugging and support compliance standards through detailed version histories.

- *Scalability:* Argo CD is adept at managing numerous application deployments across large Kubernetes clusters. Support for multi-cluster operations simplifies orchestration across distributed infrastructure, essential for scaling cloud-native applications.

- *Security:* With RBAC, the granular control of access and policies ensures that deployments are secure, and the pipeline ecosystem is governance-compliant, critical for regulated industries.

Argo CD and GitOps

Argo CD's approach to GitOps innovation is rooted in applying the principles of Git-centric workflows to operations, bridging development, and infrastructure seamlessly. GitOps enables all changes to be observable, auditable, and reversible, adhering to strict pull request (PR) processes before updates shift the desired state.

- *Reliability and Recovery:* Using GitOps alongside Argo CD ensures reliable recovery paths for infrastructure. Git can track every code and configuration change applied, empowering teams to confidently revert or recreate states in the event of an outage.

- *Comprehensive Software Delivery:* The GitOps model combines CI practices with CD mechanics, orchestrating deployments that prioritize stability and quality. Argo CD acts as the execution engine, executing GitOps principles by asserting desired cluster states reliably.

- *Feedback and Observability:* GitOps supports rapid feedback mechanisms integrated into Argo CD's processes, expediting the identification of discrepancies and supporting quick course corrections, leading to consistently reliable systems.

Conclusion on Argo CD's Role

By leveraging Argo CD's advanced GitOps capabilities, organizations acquire an unprecedented edge in agile and cloud-native application management. As a toolset ingrained with declarative configurations, version-controlled insights, and automated reconciliations, Argo CD represents a pivotal stride forward in the continuous delivery landscape.

Adopting Argo CD propels organizations into a future where deployments are more predictable, traceable, and inherently simplified. Through a steadfast alignment with GitOps methodologies and robust Kubernetes integrations, Argo CD is poised to continue evolving the landscape of software delivery with pragmatism and precision at its helm.

1.4 How Argo CD Fits into the CD Ecosystem

Argo CD emerges as a significant player within the Continuous Delivery (CD) ecosystem, particularly for Kubernetes environments. Its declarative approach to managing infrastructure and application runtimes offers a noteworthy paradigm shift in how continuous delivery is executed. By capitalizing on GitOps principles, Argo CD facilitates seamless integration with existing tools and processes, enhancing deployment strategies, system resilience, and application lifecycle management. In this section, we explore Argo CD's position within the CD framework, its interoperability with complementing tools, and its contribution to advancing DevOps and GitOps practices.

Integration within the CD Pipeline

The CD ecosystem encompasses a myriad of stages, from code commits and integration to testing, deployment, and monitoring. Argo CD seamlessly integrates into these processes by functioning as an orchestrator for deployments, ensuring that the final application state reflects the source of truth defined in Git repositories.

- *Post-CI Integration:* Argo CD fits naturally after the Continuous Integration (CI) stage, where code has been built and tested. It leverages the output artefacts from CI systems, using them as inputs for deploying applications to Kubernetes clusters.

- *Declarative Deployments:* The core advantage offered by Argo CD is its ability to manage applications declaratively. By pointing Argo CD to a Git repo containing the desired state manifest files, teams can streamline deployments across environments, ensuring consistency and version control.

- *Feedback and Observability:* Integration with observability and monitoring tools like Prometheus and Grafana enhances feedback loops. Argo CD's APIs expose metrics that are vital for assessing application health and synchronizing status between Git and live environments.

Interoperability with Complementary Tools

Argo CD does not operate in isolation; rather, it complements an array of tools and services across the DevOps spectrum, enhancing its capabilities and empowering teams to adopt a holistic CD pipeline.

- *CI Toolchains:* Jenkins, GitHub Actions, and GitLab CI/CD platforms can precede Argo CD, handling the build and initial test phases. The artefacts and container images generated are subsequently utilized by Argo CD for deployment.

- *Kubectl and Helm:* Argo CD accommodates native Kubernetes tools like kubectl and Helm for advanced resource management. It can serve as a mechanism to manage and deploy Helm charts, alleviating complexity in handling application dependencies and upgrades.

- *Security Tools:* Security tools like Snyk and Aqua Security can be integrated into the pipeline to scan applications for vulnerabilities before Argo CD conducts deployments, ensuring compliance and safeguarding application integrity.

- *Service Meshes:* Integration with service meshes like Istio and Linkerd enables network traffic management and visibility, contributing to high availability and reliability of deployed microservices.

Case Study: Argo CD in Practice

Consider a software development team responsible for deploying a microservices-based application across multiple Kubernetes clusters. By implementing Argo CD, the team can achieve greater agility and control over their deployment pipelines. Here's a detailed examination:

Scenario: The team uses Jenkins for CI, which produces Docker images stored in Docker Hub, and Argo CD to automate deployments.

```
apiVersion: argoproj.io/v1alpha1
kind: Application
metadata:
  name: microservice-app
  namespace: argocd
spec:
  project: default
  source:
    repoURL: 'https://github.com/company/microservices-helm'
    targetRevision: main
    helm:
      valueFiles:
        - values.yaml
  destination:
    server: 'https://k8s-cluster.local'
    namespace: production
  syncPolicy:
```

1.4. HOW ARGO CD FITS INTO THE CD ECOSYSTEM

```
automated:
  prune: true
  selfHeal: true
```

Here the application spec points to a Git repository containing the Helm charts defining microservices. The `syncPolicy` ensures that the application is continually validated and corrected to match the Git-defined state.

Process:

- Jenkins builds each service, running unit and integration tests, then pushes Docker images.

- Argo CD detects changes in the Git repository (Helm chart updates) and automatically synchronizes those to Kubernetes clusters.

- Integrated monitoring tools provide visibility, ensuring minimal latency in resolving issues.

Advantages of Argo CD in the CD Ecosystem

Argo CD contributes distinctive benefits to the overall CD ecosystem, enhancing efficiencies and enabling practices that align with modern Software Development Lifecycle (SDLC) methodologies.

- *Declarative Management and Source Control:* By maintaining infrastructure as code, Argo CD ensures that every aspect of the application's lifecycle is declaratively controlled and versioned in Git. This enhances reliability and facilitates audits and history tracking.

- *Built-in Rollbacks and Promotion Strategies:* The GitOps-based model allows straightforward rollbacks by reverting commits or merging PRs that rectify unwanted changes. Promotions can be easily executed by leveraging Git functionalities across branches for environments like staging, testing, and production.

- *Cross-Environment Harmony:* Argo CD's consistent deployment mechanism reduces the discrepancies between different environments by ensuring that applications deploy uniformly, minimizing configuration drift.

- *Reduced Human Error and Improved Productivity:* Automating repetitive deployment tasks frees up developers and operations staff to focus on higher-value initiatives, enhancing overall team productivity.

Advanced Feature Set of Argo CD

Argo CD boasts an expansive range of features, accommodating various use cases and deployments beyond simple applications.

- *Sync Waves and Hooks:* Sync waves enable users to dictate the order in which resources should be applied during a deployment, while hooks can execute custom logic pre- or post-sync, enriching deployment strategies.

- *Application Set Controller:* By leveraging the ApplicationSet, users can automate the creation and management of multiple applications in Argo CD, particularly useful in multi-tenant environments or where numerous instances of an application exist.

- *Multi-Cluster Support:* Argo CD extends capabilities across multiple Kubernetes clusters, allowing for intricate orchestration and management. This is vital for hybrid cloud strategies or multi-region deployments.

Conclusion on Argo CD's Role in the CD Ecosystem

Argo CD's introduction into the CD ecosystem signifies a notable advancement in how applications are deployed and managed in Kubernetes environments. By harmonizing the deployment state with Git repositories, Argo CD ensures a streamlined, reliable, and efficient process that complements existing CI/CD toolchains. As continuous delivery processes mature and Kubernetes adoption rises, Argo CD will continue to play a critical role in enabling organizations to achieve agile, scalable, and resilient software delivery.

1.5 Advantages of Using Argo CD for Continuous Delivery

Argo CD provides a comprehensive solution for Continuous Delivery (CD) in Kubernetes environments, leveraging GitOps practices to enhance deployment processes, ensure consistency, and streamline operations. In the context of modern DevOps practices, Argo CD offers multifaceted benefits that align closely with the demands for agility, reliability, and efficiency in software delivery pipelines. This section delves into the key advantages of using Argo CD for continuous delivery, providing an in-depth exploration of how it contributes to enhanced operational workflows and sustainable innovation in software engineering.

Declarative Configuration Management

At the core of Argo CD's offerings is its reliance on declarative configuration through Git repositories. This approach ensures that both application definitions and their operational states are stored as version-controlled documents, enhancing traceability and ease of replication.

- *Version Control and Transparency:* By leveraging Git, every application's desired state, from configurations to deployment specifications, is auditable and traceable. Historical changes can be examined and reverted if necessary, promoting transparency across the software delivery lifecycle.

- *Reproducibility:* Storing configurations as code in Git enables the replication of environments effortlessly, ensuring consistent deployments across development, staging, and production without significant manual intervention.

- *Collaboration and Change Management:* The Git-based workflow encourages collaborative Change Management practices within DevOps teams. By adopting pull-request mechanisms, multiple stakeholders can provide reviews and approve changes before a commit is deemed ready for deployment.

Automatic and Consistent Deployments

One of Argo CD's key strengths is its ability to continuously synchronize the desired state from Git repositories to Kubernetes clusters. This synchronization eliminates manual deployments, reduces the potential for human errors, and ensures consistent application behavior across environments.

- *Automated Synchronization:* Argo CD actively monitors specified repositories for changes, triggering automatic synchronization processes to align the live state with the declared state in Git. This automation significantly reduces deployment times and minimizes disruptions.

- *Environment Consistency:* Automatically synchronizing environments ensures configuration consistency, thereby reducing the risk of "environment drift" where differences between stages lead to unforeseen issues or defects at later stages.

- *Reduced Downtime:* By enabling rolling updates, blue-green deployments, and canary releases, Argo CD provides flexible deployment strategies that dynamically reduce application downtime and mitigate risks associated with introducing new updates.

```
apiVersion: argoproj.io/v1alpha1
kind: Application
metadata:
  name: blue-green-app
  namespace: argocd
spec:
  project: default
  source:
    repoURL: 'https://github.com/company/blue-green-repo'
    targetRevision: 'release'
    path: manifests/blue-green
  destination:
    server: 'https://k8s-cluster.local'
    namespace: production
  syncPolicy:
    automated:
      prune: true
      selfHeal: true
    syncOptions:
    - CreateNamespace=true
    - "applyOutOfSyncOnly=true"
    - "pruneLast=true"
```

Enhanced Security and Compliance

Argo CD's integration within the GitOps paradigm ensures a robust security model which enhances the overall security posture of software delivery processes.

- *Access Controls:* Argo CD utilizes Role-Based Access Control (RBAC) to manage and enforce fine-grained policies, determining who has permission to deploy applications, make changes, or enforce synchronization.

- *Secure Pipelines:* The declarative nature ensures that there is a singular flow to deployment processes, reducing indirect risks such as unauthorized changes or infrastructure misconfigurations, thus preserving system integrity.

- *Compliance and Auditing:* With all changes tracked and documented in Git, Argo CD facilitates stringent compliance with industry standards and regulations. Comprehensive audit trails and histories help verify that compliance benchmarks are consistently met.

Flexibility and Adaptability

Argo CD provides a high degree of flexibility, allowing bespoke deployments and integrations tailored to specific organizational needs, thereby enhancing adaptability.

- *Integration with Existing Toolsets:* Argo CD works synergistically with existing tools and processes, such as Terraform, Helm, and Kubernetes-native policies, ensuring seamless integrations across the software delivery pipeline.

- *Support for Various Deployment Approaches:* With robust support for Helm charts, Kustomize configurations, and Custom Resource Definitions (CRDs), Argo CD accommodates diverse deployment needs and strategies, from microservices architectures to monolith migrations.

- *Multi-Cluster Deployments:* In hybrid cloud or multi-region setups, Argo CD's capabilities extend across numerous clusters, ensuring that scaling strategies are effectively managed without additional complexity.

```yaml
apiVersion: argoproj.io/v1alpha1
kind: Application
metadata:
  name: multi-cluster-app
  namespace: argocd
spec:
  source:
    repoURL: 'https://github.com/multi-cluster/repo'
    path: 'applications'
    targetRevision: HEAD
  destination:
    server: 'https://asia-cluster.local'
    namespace: production
---
apiVersion: argoproj.io/v1alpha1
kind: Application
metadata:
  name: multi-cluster-app-us
  namespace: argocd
spec:
  source:
    repoURL: 'https://github.com/multi-cluster/repo'
    path: 'applications'
    targetRevision: HEAD
  destination:
    server: 'https://us-cluster.local'
    namespace: production
```

Improved Developer and Operations Productivity

By automating operational tasks and reducing the manual overhead of deployments, Argo CD allows teams to prioritize core activities essential for business growth and development.

- *Focus on Innovation:* Freed from monotonous or error-prone deployment steps, developers and operations teams can refocus efforts on innovation, feature development, and system optimization.

- *Rapid Feedback Loops:* Integrated feedback mechanisms, including automated tests and seamlessly connected monitoring tools, provide real-time insights into applications' performance, reducing the cycle time for fixing bugs or deploying urgent updates.

- *Self-Healing Capabilities:* The ability to automatically reconcile changes and resolve drift enables systems autonomously preserve their intended operational state, requiring minimal manual intervention even as conditions evolve.

Case Study: Implementing Argo CD in a Real-world Scenario

Consider a mid-sized retail company focusing on digital transformation to enhance its online presence via Kubernetes-based microservices architecture. Implementing Argo CD permits seamless deployment of service updates, ensuring their website and application maintain high availability and performance.

Application Specifications:

- **Services:** Product Catalog, Order Processing, User Authentication
- **CD Pipeline:** Jenkins CI → Docker Registry → Argo CD

Benefits Realized:

- **Reduced Deployment Frequency:** From twice per month to continuous delivery upon successful CI builds with immediate synchronization.
- **Downtime Reduction:** Downtime incidents fell by 70% due to Argo CD's automated reconciliation and rollback capabilities.
- **Improved Developer Efficiency:** Developers achieved 20% more focus on building new features rather than handling operations, contributing to quicker market adaptations.

Thus, transitioning to Argo CD offered substantial gains by empowering automation, improving reliability, and enabling the retail company to better meet consumer demands with agility.

Conclusion on Advantages of Argo CD

Argo CD stands out as a significant enabler of effective Continuous Delivery practices, particularly within Kubernetes environments. By embracing declarative configuration and automation, it provides a robust platform for minimizing deployment risks, accelerating software releases, and improving the overall integrity and security of application management. The distinct benefits Argo CD provides highlight its role as an indispensable component of modern DevOps strategies, ensuring that evolving business needs are met with precision, scalability, and resilience.

1.6 Real-world Use Cases of Argo CD

In various real-world applications, Argo CD has proven to be an invaluable tool within the domain of continuous delivery, particularly within Kubernetes-centric environments. Its capabilities facilitate a unique approach to handling large-scale deployments, multi-environment orchestration, and effective Docker container management across diverse industries. This section elucidates several case studies that demonstrate the practical applications and transformative impact of Argo CD on software development processes.

Case Study 1: Financial Services Firm

A leading financial services firm adopted Kubernetes for its digital platform to enhance its resilience and scalability. With an ever-growing suite of applications, ranging from customer-facing mobile tools to back-office data processing systems, the firm faced significant deployment challenges. Traditionally, releases were complex, highly manual, and risk-laden, often resulting in downtime and transaction failures.

Challenges Addressed:

- Frequent deployment errors due to manual processes.

- Long lead times for feature updates, impacting agility.

- High operational overhead to maintain environment consistency.

- *Deployment Automation with Argo CD:* By incorporating Argo CD, the financial firm automated their application deployment pipelines. They leveraged Argo CD's declarative GitOps model to ensure the desired state was consistently synchronized across environments.

- *Improved Compliance and Traceability:* The firm used Git as a single source of truth for application configurations, aligning with stringent regulatory requirements. Argo CD provided audit trails for all deployments, simplifying compliance reporting.

- *Decreased Downtime:* Automated rollback features reduced the impact of failed deployments, consequently lowering downtime incidents by 60%.

Implementation Insight:

The firm orchestrated multi-tenant configurations and rolled out complex deployments with Helm charts through Argo CD. Here's a segment of their Helm integration configuration:

```
apiVersion: argoproj.io/v1alpha1
kind: Application
metadata:
  name: transaction-service
  namespace: argocd
spec:
  project: financial-app
  source:
    repoURL: 'https://github.com/financial-firm/helm-charts'
    targetRevision: main
    helm:
      valueFiles:
      - values-production.yaml
  destination:
    server: 'https://production-cluster.local'
    namespace: services
  syncPolicy:
    automated:
      prune: true
      selfHeal: true
```

The deployment approach enabled efficient use of infrastructure and improved response times for financial transactions backed by real-time updates.

Case Study 2: E-commerce Platform

An e-commerce giant, aiming to manage high traffic volumes and dynamic consumer demands, implemented Argo CD to navigate the complexity of rapid feature rollouts and high reliability needs. The platform, composed of numerous microservices architectures, struggled with synchronized releases amid peak periods like Black Friday sales.

Challenges Addressed:

- Maintaining uptime during high-traffic periods.
- Coordinating multi-regional deployments without excess manual intervention.

- Ensuring swift rollbacks in case of deployment failures.

- *Scalable Multi-Cluster Management:* Argo CD provided automated synchronization across geographically distributed clusters, enabling seamless and uniform deployments.

- *Enhanced Speed through GitOps:* Adoption of GitOps improved deployment times by 70%, facilitating the release of new features and seasonal updates in near real-time to meet market demands.

- *Monitoring and Feedback Integration:* Integrating Argo CD with Prometheus and Grafana enabled proactive monitoring and provided rapid feedback loops for anomaly detection.

Implementation Insight:

Deployments utilized Argo CD's application sets for scalable multi-region setups, as demonstrated below:

```
apiVersion: argoproj.io/v1alpha1
kind: ApplicationSet
metadata:
  name: microservices-deployment
  namespace: argocd
spec:
  generators:
  - list:
      elements:
        - clusterName: east-coast
          server: 'https://east-coast-cluster.local'
        - clusterName: west-coast
          server: 'https://west-coast-cluster.local'
  template:
    metadata:
      name: '{{clusterName}}-app'
    spec:
      project: e-commerce
      source:
        repoURL: 'https://github.com/ecommerce-platform/microservices'
        path: services/app
      destination:
        server: '{{server}}'
        namespace: production
      syncPolicy:
        automated:
          prune: true
          selfHeal: true
```

This configuration managed synchronized application rollouts across

1.6. REAL-WORLD USE CASES OF ARGO CD

regions, streamlining multi-cluster orchestration and optimizing resource utilization.

Case Study 3: Telecommunications Company

A telecommunications provider shifted towards a cloud-native architecture to support its expanding network infrastructure and customer service applications. The complexity of integrating numerous third-party APIs and maintaining regulatory compliance posed significant challenges.

Challenges Addressed:

- Ensure regulatory compliance across distributed systems.
- Integrate a diverse array of third-party APIs seamlessly.
- Manage lifecycle operations for complex network functions.

- *Unified Compliance Management:* Argo CD's role-based access control (RBAC) and audit capabilities satisfied the compliance mandates needed across telecommunications infrastructure.
- *Efficient API Integrations:* Leveraging Argo CD's synchronization capabilities, the company effortlessly integrated APIs, while maintaining coherent application states across development lifecycles.
- *Reduced Operational Complexity:* Automated lifecycle management of network functions led to a 40% reduction in operational overhead, aligning with improved service delivery benchmarks.

Implementation Insight:

The firm utilized custom resource definitions (CRDs) and Argo CD's advanced sync hooks to automate lifecycle operations for critical network services:

```
apiVersion: argoproj.io/v1alpha1
kind: Application
metadata:
  name: network-service
  namespace: argocd
spec:
  project: telecom-net
```

```
source:
  repoURL: 'https://github.com/telecom-services/network-configs'
  path: networking
destination:
  server: 'https://network-cluster.local'
  namespace: network-ops
syncPolicy:
  automated:
    prune: true
    selfHeal: true
syncHooks:
- action: PreSync
  hook: "kubectl apply -f pre-sync-hook.yaml"
```

By automating the initiation and synchronization of network services, the provider achieved elevated efficiencies in the management of extensive, real-time communication infrastructures.

Advantages Demonstrated Across Case Studies

Across these diverse use cases, Argo CD's advantages in real-world applications are evident. These include:

- *Operational Efficiency:* Automated synchronization and deployment reduce time-consuming manual interventions, fostering an environment for rapid feature delivery and improved system reliability.

- *Enhanced Security and Compliance:* With built-in compliance support and secure workflows, enterprises maintain adherence to regulatory standards effortlessly, decreasing the risk of breaches and policy violations.

- *Scalability and Adaptability:* Support for multi-cluster deployments and dynamic orchestration delivers scalable solutions, whether managing multi-regional e-commerce platforms or extensive telecom networks.

- *Transparency and Traceability:* The GitOps mechanism offers clear traceability for changes, empowering organizations to maintain accountability and comprehensive understanding of their deployment versions and history.

Conclusion on Argo CD Use Cases

Argo CD has emerged as a transformative continuous delivery tool, with a marked impact on Kubernetes management and operations across industries. These case studies illustrate its capability to streamline complex deployments, enhance operational integrity, and provide a robust framework that aligns with modern software development paradigms. As digital transformation accelerates and the demand for efficient deployment pipelines grows, Argo CD continues to play a critical role in enabling businesses to innovate, adapt, and thrive on the global stage.

1.7 Setting the Stage for Learning Argo CD

As organizations continue to embrace DevOps methodologies and cloud-native technologies, the necessity for advanced tools that streamline software delivery processes becomes increasingly evident. Argo CD has emerged as a pivotal component within the continuous delivery landscape, particularly for Kubernetes-centric environments. This section aims to provide a comprehensive foundation for those embarking on learning Argo CD, outlining key concepts, preparing environments, and identifying prerequisites to facilitate efficient mastery of this transformative technology.

Foundational Concepts in GitOps and Kubernetes

Before diving into Argo CD, it is critical to have a solid understanding of the foundational principles that underpin its operation, primarily GitOps and Kubernetes:

- *GitOps Principles:* GitOps is a framework that utilizes Git repositories as the single source of truth for declarative infrastructure and application state management. Changes are managed through version-controlled commits, promoting an immutable infrastructure approach that enhances transparency, traceability, and rollback capabilities.

- *Kubernetes Concepts:* Kubernetes is an extensible, open-source platform for managing containerized workloads. Understanding key Kubernetes concepts, such as pods, deployments, services, namespaces, and Custom Resource Definitions (CRDs), is essential, as Argo CD leverages these constructs to function within Kubernetes clusters.

To effectively engage with Argo CD, proficiency in Kubernetes operations and fundamental CI/CD processes is expected. Deployment strategies such as blue-green deployments, canary releases, and rolling updates should also be familiar to enhance the learning experience.

Setting Up the Learning Environment

Preparing a suitable environment is crucial for acquiring hands-on experience with Argo CD. This preparation involves setting up Kubernetes clusters, installing necessary tools, and configuring repositories to simulate a real-world continuous delivery scenario:

- *Kubernetes Cluster Setup:* Beginners can start with minikube or kind (Kubernetes IN Docker) for lightweight local clusters, while advanced users might opt for a more robust managed service like Google Kubernetes Engine (GKE) or Amazon EKS for larger scale learning exercises.

```
minikube start --cpus=4 --memory=4096 --driver=virtualbox
```

- *Installing Argo CD:* Installation involves deploying the Argo CD components within a Kubernetes namespace. It is advisable for learners to install Argo CD on a fresh cluster to avoid complications with existing applications.

```
kubectl create namespace argocd
kubectl apply -n argocd -f https://raw.githubusercontent.com/argoproj/argo-cd/
    stable/manifests/install.yaml
```

- *Git Repository Configuration:* Set up a public or private Git repository to host application manifests. This repository acts as the source of truth, where GitOps workflows will be demonstrated and tested.

- *CLI and UI Access:* Familiarize yourself with the Argo CD command-line tool ('argocd cli') and the web-based user interface. These tools offer comprehensive management capabilities and visualization of the application state.

1.7. SETTING THE STAGE FOR LEARNING ARGO CD

```
VERSION=$(curl --silent "https://api.github.com/repos/argoproj/argo-cd/
    releases/latest" | grep '"tag_name":' | sed -E 's/.*"([^"]+)".*/\1/')
curl -sSL -o argocd https://github.com/argoproj/argo-cd/releases/download/${
    VERSION}/argocd-linux-amd64
chmod +x argocd
mv ./argocd /usr/local/bin/
```

Key Learning Objectives for Argo CD

To maximize the effectiveness of learning Argo CD, it is essential to define clear learning objectives. These objectives guide the learning process, ensuring that foundational skills are acquired and evolving to support more advanced operational goals.

- *Understand Declarative Application Management:* Develop an in-depth comprehension of how declarative application management using Argo CD benefits continuous delivery processes. Learn to create applications using YAML manifests, defining repositories, paths, synchronization policies, and destinations.

- *Implement Synchronization Policies:* Master the use of synchronization policies within Argo CD to automate deployments, including strategies like self-healing and automatic pruning.

```
syncPolicy:
  automated:
    prune: true
    selfHeal: true
  syncOptions:
  - CreateNamespace=true
```

- *Deploy Multi-Cluster Applications:* Gain expertise in deploying applications across multiple Kubernetes clusters, leveraging Argo CD's multi-cluster management features.

- *Integrate Monitoring and Logging Tools:* Explore the integration of monitoring and logging tools with Argo CD applications to provide real-time observability and insights into application performance.

- *Explore Advanced GitOps Workflows:* Engage in advanced GitOps workflows, managing complex applications with branching strategies, canary deployments, rollbacks, and multi-service orchestration.

```
kubectl apply -f https://raw.githubusercontent.com/argoproj/argo-rollouts/
    stable/manifests/install.yaml
# Define rollouts in application manifests
```

Learning Resources and Community Engagement

Leveraging resources and engaging with the community play a fundamental role in deepening knowledge and troubleshooting effectively during learning:

- *Documentation and Tutorials:* The official Argo CD documentation is a critical resource, offering insights into installation, configuration, and operation. Supplement this learning with tutorials and walkthroughs provided by the community and seasoned practitioners.

- *Argo CD GitHub Repository:* The source code and issues page on GitHub provide a deeper understanding of Argo CD's inner workings, including contributing to the open-source project and resolving technical hurdles.

- *Online Courses and Webinars:* Numerous online platforms like Udemy, Coursera, and free webinars by CNCF or related conferences offer structured courses and up-to-date discussions on GitOps and Argo CD concepts.

- *Community Forums and Discussion Groups:* Join forums like Argo CD's official Slack channel, Stack Overflow, and Kubernetes subreddits, actively participating in discussions and exchanging knowledge or querying practices.

Real-World Scenario Simulation

Simulating real-world scenarios during learning accelerates understanding by applying theoretical knowledge to practical tasks. This involves creating realistic application environments and deployments, identifying and resolving typical challenges:

- *Simulating Production Workloads:* Set up applications that mirror production-scale workloads, involving traffic distribution

1.7. SETTING THE STAGE FOR LEARNING ARGO CD

tests, variable data loads, and failure recovery processes to identify potential performance bottlenecks.

- *Cross-Environment Synchronization:* Practice deploying consistent applications across staging, development, and production environments to highlight the intricacies of Argo CD's synchronization capabilities.

- *Failover Procedures and Rollbacks:* Test and validate failover procedures, simulating application breaches or deployment rollbacks to understand system resilience and disaster recovery strategies.

```
argocd app rollback <app-name>
```

- *CI/CD Integration Exercises:* Integrate Argo CD with continuous integration tools like Jenkins or GitHub Actions, creating full-stack automated pipelines to curate proficiency in a cohesive GitOps workflow.

These simulations not only solidify technical skills but result in a clearer understanding of how Argo CD functions within a broader ecosystem of enterprise applications and modern development practices.

Conclusion on Preparing for Argo CD Learning

Setting the stage for learning Argo CD involves a careful blend of theoretical groundwork, practical experimentation, and community engagement. Mastering foundational concepts in GitOps and Kubernetes, establishing a development environment, and defining clear learning objectives are crucial steps toward efficient skill acquisition. As learners progress, ongoing engagement with community resources and the simulation of complex scenarios will provide the knowledge and insight necessary to leverage Argo CD effectively within contemporary DevOps practices. With these tools and perspectives in hand, the path to becoming proficient in Argo CD is both accessible and rewarding.

Chapter 2

Getting Started with Kubernetes

Kubernetes serves as a powerful orchestration platform, pivotal for managing containerized applications in dynamic environments. This chapter is designed to provide foundational knowledge on Kubernetes, covering essential concepts such as pods, nodes, and clusters, and equipping the reader with the skills necessary to set up a local Kubernetes environment. From exploring key components and networking capabilities to deploying and managing applications, readers will develop a comprehensive understanding of Kubernetes operations. Additionally, insights into using tools like kubectl and techniques for logging and monitoring establish a solid groundwork for more advanced practices.

2.1 Kubernetes Basics and Fundamental Concepts

At the core of Kubernetes are several fundamental concepts that serve as building blocks for orchestrating containerized applications. Understanding these components is pivotal to leveraging the full power of the platform. This section delves into the architecture and crucial elements such as pods, nodes, and clusters.

A **Kubernetes Cluster** is a set of nodes that run containerized applications managed by Kubernetes. It is composed of one or more *control planes* and a set of *worker nodes*. The control plane administers the cluster, maintaining overall management tasks such as scheduling, state management, and providing an API surface for interaction.

Nodes are the worker machines, which can be either virtual or physical, hosting the Pods. A node performs the necessary actions to run container workloads. Each node contains the following components:

- kubelet: An agent that manages containers running on the host.
- kube-proxy: A network proxy that enables Kubernetes networking services.
- Container runtime: Software that runs the containers (e.g., Docker, containerd).

The **Control Plane** is responsible for making global decisions about the cluster's working condition (e.g., scheduling), and detecting and responding to cluster events (e.g., starting up a new pod).

Key components of the control plane include:

- kube-apiserver: The API server is a component of the Kubernetes control plane that exposes the Kubernetes API. The API server is the front-end for the Kubernetes control plane.
- etcd: A consistent and highly-available key-value store used as Kubernetes' backing store for all cluster data.

- kube-scheduler: Watches for newly created Pods with no assigned node, and selects a node for them to run on.

- kube-controller-manager: Runs controller processes that regulate the state of the cluster, handling tasks such as replication and scaling.

Pods are the smallest and simplest Kubernetes objects. A Pod represents a single instance of a running process in the cluster. Pods encapsulate one or more containers, storage resources, and a unique network IP. Pods in a Kubernetes cluster can be treated similarly to a logical host; they can contain multiple application containers which are relatively tightly coupled.

```
apiVersion: v1
kind: Pod
metadata:
  name: nginx
  labels:
    app: nginx
spec:
  containers:
  - name: nginx
    image: nginx:1.14.2
    ports:
    - containerPort: 80
```

This YAML declaration describes a simple Pod consisting of a single container that runs the Nginx web server. The label helps identify this particular Pod within the cluster.

Namespaces provide a mechanism for isolating groups of resources within a single cluster. Namespaces are intended for use in environments with many users spread across multiple teams, or projects. They work as a virtual cluster, intended for separating and organizing resources in large-scale deployments.

The following command can be used to create a new namespace:

```
kubectl create namespace my-new-namespace
```

Deployments describe the desired state of application and controller objects and manage the scaling and updating of Pods in Kubernetes. They provide declarative updates for both Pods and ReplicaSets. Here is a basic example of a Deployment:

```yaml
apiVersion: apps/v1
kind: Deployment
metadata:
  name: nginx-deployment
spec:
  replicas: 3
  selector:
    matchLabels:
      app: nginx
  template:
    metadata:
      labels:
        app: nginx
    spec:
      containers:
      - name: nginx
        image: nginx:1.14.2
        ports:
        - containerPort: 80
```

This example specifies a Deployment of three replicas of the Nginx Pod. Kubernetes will ensure that the specified number of replicas are running and available at all times.

Services are responsible for enabling network access to a set of Pods within a cluster. They define a logical set of Pods and a policy by which to access them. Kubernetes service types include ClusterIP, NodePort, and LoadBalancer, each providing different levels of accessibility.

A ClusterIP Service example:

```yaml
apiVersion: v1
kind: Service
metadata:
  name: my-service
spec:
  selector:
    app: MyApp
  ports:
    - protocol: TCP
      port: 80
      targetPort: 9376
```

This YAML configuration describes a Service resource that targets Pods with the label app: MyApp. The Service will route traffic on port 80 to port 9376 on the target Pods.

Understanding these basic Kubernetes concepts equips practitioners with the foundational knowledge required to manage more complex architectures. Familiarity with these building blocks enables optimization of workflows, hence supporting large-scale, dynamic application environments effectively. By integrating these components, Kubernetes provides a resilient, scalable platform for modern application deployment. This architecture ensures that resources are efficiently managed while maintaining a seamless scalability model, ultimately meeting the demands of any deployment size.

2.2 Setting Up a Local Kubernetes Environment

Installing and configuring a local Kubernetes environment is an essential step in experiencing firsthand the orchestration capabilities that Kubernetes offers. Such an environment provides a safe and efficient platform to experiment with Kubernetes without needing a full cloud infrastructure. This section outlines the process using popular tools like Minikube and Kind (Kubernetes IN Docker), highlighting their features, installation steps, and configurations.

Minikube is one of the most common tools for creating a local Kubernetes cluster. It runs a single-node Kubernetes cluster inside a virtual machine on your personal computer. Minikube supports features such as:

- Support for Kubernetes API objects and enabling features extensions and applications to small scale.

- Providing a graphical dashboard to visualize and manage cluster resources.

- Compatibility with a wide range of hypervisors such as VirtualBox, KVM, Hyper-V, and Docker.

To set up Minikube, follow these steps:

1. **Install the required dependencies:** Ensure you have a compatible hypervisor and Docker installed on your machine. For example, on macOS, you can install VirtualBox or use Docker Desktop.

2. **Install Minikube:** You can download and install Minikube via package managers or using a direct binary. For instance, using Homebrew on macOS, the command is:

```
brew install minikube
```

3. **Start Minikube:** Once installed, start Minikube with:

```
minikube start
```

This command initializes a VM and starts a Kubernetes cluster running inside. Minikube will download the necessary images and create a local cluster.

4. **Access the Kubernetes dashboard:** Provide a visual interface for managing resources within the cluster by enabling the dashboard addon:

```
minikube dashboard
```

5. **Verify installation:** Confirm that Minikube has been properly installed and the cluster is running with:

```
kubectl cluster-info
```

Kubernetes IN Docker (Kind) is another effective tool designed for testing Kubernetes clusters locally. Kind utilizes Docker containers as "nodes" and is useful for CI environments or local development. Key properties include:

- Running Kubernetes cluster entirely inside Docker containers.
- Facilitating lightweight clusters suitable for development and testing.
- Providing compatibility with continuous integration workflows.

To set up Kind, follow these steps:

1. **Ensure Docker is installed:** Docker is fundamental for Kind operation. Verify by running:

```
docker --version
```

2. **Install Kind:** You can install Kind via Go, direct binary, or by using package managers. A direct download and install method is:
   ```
   curl -Lo ./kind https://kind.sigs.k8s.io/dl/v0.11.1/kind-$(uname)-amd64
   chmod +x ./kind
   mv ./kind /usr/local/bin/kind
   ```

3. **Create a Kind cluster:** Initiate a local Kubernetes cluster using:
   ```
   kind create cluster
   ```
   This command sets up a multi-node cluster using Docker containers as nodes.

4. **Verify the installation:** Check if your Kind cluster is operational by:
   ```
   kubectl get nodes
   ```
   This should display a list of nodes in the cluster.

5. **Clean up:** You can delete the cluster when no longer needed using:
   ```
   kind delete cluster
   ```

Both Minikube and Kind allow users to interact with their clusters using **kubectl**, a command-line tool integral to Kubernetes management. Understanding **kubectl** command syntax and options is crucial as it serves as the primary interface for performing actions on a cluster.

```
kubectl get pods --all-namespaces
```

The above command lists the pods running in all namespaces, confirming visibility into cluster workloads.

Configuring your local Kubernetes environment permits you to explore unique features such as persistent storage, network policies, and custom resource definitions (CRDs). Minikube supports addons, which enable extended Kubernetes capabilities on your local machine. These include metrics-server for resource usage tracking, ingress for managing external access, and volumes for persistent storage.

```
minikube addons enable ingress
```

Executing the above command configures Minikube to manage Ingress resources, pivotal for routing external traffic into the cluster. Alternatively, using Kind's advanced configuration capabilities, you can create complex cluster architectures by defining YAML configurations that describe multi-node arrangements.

```
kind: Cluster
apiVersion: kind.x-k8s.io/v1alpha4
nodes:
- role: control-plane
- role: worker
- role: worker
```

The above configuration establishes a cluster using Kind with one control plane node and two worker nodes, reflecting a more realistic Kubernetes setup.

Networking in a local Kubernetes environment can present unique challenges. Local environments often differ significantly from cloud providers due to their underlying network implementations. Minikube uses NAT (Network Address Translation) or bridge networking for local access while Kind leverages Docker's built-in network functionality. Hence, networking configurations such as service types, Ingress, or routes can behave differently or require additional setup for local environments.

The setup of local monitoring and logging tools is also possible in Minikube and Kind environments. These include Prometheus, Grafana, or ELK (Elasticsearch, Logstash, Kibana) stack. They aid in gaining insights into cluster operations and performance benchmarks.

Establishing a local Kubernetes environment with Minikube or Kind provides the flexibility needed to explore Kubernetes in a controlled space. With a basic setup, you possess the power to deepen your understanding of Kubernetes architecture, experiment with features, and prepare for larger-scale deployments. Such an environment serves as a crucial stepping stone towards mastering Kubernetes management and orchestration in more complex and dynamic distributed systems.

2.3 Working with Kubernetes Objects

Kubernetes provides a wide array of objects that are crucial for defining and managing workloads in a cluster. Understanding Kubernetes objects and their relationships is fundamental to deploying and managing applications effectively. A Kubernetes object is a persistent entity in the Kubernetes system, serving as a record of intention or the desired state.

This section will delve into various Kubernetes objects, including **Pods**, **ReplicaSets**, **Deployments**, **Services**, **ConfigMaps**, **Secrets**, and **Ingress**. Each object plays a unique role in the orchestration ecosystem and contributes to the scalable, resilient management of applications.

Pods are the most basic deployable objects in Kubernetes. A pod encapsulates one or more containers that share the same network namespace, and may also share storage resources. Pods provide an abstraction layer over containers, allowing Kubernetes to manage containers as a single entity.

```
apiVersion: v1
kind: Pod
metadata:
  name: sample-pod
spec:
  containers:
  - name: myapp-container
    image: alpine
    command: ['sh', '-c', 'echo Hello Kubernetes! && sleep 3600']
```

In this pod definition, a single container runs a simple Alpine Linux image. The pod demonstrates key aspects such as defining containers, setting the command sequence, and running processes.

ReplicaSet is a higher-level concept that ensures a specified number of pod replicas are running at any given time, thereby providing redundancy and availability.

```
apiVersion: apps/v1
kind: ReplicaSet
metadata:
  name: frontend
spec:
  replicas: 3
  selector:
```

```
    matchLabels:
      tier: frontend
  template:
    metadata:
      labels:
        tier: frontend
    spec:
      containers:
      - name: nginx
        image: nginx:1.14.2
```

This ReplicaSet maintains three instances of an nginx pod, guaranteeing that the defined number of replicas is consistently running. If a pod fails, the ReplicaSet controller recognizes the discrepancy and creates additional pods to meet the specified requirement.

Deployments provide declarative updates for Pods and ReplicaSets, offering robust features for application lifecycle management, such as rolling deployments, rollbacks, and scaling.

```
apiVersion: apps/v1
kind: Deployment
metadata:
  name: frontend-deployment
spec:
  replicas: 3
  selector:
    matchLabels:
      app: frontend
  template:
    metadata:
      labels:
        app: frontend
    spec:
      containers:
      - name: nginx
        image: nginx:1.14.2
```

A Deployment manages pods through ReplicaSets, facilitating controlled rollouts and version management, crucial for continuous deployment systems.

Services create an abstraction for networking, enabling an entry point to reach a set of pods defined by a selector.

```
apiVersion: v1
kind: Service
metadata:
  name: frontend-service
spec:
  type: ClusterIP
  selector:
```

```
    app: frontend
ports:
  - protocol: TCP
    port: 80
    targetPort: 80
```

This configuration sets up a ClusterIP Service, accessible only within the cluster, which routes traffic to the set of pods labeled with 'app: frontend'. Services support multiple internal service discovery mechanisms and load balancing.

ConfigMaps are opaque repositories of configuration data for configuring pods. They serve to decouple configuration artifacts from image content, ensuring portability and flexibility.

```
apiVersion: v1
kind: ConfigMap
metadata:
  name: example-config
data:
  key1: value1
  key2: value2
```

Incorporating this ConfigMap into pods allows Kubernetes to inject configuration data as environment variables or populate configuration files within a container filesystem.

Secrets offer a secure method for managing sensitive information, such as passwords, OAuth tokens, and SSH keys.

```
apiVersion: v1
kind: Secret
metadata:
  name: mysecret
type: Opaque
data:
  username: c3RhcmxvcmQ=
  password: MWYyZDFlMmU2N2Rm
```

Secrets differ from ConfigMaps in that they are designed to keep sensitive information private. The data field contains base64-encoded values to be decoded before use.

Ingress manages external access to the services in a cluster, typically through HTTP/S. Ingress can provide load balancing, SSL termination, and name-based virtual hosting.

```
apiVersion: networking.k8s.io/v1
kind: Ingress
```

```
metadata:
  name: example-ingress
spec:
  rules:
  - host: www.example.com
    http:
      paths:
      - path: /
        pathType: Prefix
        backend:
          service:
            name: frontend-service
            port:
              number: 80
```

An Ingress specification provides a router between the internet and Kubernetes services, routing requests to 'frontend-service' based on defined HTTP rules.

The integration of Kubernetes Objects is facilitated by identifiers such as **labels** and **selectors**, which classify and group resources. Labels are arbitrary key/value pairs attached to objects, and selectors enable matching of resource sets based on these labels.

Taken together, these Kubernetes objects underpin the architecture of scalable, efficient, and resilient containerized applications. They provide a comprehensive API for defining desired states and managing application lifecycles, rendering Kubernetes an efficient platform for cloud-native application orchestration. Mastery of these objects is imperative for orchestrating complex distributed systems, implementing effective DevOps workflows, and optimizing application deployments across diverse environments.

2.4 Understanding Kubernetes Networking

Kubernetes networking is a critical pillar within the orchestration framework, crucial for managing communications in a distributed environment. It abstracts the underlying hardware, providing a seamless and scalable means of communication for containers within a cluster. Kubernetes networking encompasses several key concepts, including Pod networking, Service networking, Ingress, and network policies.

2.4. UNDERSTANDING KUBERNETES NETWORKING

Understanding these components is imperative for deploying robust and resilient applications.

Pod Networking is fundamental in Kubernetes, establishing how pods interact with each other and with external components. Each pod in a Kubernetes cluster is assigned a unique IP address. Therefore, Pod-to-Pod communication is typically straightforward, with each pod capable of reaching any other pod in the cluster via its IP address without the need for Network Address Translation (NAT). This model ensures a clean, efficient, and simplified networking environment as all pods are in a flat address space, similar to nodes on an overlay network.

The Kubernetes networking model is based on the following principles:

- Pods can communicate with all other pods in the cluster without having to know if they are on the same node.
- Nodes can run a different OS and may have different kinds of hardware, but they can communicate without translating the pod's address.
- The IP a pod sees itself as is the same IP that others see it as; this symmetry simplifies development.

Network Plugins such as Flannel, Calico, and Weave provide the network interface necessary for implementing Kubernetes networking requirements. These plugins operate within the Container Network Interface (CNI), facilitating a consistent network abstraction across different environments:

1. **Flannel** is a simple and stable solution that creates an overlay network to allow pods across different nodes to communicate.
2. **Calico** operates under the principle of a pure layer 3 approach for routing, providing advanced capabilities like network policy enforcement.
3. **Weave** provides a network for deploying microservices, focusing on simplicity and speed.

These plugins manage the allocation of network addresses and ensure packet forwarding between the Nodes.

Service Networking is integral to allow seamless inter-pod communications inside and outside the Kubernetes cluster. Services in Kubernetes expose a set of Pods as a network service. In Kubernetes, Services abstract network proxies that manage traffic directed to a set of Pods.

A Service can be defined in several ways:

- **ClusterIP (default)**: Exposes the service on an internal IP in the cluster; the service is only reachable from within.

- **NodePort**: Exposes the service on the IP of each Node at a static port, which makes the service reachable externally.

- **LoadBalancer**: Exposes the service externally using a cloud provider's load balancer.

- **ExternalName**: Maps a Service to a DNS name.

To illustrate, consider the following example of setting up a ClusterIP Service:

```
apiVersion: v1
kind: Service
metadata:
  name: my-clusterip-service
spec:
  selector:
    app: MyApp
  ports:
    - protocol: TCP
      port: 80
      targetPort: 9376
```

This configuration routes internal traffic on TCP port 80 to a set of Pods identified by the label `app: MyApp` at port 9376.

Ingress is a powerful API allowing external HTTP and HTTPS routing to Kubernetes services. It provides load balancing, SSL termination, and name-based virtual hosting:

```
apiVersion: networking.k8s.io/v1
kind: Ingress
metadata:
  name: example-ingress
spec:
  rules:
  - host: example.com
    http:
```

2.4. UNDERSTANDING KUBERNETES NETWORKING

```
      paths:
      - path: /
        pathType: Prefix
        backend:
          service:
            name: example-service
            port:
              number: 8080
```

This Ingress configuration directs requests for example.com to example-service's Pod on port 8080, illustrating how Ingress Controllers facilitate consistent routing while decoupling application logic from infrastructure details.

Network Policies are used to specify how groups of Pods interact. Kubernetes allows for fine-grained control over communication channels, enhancing security and compliance by way of network constraints. Policies define rules using label selectors, creating a network security model that can restrict or permit traffic to Kubernetes resources.

```
apiVersion: networking.k8s.io/v1
kind: NetworkPolicy
metadata:
  name: allow-specific-ingress
spec:
  podSelector:
    matchLabels:
      role: app
  ingress:
  - from:
    - podSelector:
        matchLabels:
          role: api
```

The above Network Policy permits ingress traffic to Pods labeled with role: app only from Pods labeled with role: api, showing the precise control possible over pod communications.

A practical understanding of Kubernetes networking also involves consideration of DNS within the cluster. Kubernetes automatically configures DNS to provide request routing by default via a DNS server running alongside the kube-dns or CoreDNS service. This setup ensures that internal Services resolve to their ClusterIP, allowing other Pods to access them via DNS.

Service Discovery in Kubernetes operates inherently with DNS, making it seamless for services to find one another. Without any configuration changes, every ClusterIP Service gets a DNS entry of the form service.namespace.svc.cluster.local.

Kubernetes networking extends further into challenge areas like multi-cluster workloads and cross-cluster communications. Addressing these enables a decentralized architecture where applications communicate across geographical boundaries, achieving high availability and disaster recovery.

Multi-Networking enables communication through hybrid models, mixing and matching networking strategies to connect Kubernetes clusters over WANs with tools such as Istio, Linkerd, or service mesh architectures. These tools provide more advanced networking requirements such as secure service-to-service communications and policy-driven traffic control.

Understanding and configuring Kubernetes networking is essential to building scalable, high-performance applications, ensuring that services communicate efficiently while adhering to security and compliance standards. Equipped with these insights, you can architect networks that meet business needs, future-proof deployments, and optimize the operational governance of containerized applications.

2.5 Managing Kubernetes with kubectl

The **kubectl** command-line tool is a critical instrument for interacting with Kubernetes clusters. It provides the primary interface where users can explore resources, deploy applications, inspect and modify cluster configurations, and delve into the status of various cluster components. Mastering kubectl is essential for efficiently managing Kubernetes environments, from basic deployments to complex, high-availability configurations.

Kubectl Basics begin with understanding its syntax. A typical command follows the structure 'kubectl <command> <type> <name> [flags]'. The command specifies the operation (like 'get', 'describe', 'create', or 'delete'), the type refers to the Kubernetes resource (such as pods, deployments, services), and the name designates the specific resource you're targeting.

To list all resources in a namespace, the 'get' command is utilized as follows:

```
kubectl get all
```

Using 'kubectl get' with different resource types allows users to view existing deployments, pods, services, and more, providing a quick overview of the active components within a Kubernetes namespace.

For a more detailed examination of a specific resource, the 'describe' command is valuable:

```
kubectl describe pods my-pod
```

This command provides detailed information about a specific pod, including events, conditions, and configurations, which is critical for debugging and understanding the state of pod operations.

Managing Lifecycle with apply, create, and delete

Kubectl can create resources from either command options or configuration files. The 'apply' command is used for declarative configurations and is idempotent, meaning it applies the desired state described in configuration files without unintended side effects:

```
kubectl apply -f my-deployment.yaml
```

Here, a deployment is created or updated based on the specification provided in 'my-deployment.yaml'.

Conversely, the 'create' command is imperative, directly creating objects without checking if they already exist:

```
kubectl create deployment httpd --image=httpd
```

This imperative command creates a new deployment running the 'httpd' image.

For deleting resources, kubectl offers the 'delete' command, which requires the type and name of the resource or a specification file:

```
kubectl delete pod my-pod
```

This command deletes a specific pod by name, removing it and its associated resources.

Namespaces and Context Management

Namespaces in Kubernetes provide a scope for resource names, supporting organizational needs in complex clusters. Kubectl interacts with namespaces through the '-n' flag to specify the target namespace:

```
kubectl get pods -n my-namespace
```

Listing resources in a specific namespace helps manage environments efficiently, especially as clusters grow in complexity.

Contexts in Kubernetes simplify management further by allowing users to switch between cluster configurations easily. A context is a group of access parameters, including the cluster, namespace, and authentication information. Switch between contexts using:

```
kubectl config use-context my-context
```

Managing multiple clusters becomes straightforward with contexts, optimizing operations and ensuring secure, accurate updates.

Labeling and Selection

Kubectl provides advanced resource selection capabilities through labels. Labels are key/value pairs that provide identification for Kubernetes objects.

To apply a label, use:

```
kubectl label pods my-pod app=myapp
```

This action assigns the label 'app=myapp' to a specific pod. Selection using labels aids in grouping resources for batch operations:

```
kubectl get pods -l app=myapp
```

Such queries return all pods matching the 'app=myapp' label, streamlining management for operators.

Advanced Operations: Scaling, Rolling Updates, and Rollbacks

Pod scaling, an essential aspect of deployment management, uses the 'scale' sub-command to adjust replicas as workload demands.

```
kubectl scale deployment my-deployment --replicas=5
```

Here, the deployment 'my-deployment' is scaled to five replicas, facili-

2.5. MANAGING KUBERNETES WITH KUBECTL

tating responsiveness to changes in resource demands.

Rolling updates ensure minimal downtime and graceful transitions between application versions. Accomplish via:

```
kubectl set image deployment/my-deployment nginx=nginx:1.19.1
```

This updates images in a running deployment, keeping services available as the update progresses.

In case a deployment update introduces issues, swift rollbacks are possible:

```
kubectl rollout undo deployment/my-deployment
```

This command reverts a deployment to its previous configuration, safeguarding applications from faulty updates.

Debugging with kubectl

Kubectl aids significantly in diagnosing and resolving issues in Kubernetes deployments. Retrieve logs to investigate application behavior:

```
kubectl logs my-pod
```

Logging provides insights into container operations, vital for troubleshooting runtime errors or unexpected behaviors.

The 'exec' command allows operators to run arbitrary commands in a container, facilitating direct intervention and debugging:

```
kubectl exec -it my-pod -- /bin/bash
```

This interactive session permits examination of the container's filesystem and processes, proving invaluable for intricate debugging tasks.

Integrating with Automation and Scripting

Kubectl integrates into scripts and automation workflows seamlessly, enhancing DevOps practices. Here is an example of how kubectl can be integrated into a Bash script:

```
#!/bin/bash

NAMESPACE="default"
PODS=$(kubectl get pods -n $NAMESPACE --no-headers -o custom-columns=":
    metadata.name")

for POD in $PODS; do
```

```
echo "Processing pod: $POD"
kubectl logs $POD -n $NAMESPACE
done
```

The script above retrieves logs for all pods in a specified namespace, automating data collection and reducing manual intervention.

Understanding and mastering kubectl command intricacies equip users with the capabilities necessary for effective cluster management. Beyond basic interaction, kubectl entrenches itself within the broader Kubernetes ecosystem, forming the backbone of standard operating procedures, securing environments, managing deployments, and ensuring application health and scalability.

2.6 Deploying Your First Application on Kubernetes

Deploying applications on Kubernetes involves defining and managing multiple objects that collectively ensure an application is properly run and managed within a cluster. This process represents a fusion of infrastructure as code, orchestration, and continuous deployment principles. In this section, we will explore a step-by-step guide on deploying a simple web application, highlighting each phase and illustrating essential Kubernetes objects like Deployment, Service, and Ingress.

The chosen application for deployment is a basic Nginx web server serving static content, representing a typical web server setup. Our deployment will encompass defining resource requirements, exposing the application to receive traffic, and ensuring the application remains available through rolling updates and redundancy strategies.

Step 1: Defining a Deployment

The first step in deploying an application on Kubernetes involves creating a Deployment object, which specifies the desired state of application Pods and manages updates and scaling:

```
apiVersion: apps/v1
kind: Deployment
metadata:
  name: nginx-deployment
spec:
```

2.6. DEPLOYING YOUR FIRST APPLICATION ON KUBERNETES

```
replicas: 2
selector:
  matchLabels:
    app: nginx
template:
  metadata:
    labels:
      app: nginx
  spec:
    containers:
    - name: nginx
      image: nginx:1.21.3
      ports:
      - containerPort: 80
```

In this YAML configuration file, a Deployment named 'nginx-deployment' is defined with two replicas of an Nginx containerized application. The 'spec.selector' ensures the system selects Pods labeled with 'app: nginx', and the 'template.spec' specifies the container image and the port it listens on, reflecting fundamental configurations for running a web server.

Step 2: Application Deployment using kubectl

With the deployment configuration set, the next phase is to deploy the application using the 'kubectl apply' command. This command applies the configuration specified in the deployment YAML file to the cluster:

```
kubectl apply -f nginx-deployment.yaml
```

This command instructs the Kubernetes API server to create the resources described in the YAML file. Kubernetes will subsequently manage the application lifecycle, enforcing the desired state.

Step 3: Exposing the Application with a Service

For external access, a Service object is needed to route traffic to the Pods. Services provide stable endpoints to Pod sets, even as Pods get rescheduled or scaled:

```
apiVersion: v1
kind: Service
metadata:
  name: nginx-service
spec:
  type: LoadBalancer
  selector:
    app: nginx
  ports:
    - protocol: TCP
```

```
port: 80
targetPort: 80
```

This Service configuration routes external traffic to Nginx Pods. With 'type: LoadBalancer', it provides an external IP address for accessing the service outside the cluster, assuming a cloud provider is present that supports it.

```
kubectl apply -f nginx-service.yaml
```

Applying this service definition with 'kubectl' creates a network path to access the application globally.

Step 4: Configuring Ingress for HTTP Routing

To handle HTTP routing and traffic management, an Ingress resource complements the service, offering a bridge between external requests and service endpoints using HTTP:

```
apiVersion: networking.k8s.io/v1
kind: Ingress
metadata:
  name: nginx-ingress
spec:
  rules:
  - host: nginx.example.com
    http:
      paths:
      - path: /
        pathType: Prefix
        backend:
          service:
            name: nginx-service
            port:
              number: 80
```

With this configuration, an Ingress controller routes requests sent to 'nginx.example.com' to 'nginx-service', finessing control over HTTP traffic patterns. Proper domain name setup and Ingress controller deployment are prerequisites for leveraging Ingress routing capabilities.

Step 5: Verifying the Deployment and Monitoring

Deployment verification is a critical phase, implementing commands to inspect resource allocations and check system health using 'kubectl':

```
kubectl get deployments
kubectl get services
kubectl get pods
kubectl describe deployment nginx-deployment
```

By issuing these commands, an operator obtains vital statistics and descriptive overviews of resource status and conditions, enabling troubleshooting and compliance with expected behavior.

Integration of logging and monitoring tools provides valuable insights into application performance and cluster operations. Systems like Prometheus and Grafana connect with Kubernetes to deliver detailed analysis on resource consumption and service uptime.

Step 6: Implementing Rolling Updates and Scaling

Kubernetes naturally accommodates rolling updates, minimizing downtime by sequentially updating Pods. Execute an updated container execution using:

```
kubectl set image deployment/nginx-deployment nginx=nginx:1.21.4
```

This command initiates a rolling update, applying changes incrementally, confirming a successful deployment before progressing. For scaling, Pod replicas are adjusted using:

```
kubectl scale deployment/nginx-deployment --replicas=3
```

Adjusting the replicas maintains availability and performance under varying loads by horizontally scaling resources.

Deploying applications on Kubernetes unfurls dynamic capabilities for managing modern cloud-native projects. The orchestration and resource control facilitated by Kubernetes, in close concert with its extensive ecosystem, empower development and operations teams to continuously deliver and iterate applications proficiently.

Effective Kubernetes deployment transcends simple configurations, demanding an astute appreciation of infrastructure as code principles, resource constraints, and scalable architectures. Mastery of initial deployment steps provides a robust foundation upon which complex distributed systems can be architected, delivering innovative and resilient services to clients globally.

2.7 Exploring Kubernetes Logging and Monitoring

Kubernetes logging and monitoring are critical components for maintaining application health and operational performance within a cluster. These facets provide insights into system behavior, detect anomalies, and ensure infrastructure transparency, facilitating troubleshooting and resource management. Effective logging and monitoring are paramount to managing complex, distributed applications running on Kubernetes. This section explores methodologies, tools, and configurations essential for capturing, analyzing, and visualizing logs and metrics in Kubernetes environments.

Understanding Kubernetes Logging

Logging in Kubernetes involves capturing and storing logs produced by the application as well as the platform itself. These logs are invaluable for diagnosing issues, understanding application performance, and tracking historical usage patterns. Kubernetes categorizes logs into various sections depending on their origin:

- **Application Logs**: Generated by applications running in Pods. They reflect the application's internal states, errors, and event sequences.

- **System Logs**: Produced by Kubernetes system components like kubelet and the API server, describing the state and health of Kubernetes services.

- **Node Logs**: Collected at the infrastructure level, including kernel logs and daemon logs, providing insights into underlying hardware and OS performance.

Applications often write their logs to standard output (stdout) and standard error (stderr). Kubernetes grants access to these outputs using 'kubectl logs':

```
kubectl logs my-pod
```

This command retrieves logs from the specified pod, key to understanding runtime behavior and identifying errors.

2.7. EXPLORING KUBERNETES LOGGING AND MONITORING

Centralized Logging Solutions

While Kubernetes provides native logging capabilities, configuring a centralized logging solution is often essential for scalability and streamlined operations, especially in multi-node clusters. Common logging architectures involve tools like the Elastic Stack (ELK: Elasticsearch, Logstash, and Kibana) or the EFK stack (Elasticsearch, Fluentd, and Kibana):

- **Elasticsearch**: A search and analytics engine to index and store logs.

- **Fluentd/Logstash**: Daemons that collect logs from various sources and forward them to Elasticsearch or another data repository.

- **Kibana**: A user interface for visualizing logs and creating interactive dashboards.

Setting up a centralized EFK logging implementation involves deploying Fluentd as a DaemonSet to aggregate logs from each node:

```
apiVersion: apps/v1
kind: DaemonSet
metadata:
  name: fluentd
spec:
  selector:
    matchLabels:
      name: fluentd
  template:
    metadata:
      labels:
        name: fluentd
    spec:
      containers:
      - name: fluentd
        image: fluent/fluentd-kubernetes-daemonset:v1.11.5
        resources:
          limits:
            memory: "200Mi"
            cpu: "100m"
```

Fluentd collects logs from containers and nodes, processes them, and sends the data to Elasticsearch, indexed for search utilities and analysis.

Kubernetes Monitoring Configuration

Kubernetes monitoring extends beyond logs, providing visibility into resource usage and performance metrics. These metrics encompass CPU and memory utilization, network bandwidth, and latencies. Implementing a robust monitoring strategy ensures clusters operate optimally, supporting resource planning and incident management.

A prevalent choice for monitoring Kubernetes clusters is the Prometheus monitoring stack, accompanied by Grafana for visualization:

- **Prometheus**: An open-source metrics collector that scrapes metrics in time-series format from configured endpoints.

- **Grafana**: A visualization tool that interfaces with Prometheus to present metrics via dashboards. Grafana supports alerting across diverse data source integrations.

To deploy Prometheus in Kubernetes, use the Prometheus Operator, simplifying the setup and configuration:

```
apiVersion: monitoring.coreos.com/v1
kind: Prometheus
metadata:
  name: k8s-prometheus
spec:
  serviceMonitorSelector:
    matchLabels:
      team: frontend
  resources:
    limits:
      memory: 400Mi
      cpu: 200m
```

The Prometheus Operator manages Prometheus instances within the cluster, facilitating the auto-discovery of service endpoints to gather metrics.

Integrating with Grafana allows for intuitive and customizable metric dashboards. Deploy Grafana using Kubernetes Deployments:

```
apiVersion: apps/v1
kind: Deployment
metadata:
  name: grafana
spec:
  replicas: 1
  selector:
    matchLabels:
```

```
      app: grafana
  template:
    metadata:
      labels:
        app: grafana
    spec:
      containers:
      - name: grafana
        image: grafana/grafana
        ports:
        - containerPort: 3000
```

After Grafana deployment, dashboards can be configured to reflect meaningful insights into system operations and performance metrics, effectively aiding decision-making processes.

Best Practices in Logging and Monitoring

Implementing best practices optimizes the logging and monitoring setup for Kubernetes, ensuring ample coverage and reliability:

- **Structured Logging**: Implement structured logging, capturing logs in JSON format to enable detailed querying and more robust analytics.

- **Log Retention Policies**: Define clear retention policies for log storage, balancing historical access needs and storage costs.

- **Alerts and Notifications**: Establish alert rules within Prometheus to trigger notifications via email, Slack, or other systems when performance thresholds are exceeded or anomalies detected.

- **Resource Tagging**: Consistently use labels and annotations for resources, aiding in log correlation and simplifying monitoring views.

- **Scalable Architecture**: Design a scalable logging and monitoring setup, adapting to growth in cluster size and application components without bottlenecking performance.

Kubernetes logging and monitoring ensure systemic transparency and traceability, facilitating root cause analysis and operational excellence. By adopting a strategic approach, engineers maintain visibility across the diverse array of workloads within a Kubernetes environment, ensuring applications remain healthy and responsive under varying demands. Continued refinement of these strategies fortifies the infrastructure's resilience, optimizing systems for both present and future operational landscapes.

Chapter 3

Understanding Argo CD Architecture

Argo CD's architecture is uniquely designed to facilitate seamless continuous delivery within Kubernetes environments, leveraging GitOps principles. This chapter delves into the core components of Argo CD, including the API server, repository server, and application controller, each integral to its operations. It elucidates how Git serves as the cornerstone for application configuration management and synchronization. By exploring config management via tools like Helm and Kustomize, and discussing network and security considerations, readers will gain a detailed understanding of Argo CD's structural and operational dynamics. Additionally, insights into the user interface demonstrate how Argo CD offers intuitive management capabilities.

3.1 Core Components of Argo CD

Argo CD is a declarative continuous delivery tool for Kubernetes designed to manage and automate application deployments. At its core,

Argo CD operates on the principles of GitOps, wherein the desired state of the application, represented within a Git repository, serves as the single source of truth. Argo CD's architecture is composed of several integral components: the API server, repository server, application controller, and others, operating in tandem to facilitate efficient application delivery and management.

The **API Server** acts as the entry point for user requests, facilitating interactions between users and Argo CD through a REST API. It serves as a bridge between external clients, like the Web UI or CLI, and the core functionalities of Argo CD. The API server handles authentication and authorization, ensuring secure access control to resources and operations within Argo CD.

The following is an example of how an interaction with the API server might look when fetching an application status:

```
curl -X GET \
 -H "Authorization: Bearer <token>" \
 https://argocd.example.com/api/v1/applications/my-app
```

The **Repository Server** is tasked with managing interactions with source code repositories, primarily Git. It is responsible for fetching application manifests and identifying differences between the desired state (in Git) and the live state (in the Kubernetes cluster). Unlike traditional deployment tools, where configurations may reside outside version control, Argo CD centers its deployment strategy around Git management, aligning with the GitOps methodology.

A typical configuration file for an application managed by Argo CD might be stored in a Git repository as follows:

```
apiVersion: argoproj.io/v1alpha1
kind: Application
metadata:
  name: my-app
spec:
  project: default
  source:
    repoURL: 'https://github.com/example/my-app-repo'
    targetRevision: HEAD
    path: helm/myapp
  destination:
    server: 'https://kubernetes.default.svc'
    namespace: default
```

The **Application Controller** is the component responsible for moni-

3.1. CORE COMPONENTS OF ARGO CD

toring the live state of applications as deployed in the Kubernetes cluster and reconciling it against the desired state defined in the Git repositories. It systematically applies changes by synchronizing resources. The controller continuously validates the application's real-time configuration against the declared configurations, ensuring drift detection and automatic synchronization as required.

Within the heart of Argo CD's operation, synchronization processes can be critical. Here's an example of invoking a manual synchronization process, which can be executed when automatic synchronization is disabled:

```
argocd app sync my-app
```

Central to reconciliation efforts, the application controller employs a robust reconciliation loop—a feedback cycle designed to log application states, detect discrepancies between desired and actual deployment manifests, and implement corrective actions.

The diagram below illustrates a simplified structure of Argo CD's architecture, showcasing how external inputs alter the system's state through coordinated interactions among its components:

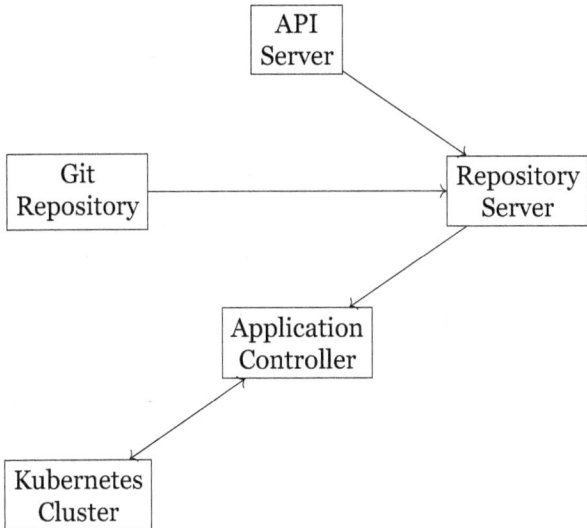

Each component of this architecture operates cohesively to ensure the integrity and accuracy of deployments. The entire workflow aligns closely with the principles of GitOps, emphasizing a declarative, automated, and secure approach to continuous delivery.

Reflecting on the functional dynamics of Argo CD, the **Controller-Scheduler Component** emerges as another fundamental piece, although it often exists in a more auxiliary role. This entity handles deployment scheduling tasks and resource utilization optimizations. By judiciously timer-scheduling synchronization tasks, it manages to maintain a balance between deployment agility and resource availability.

Furthermore, the **Dex and RBAC components** oversee authentication and authorization. Dex operates as an OpenID Connect identity (OIDC) provider, integrating single sign-on (SSO) capabilities into Argo CD's user management for simplified user interactions. Meanwhile, Role-Based Access Control (RBAC) policies further delineate permissions and capabilities within the system, enabling multitenancy and secure segregation among various project spaces.

For instance, an RBAC policy for an Argo CD project might be articulated as follows:

```
apiVersion: v1
kind: ConfigMap
metadata:
  name: argocd-rbac-cm
data:
  policy.default: role:readonly
  policy.csv: |
    p, role:org-admin, applications, *, *, *, allow
    g, alice, role:org-admin
```

This configuration explicitly assigns administrative privileges to certain users for all applications within the organization, implementing access control practices vital for maintaining secure environments.

To encapsulate state visibility, Argo CD also leverages **Prometheus metrics**, affording an ongoing inward view of application health, performance, and event logging. This integration permits a granular level of monitoring, potentially coupled with alerting mechanisms to preemptively address system anomalies.

Within the paradigm of GitOps, Argo CD's architecture and components are strategically designed to harness Kubernetes' capabilities, aligning orchestrated efforts with foundational tenets of modern application deployment strategies. Its operation centers on a Git-centric approach, reinforcing the seamless synthesis of configuration management, resource optimization, security facilitation, and relentless intent verification.

By internalizing its core component frameworks and operational principles, practitioners can adeptly navigate and exploit Argo CD's potential across diversified deployment scenarios, achieving scalable, resilient, and efficient application delivery in cloud-native ecosystems.

3.2 Exploring Application Repositories

Application repositories are a foundational facet of Argo CD, anchoring its operational philosophy within the GitOps framework. The integration of source code and configurations within Git repositories underscores a paradigm shift toward declarative and version-controlled application delivery. Argo CD leverages these repositories to maintain the consistency and integrity of deployments across distributed Kubernetes environments.

Fundamentally, application repositories in Argo CD serve as the definitive source of truth, encapsulating both infrastructure and application configurations. These repositories are diligently monitored for changes, triggering automated synchronization processes that align the live application state with the desired state outlined within. This continuous integration and continuous deployment (CI/CD) cycle minimizes manual oversight, optimizing reliability, and security.

Repository Structure

An understanding of repository structure is critical to effective deployment using Argo CD. Repositories can be organized using various conventional structures based on application needs, often employing monorepos or polyrepos strategies.

Monorepo Strategy: A monorepo contains multiple projects or components within a single repository. This structure facilitates cross-team collaboration and simplifies dependency management. However, it demands stringent governance to ensure scalability.

```
my-monorepo/
   microservice-A/
      Dockerfile
      app-config.yml
      ..
   microservice-B/
      Dockerfile
      app-config.yml
      ..
   shared-libs/
      common-util.js
```

Polyrepo Strategy: A polyrepo approach distributes projects or components across multiple repositories, offering greater modularity and reduced complexity per repo. This eases versioning and change isolation.

```
microservice-A-repo/
   Dockerfile
   app-config.yml
   ..

microservice-B-repo/
   Dockerfile
   app-config.yml
   ..
```

Argo CD supports both strategies, enabling seamless synchronization and deployment across varying repository architectures.

Configuration Management

Within application repositories, configurations are typically articulated using predefined templates and manifests. Choices such as Helm charts and Kustomize overlays are widely used due to their modular and hierarchical structuring.

Helm Charts: Helm charts simplify Kubernetes resource management through parameterized templates, automating the creation and versioning of consistent deployment artifacts.

A sample values.yaml file from a Helm chart might look as follows:

```
replicaCount: 3
image:
  repository: nginx
  tag: stable
service:
  type: ClusterIP
  port: 80
```

```
resources: {}
```

Upon updates to the chart or the values.yaml, Argo CD can detect modifications and apply them within the cluster environment.

Kustomize Overlays: Kustomize allows for declarative management and modification of Kubernetes configurations independently from base manifests, ideal for environment-specific customization without altering original files.

Here's an example of a Kustomization.yaml file for a staging environment:

```
bases:
  - ../../base
patchesStrategicMerge:
  - replica-count-overrides.yaml
images:
  - name: nginx
    newTag: 1.19.6
```

Changes in overlays or image versions quickly propagate through environments, maintaining application integrity.

Git Repository Integration

Git repositories integrated with Argo CD must be properly configured to accommodate robust and secure deployment strategies. Public and private repositories provide distinct authentication challenges. Whereas public repositories may employ straightforward HTTPS cloning methods, private repositories often mandate SSH keypair configurations or personal access tokens to safeguard access.

To configure a private repository with an SSH key in Argo CD:

```
argocd repo add git@github.com:example/private-repo.git \
  --ssh-private-key-path ~/.ssh/id_rsa
```

Here, Argo CD requires explicit identification of the SSH key, enabling secure repository access in conformance with principles of least privilege in security protocols.

Branch Management and Target Revisions

Argo CD permits deployment from specific branches or tags within the repository, affording flexibility across staging and production workflows. The spec.source.targetRevision field dictates the target branch or commit hash.

An application manifest utilizing a specific tag might appear as:

```
apiVersion: argoproj.io/v1alpha1
kind: Application
metadata:
  name: feature-release
spec:
  project: default
  source:
    repoURL: 'https://github.com/example/app-repo.git'
    targetRevision: 'v1.0.0'
    path: charts/myapp
  destination:
    server: 'https://kubernetes.default.svc'
    namespace: production
```

This approach ensures deterministic deployments aligned precisely with pre-validated and versioned iterations of application code.

Managing Large Repositories

For substantial projects, the repository size and performance can become bottlenecks. Effective strategies such as employing shallow clones or archive artifacts can mitigate download and processing times. Notably, Argo CD abstracts these complexities from end-users, handling efficient resource acquisition and management in the background.

Automated Deployments and Observability

Adhering to GitOps tenets, Argo CD continuously watches repository states. Any committed changes automatically trigger reconciliation processes through webhook integrations or polling mechanisms (with configured intervals).

This innate feedback loop roadmap facilitates high observability across the entire application lifecycle via metrics and logs exported through integrated Prometheus services. Notably, operators configure alerting on divergence or synchronization failure events, maintaining strict adherence to defined application states.

Security Implementations

Security is pivotal in handling application repositories, impacting not just access control mechanisms but also the verification and validation of manifests and configurations deployed. GPG signature checks or external security scanners may optionally operate alongside Argo CD, providing an additional layer of trust.

Argo CD's robust management of application repositories encapsulates critical aspects of modern continuous delivery. From structuring and configuring development environments, managing Git-oriented processes, to ensuring cross-environment cohesion—Argo CD takes full advantage of Git repositories as its operational fulcrum. This alignment fosters a seamless and comprehensive delivery experience across multiple Kubernetes environments.

3.3 The Role of GitOps in Argo CD

The advent of GitOps has redefined the paradigms of application deployment and management within Kubernetes-based infrastructures. By employing Git as the single source of truth, GitOps has seamlessly integrated the principles of Infrastructure as Code (IaC) with modern CI/CD practices. Argo CD is a compelling implementation of GitOps methodology, providing a cohesive platform for automating and streamlining application delivery. This section delves into the fundamentals of GitOps, how Argo CD embodies these principles, and examines the manifold benefits derived from its implementation in cloud-native workflows.

Principles of GitOps

The inception of GitOps, pioneered by Weaveworks, brought forth a revolutionary approach to operational consistency and agility. At its core, GitOps is founded on several key principles that distinguish it from traditional configuration management and deployment models:

- **Declarative Configuration:** All configuration states and application parameters are explicitly defined and stored within version-controlled repositories. By using declarative syntax, it becomes feasible to mold infrastructure and applications through automated reconciliation rather than imperative commands.

- **Automatic Drift Detection and Reconciliation:** As Kubernetes environments are dynamic and prone to manual changes,

GitOps ensures infrastructure consistency by automatically detecting and reconciling state drifts—the discrepancies between the live environment and the desired state defined in Git.

- **Version Control as Source of Truth:** By leveraging the capabilities of version control systems like Git, GitOps enables a seamless record of changes, rollbacks, and collaborative contributions to infrastructure and application source.

- **CI/CD with Enhanced Security:** With verifiable event logs, role-based access control, and robust security protocols, GitOps restricts who can modify or apply changes, enforcing security across deployments.

GitOps in Action with Argo CD

Argo CD embodies GitOps principles, applying its methodologies to streamline the deployment process by tightly integrating Git-based workflows with Kubernetes orchestration. Its architecture is inherently designed to reconcile application states automatically, offering an efficient pathway from declarative configuration to automated deployment.

Declaring Application State in Git

In Argo CD, applications are represented as Kubernetes custom resources managed within Git repositories. This architecture follows a structured approach where manifests, Helm charts, or Kustomize overlays are maintained and versioned within these repositories. The application's desired state is directly harvested from these resources, obviating external state configurations.

An example manifest that Argo CD would monitor might use Kustomize to orchestrate the desired state:

```
apiVersion: argoproj.io/v1alpha1
kind: Application
metadata:
  name: web-service
spec:
  project: default
  source:
    repoURL: 'https://github.com/example/web-service-config.git'
    targetRevision: master
    path: overlays/production
  destination:
```

```
    server: 'https://kubernetes.default.svc'
    namespace: production
```

Here, Argo CD continuously reconciles the web-service application to reflect the configurations defined within the production overlay directory of the Git repository, automating resource adjustments as needed.

Drift Detection and Automated Reconciliation

Drift detection is a critical aspect of GitOps. Argo CD continuously observes the live cluster state and compares it against the intended configurations as delineated in the repository. In doing so, any inconsistencies – either due to unintentional changes or infrastructure variability – trigger automated reconciliation processes to bring the live state back into alignment.

This reconciliation mechanism operates with precision, executing discrete actions such as rolling updates for deployment, configuration regeneration, or even rolling back to stable configuration states as necessary.

Consider an automation scenario where a deployment YAML has its image version updated within the repository:

```
apiVersion: apps/v1
kind: Deployment
metadata:
  name: web-frontend
spec:
  containers:
    - name: frontend
      image: nginx:1.19.6
```

When the version is changed to nginx:1.19.6 in Git, Argo CD orchestrates a synchronized update on live deployments without the need for manual intervention or procedural deployment scripts.

Enforcing Security with Observability

Argo CD's GitOps model enhances the security fabric of application deployments through immutable audit trails intrinsic to Git itself. Every modification, commit, and merge within the repository logs an auditable action that can be traced back to contributors and the context of changes.

Moreover, Argo CD permits granular observability through standard logging and monitoring paradigms by interfacing with tools such as Prometheus and Grafana. Metrics scrapped from the system provide deep introspection into deployment successes, reconciliation status, and cluster health.

Alerts can be configured to notify operations teams of drift events, reconciliation failures, or policy violations, thereby providing reactive control over any arising issues within the deployment lifecycle.

GitOps Patterns and Practices in Argo CD

Argo CD is regularly applied within established GitOps operational patterns, such as Progressive Delivery, Environment Segregation, and Multi-repo Configurations. Each of these orchestrates distinct deployment strategies reflective of diverse organizational requirements:

Progressive Delivery: Effective usage of Canary, Blue-Green, or Feature-Flag deployments reduces risk by incrementally releasing changes to subsets of users. Through Argo Rollouts in conjunction with Argo CD, progressive delivery allows seamless experimentation with controlled exposure and rollback facilitated by GitOps control points.

Environment Segregation: Argo CD facilitates environment-specific configurations by managing multiple Git repositories or branches, each corresponding to environments such as Development, Staging, and Production. This ensures encapsulation and guarantees isolated testing.

Configuration manifests might look like this for different environments:

```
source:
  repoURL: https://github.com/example/service-configs
  path: /environments/staging
  targetRevision: HEAD
```

Multi-repo Configurations: Organizations with microservices or multi-component architectures may prefer managing discrete repositories per service. Shared libraries can be included or referenced as submodules or overlays, granting independent lifecycle management while preserving service interdependencies.

Best Practices for Implementing GitOps with Argo CD

Implementing GitOps with Argo CD can yield myriad operational efficiencies, yet mastering it necessitates a discerning application of best practices to leverage its full potential:

- **Ensure Repository Hygiene:** Structuring and organizing the repository with clear directories, naming conventions, and isolated configurations enhances readability and maintainability.
- **Automate Tests and Validation:** Employ automated testing pipelines and manifest validators to confirm the stability and correctness of configurations before they are merged.
- **Embrace Minimalist Configurations:** Avoid redundant or verbose parameters in declarative files; focus on necessary, maintainable configurations.
- **Monitor and Optimize Additional Repos:** Regularly audit and balance repository sizes, branches, and clone depths to prevent sprawl and performance lags.
- **Audit and Role Management:** Enforce access controls, audit repository logs, and strictly define RBAC protocols to secure the system from unauthorized access or unapproved changes.

Argo CD's synthesis of GitOps principles provides a resolute, effective framework for application delivery onto Kubernetes. Through declarative configurations, automated drift detection, and progressive security and observability practices, GitOps as implemented by Argo CD enhances application lifecycle management with unprecedented deployment efficiency and consistency. With its dynamic reconciliation capabilities and robust ecosystem of integration points, Argo CD presents itself as an essential asset for organizations embracing cloud-native infrastructure transformation.

3.4 Argo CD's Application Controller

At the heart of Argo CD's automated deployment process lies the Application Controller, a crucial component responsible for orchestrating and managing the synchronization of application states within Kubernetes clusters. The Application Controller's role is to ensure that the live state of applications in the Kubernetes environment mirrors the desired configuration defined in Git repositories. By applying GitOps principles, the Application Controller enables continuous delivery practices while offering operational efficiencies through a robust architecture and effective management techniques. This section explores the intricacies of the Application Controller's functionality, its operational mechanisms, configurations, and the contributions it makes toward achieving seamless application delivery.

Architecture of the Application Controller

Structurally, the Application Controller integrates tightly with other core components of Argo CD, such as the API Server and Repository Server, each contributing specific functionalities to deliver a cohesive application deployment solution. Within its architecture, the Application Controller operates as a control loop pattern, continuously monitoring the state of Kubernetes applications and reconciling them against the target state defined by application manifests stored in Git repositories.

The Application Controller executes a continuous reconciliation loop, ensuring that the cluster's active deployments accurately reflect the desired configurations. This loop encompasses stages of observation, planning, and execution, wherein the controller identifies discrepancies (or "drifts"), plans corrective actions, and executes necessary changes to restore alignment between the actual and declared states.

The architectural design of the Application Controller embodies scalability and resilience. Although it operates continuously to manage deployments, its use of Kubernetes built-in resources such as custom controllers and efficient inter-component communication protocols minimizes performance overhead and ensures robustness under varying loads.

Mechanism of Action in Application Synchronization

The Application Controller's primary function is to orchestrate synchronization activities. It periodically queries the live Kubernetes cluster to ascertain the current state of managed resources and reconcile them against desired states tracked in Git repositories. Any detected drift triggers the controller to undertake a series of adjustment operations.

1. **State Comparison**: The Application Controller initially performs a detailed comparison between the current application state in the Kubernetes cluster and the desired state as specified in the Git repository. It uses Kubernetes API queries to retrieve the live state and assess any discrepancies.

2. **Plan and Prepare Updates**: Upon detecting a drift, the Application Controller plans the execution of required changes. It does this while considering dependency management, ordering of tasks, and resource utilization strategies.

3. **Apply Changes and Reconcile**: The controller applies corrective actions to the cluster, rolling out updates, configuration adjustments, or resource deletions as necessary. The controller's operations may involve blue-green deployment strategies, canary releases, or other deployment models—as dictated by policies.

4. **Status Monitoring and Feedback**: Following the application of changes, the controller monitors the new live state to confirm successful application or detect any residual drifts. The controller logs all actions and outcomes, enabling observability and audit readiness.

A simple use case might involve updating a deployment, which previously specified version 1.0.0 of a container image, to version 1.1.0:

```
apiVersion: apps/v1
kind: Deployment
metadata:
  name: sample-deployment
spec:
  replicas: 3
  template:
    metadata:
      labels:
        app: sample
    spec:
      containers:
      - name: sample-container
        image: sample-image:1.1.0
```

The Application Controller ensures that after this change is committed to the Git repository, the Kubernetes deployment is synchronized automatically to reflect this updated image version.

Advanced Functionalities and Configuration Options

Beyond mere synchronization, the Application Controller supports nuanced configuration mechanisms that suit diverse application needs and operational considerations. These include customizing synchronization settings and implementing different application behaviors and strategies.

Sync Policies and Options

Argo CD allows the configuration of specific sync policies, defining when and how synchronization actions occur. The default behavior includes manually invoked syncs; however, automated sync can be configured for real-time updates.

- **Automatic Synchronization**: Enables continuous auto-sync of application states, immediately applying changes as they are committed to Git repositories.

- **Hooks**: Argo CD provides mechanisms for pre-sync and post-sync hooks, allowing advanced operations or conditions to be executed before or after sync processes. Hooks may be customized to perform actions like data migration, additional testing, or notifications.

```
apiVersion: argoproj.io/v1alpha1
kind: Application
metadata:
  name: app-hooks-example
spec:
  syncPolicy:
    automated:
      prune: true
    syncOptions:
    - SkipDryRunOnMissingResource=true
  hooks:
  - name: my-hook
    exec:
      command: ["sh", "-c"]
      args: ["./pre_update_script.sh"]
```

Health Assessment

The evaluation of resource health during sync operations is another attribute managed by the Application Controller. It automatically conducts health assessments based on resource types, reporting on the readiness, health, and potential issues of Kubernetes objects. This feature not only improves visibility but helps in predictive anomaly detection, triggering alerts for potential downtimes or inadequacies.

Resource Pruning

When an application state transitions result in certain resources becoming obsolete, the Application Controller employs resource pruning strategies to clean up and remove unnecessary objects. This decluttering approach keeps applications lean and aligned with designated configurations, maintaining efficiency and reducing resource wastage.

Logging, Monitoring, and Observability

To comprehensively understand the operational behavior of Argo CD's Application Controller, logging and monitoring mechanisms are indispensable. Logs capture detailed records of synchronization efforts, applied changes, and triggers encountered. These logs facilitate auditing and root cause analysis of operational discrepancies or failures.

Modern observability tools, when integrated with Argo CD, can provide real-time metrics and visualizations to monitor the Application Controller's performance:

- **Prometheus & Grafana**: Integrates seamlessly for telemetry data accumulation, offering visualization dashboards for insights into synchronization activities, resource allocation, and potential anomalies.

- **Cloud-Native Management Platforms**: Platforms like OpenShift or AWS provide out-of-the-box Argo CD integrations for enhanced observability within managed cloud environments.

Security and Role-Based Access Control

The Application Controller benefits from robust security protocols integrated within Argo CD. Through rigorous policy management and role-based access control (RBAC), administrators can safeguard application deployments against unauthorized changes or misconfigurations.

A sample RBAC policy, granting specific permissions to a user for application management, could be structured as follows:

```
apiVersion: v1
kind: ConfigMap
metadata:
```

```
name: argocd-rbac-cm
data:
  policy.csv: |
    p, role:project-admin, applications, update, *, *, allow
    g, jane-doe, role:project-admin
  policy.default: role:readonly
```

This configures user jane-doe with administrative privileges over updating applications, illustrating how sensitive operations can be assigned selectively to authorized personnel.

Real-World Implementations and Use Cases

In practice, the Application Controller can address a range of deployment scenarios, from simple stateless microservices to complex multi-tenant applications requiring bespoke resource provisioning. The flexibility and extensibility of its operational models make it well-suited to enterprise environments with diverse operational demands.

Consider real-world use cases like implementing continuous delivery for high-traffic retail platforms or facilitating real-time infrastructure updates across global financial trading systems. The Application Controller streamlines these processes, harmonizing deployments to both maximize uptime and align with operational mandates.

The Argo CD Application Controller embodies the integration of refined orchestration methodology into the field of Kubernetes-driven application delivery. Through its careful enforcement of GitOps principles, automated reconciliation, and extensive configurability, it facilitates a unified, scalable, and secure applications management ecosystem. As organizations continue to embrace cloud-native solutions and methodologies, the Application Controller will remain an imperative tool in achieving operational excellence and integrity within DevOps cycles.

3.5   Config Management in Argo CD

Configuration management is a pivotal aspect of deploying and managing applications in Kubernetes environments. Within the realm of Argo CD, configuration management is intricately linked with the foundational principles of GitOps, emphasizing declarative configurations, automation, and version control. Argo CD enables users to manage Kubernetes manifests efficiently while integrating seamlessly with configuration management tools such as Helm and Kustomize. This section delves deeply into the mechanisms and best practices for configuration management in Argo CD, highlighting its integration with external tools and exploring advanced capabilities for managing complex application configurations.

Declarative Configuration Management

The declarative approach to configuration management, as facilitated by Argo CD, entails defining the desired configuration state of applications explicitly in manifests that reside within source-controlled repositories. These manifests encompass the entirety of application components necessary for deployment, structured using YAML or JSON formats.

Key elements typically defined include:

- **Kubernetes Objects**: These represent the deployment, service, configuration maps, secrets, and other essential Kubernetes resources.

- **Parameters and Values**: Attributes defining the behavior, scale, and scope of application environments.

- **Immutable Tagging**: Immutable versions and tags ensure rollback resilience and traceability.

```
apiVersion: apps/v1
kind: Deployment
metadata:
  name: sample-app
spec:
  replicas: 2
  selector:
    matchLabels:
      app: sample-app
  template:
    metadata:
      labels:
        app: sample-app
    spec:
      containers:
      - name: sample-container
        image: sample-image:v1.0.0
```

This YAML snippet illustrates a basic declarative schema, detailing the design of a deployment and its constituent services.

GitOps and Infrastructure as Code (IaC)

Argo CD implements GitOps by situating Git repositories as the canonical source of declarative infrastructure. This convergence with IaC principles results in infrastructure and application configurations as code, fostering reproducibility, versioning, and collaborative change management.

Integration with Helm

Helm is a package manager for Kubernetes, transforming complex Kubernetes application configurations into reusable, version-controlled charts. Argo CD integrates with Helm to offer templated application deployment and environment-specific configuration overrides.

Helm Chart Structure

Helm charts encapsulate the configuration and deployment instructions for a Kubernetes application, structured with templates and values files. They provide parameterized and re-usable templates:

```yaml
# Chart.yaml
apiVersion: v2
name: myapp
version: 0.1.0

# values.yaml
replicaCount: 3
image:
  repository: nginx
  tag: stable
service:
  type: ClusterIP
  port: 8080
```

Application Definition in Argo CD using Helm

An application in Argo CD utilizing Helm may be defined as follows:

```yaml
apiVersion: argoproj.io/v1alpha1
kind: Application
metadata:
  name: my-helm-app
spec:
  source:
    repoURL: 'https://github.com/example/helm-charts.git'
    targetRevision: HEAD
    chart: myapp
```

9.5. CONFIG MANAGEMENT IN ARGO CD

```
destination:
  server: 'https://kubernetes.default.svc'
  namespace: production
project: default
```

Helm Release Strategies

Various strategies can be adopted for Helm releases, such as:

- **Rolling Upgrades**: Ensures zero downtime by updating a few pods at a time.
- **Imperative Releases**: Manual Helm CLI installations and upgrades.
- **Declarative Releases**: Argo CD automates releases to maintain desired state through GitOps, minimizing human error.

Integration with Kustomize

Kustomize provides another layer of configuration management by allowing overlay modifications over a base set of Kubernetes configurations, facilitating specialized environment deployment without altering the foundational configuration files.

Kustomization Files and Overlays

Kustomize enables users to maintain base and overlay directories, where overlays can adjust configurations tailored to specific environments:

- **Base**: Contains the essential manifest configurations.
- **Overlay**: Consists of patches or configurations specific to the environment (e.g., development, staging, production).

```
# Base Deployment (base/deployment.yaml)
apiVersion: v1
kind: Pod
metadata:
  name: sample-pod
spec:
  containers:
  - name: sample-container
    image: sample-image:latest
```

```
# Overlay (overlays/staging/kustomization.yaml)
bases:
  - ../../base
namePrefix: staging-
images:
  - name: sample-image
    newTag: 2.0.0
```

Kustomize Application in Argo CD

Argo CD applications utilizing Kustomize might appear as:

```
apiVersion: argoproj.io/v1alpha1
kind: Application
metadata:
  name: sample-kustomize-app
spec:
  source:
    repoURL: 'https://github.com/example/kustomize-configs.git'
    targetRevision: develop
    path: overlays/staging
  destination:
    server: 'https://kubernetes.default.svc'
    namespace: staging
  project: default
```

By adopting these Kustomize overlays, Argo CD streamlines deployment across multiple environments without duplicating configuration efforts.

Parameterization and Secrets Management

Parameterizing configuration files and securely managing secrets are critical components of effective configuration management.

- **ConfigMaps** and **Secrets**: Manage configuration files discretely while integrating them into the manifest structure. Utilizing tools like SealedSecrets or SOPS can enhance security by encrypting sensitive configurations.

Example Parameterization

Using ConfigMaps, users can parameterize environmental variables, enabling dynamic configurations without manifest changes.

```
# ConfigMap
apiVersion: v1
kind: ConfigMap
metadata:
  name: env-vars
```

```
data:
  APP_ENV: staging
  LOG_LEVEL: debug
```

Drift Detection and Automated Synchronization

Argo CD detects configuration drift – deviations of the live state from the desired state – and automates reconciliation through continuous synchronous operations. This proactive drift management minimizes manual intervention and corrects state misalignment.

Config Management Best Practices in Argo CD

Argo CD's configuration management, when implemented effectively, maximizes operational efficiencies. Recommended practices and strategies involve:

- **Modularization**: Design configurations to be modular and reusable to facilitate size management and minimize redundancy.

- **Version Discipline**: Maintain version discipline in repositories, tagging specific releases under immutable labels for traceability and rollback.

- **Security Hardening**: Prioritize encryption and access controls to limit configuration exposure and risks associated with unauthorized amendments.

- **Testing and Validation**: Pre-emptive testing through CI pipelines and configuration validation ensure configurations are error-free and deployment-ready.

Advanced Monitoring and Auditing Capabilities

Enhanced visibility into configuration logistics is achieved via potent monitoring tools and dashboards accessible through integrations with Prometheus and Grafana. Real-time metric evaluations facilitate quick detection of irregularities and performance thresholds, preventing potential downtimes or security lapses.

Case Studies and Real-World Applications

Through Argo CD, organizations effectively manage large-scale application configurations, where operational demands entail flexible, scalable solutions. Consider an e-commerce giant deploying microservices; Argo CD ensures synchronization across global data centers, with configuration changes consistently propagated across diverse infrastructures.

Configuration management within Argo CD is central to realizing GitOps-centric continuous deployment strategies; it enhances application delivery by employing powerful orchestration, precise integration with tools like Helm and Kustomize, and root-to-leaf management of infrastructure environments. Optimizing these strategies ensures reliable, resilient, and efficient deployment pipelines – an essential boon to cloud-native enterprises navigating complex Kubernetes ecosystems. Through Argo CD, effective configuration management thus transforms operational capabilities, adapts effortlessly to evolving needs, and drives innovation in application development and maintenance.

3.6 Networking and Security within Argo CD

In the orchestration of complex application deployments within Kubernetes environments, networking and security constitute critical layers of consideration, ensuring that deployments from Argo CD are both efficient and secure. Given the cloud-native operations facilitated by Argo CD, implementing robust security controls and networking strategies is imperative for safeguarding application integrity, confidentiality, and performance. This section delves into the multifaceted networking and security mechanisms employed in Argo CD deployments, elaborating on secure communication channels, firewall configurations, access management, secrets handling, and compliance considerations.

Networking Architecture in Argo CD

The networking architecture of Argo CD encompasses the connectivity between internal components such as the API Server, Repository Server, and Application Controller, as well as the external interfaces with users, Git repositories, and Kubernetes clusters. An efficient networking setup must ensure seamless communication across these components while maintaining robust security postures.

- **External Connectivity**: Argo CD relies on HTTP/HTTPS protocols to interact with Git repositories, users (via CLI or Web UI), and occasionally, external dependencies or third-party services.
- **Internal Communication**: The communication between Argo CD's core components is typically orchestrated through internal Kubernetes networking mechanisms. Services within the same Kubernetes namespace can communicate seamlessly using service discovery and DNS within the cluster. Network policies should be configured to isolate and securely enable necessary component interactions.
- **Ingress and Egress Management**: Managing ingress (inbound traffic) and egress (outbound traffic) rules is crucial for controlling the data flows that originate or terminate at the Argo CD deployment.

Example of an egress rule setup as a Kubernetes NetworkPolicy to restrict outbound traffic to only Git repository domains:

```
apiVersion: networking.k8s.io/v1
kind: NetworkPolicy
metadata:
  name: allow-egress-to-github
spec:
  podSelector:
    matchLabels:
      app: argocd
  policyTypes:
  - Egress
  egress:
  - to:
    - ipBlock:
        cidr: 140.82.114.0/24 # GitHub IP block
    ports:
    - protocol: TCP
      port: 443
```

Leveraging Service Meshes for Secure Networking

Service meshes, like Istio or Linkerd, can significantly enhance networking capabilities by providing features such as secure communication (mTLS), observability, and traffic management. Integrating a service mesh with Argo CD could potentially streamline network policies, automate transport-layer security, and provide enhanced telemetry.

- **Mutual TLS (mTLS)**: Ensures cryptographic authentication and confidentiality for service-to-service communications.

- **Traffic Shaping**: Implement traffic policies/directives to manage deployment canaries or staged rollouts securely.

Authentication and Authorization Mechanisms

Controlling access to Argo CD is managed primarily through authentication and authorization protocols that rigorously enforce access control.

- **Authentication**: Users or automation tools interface with Argo CD using tokens, certificates, or OIDC providers (e.g., Dex). These authenticated means confirm user identities before granting state or resource interactions.

Example CLI login using a token:

```
argocd login argocd.example.com --username admin --password MyArgoPassword
```

- **Role-Based Access Control (RBAC)**: Authorization in Argo CD entails RBAC, establishing who can perform actions such as viewing resources, modifying applications, or initiating sync processes.

Example of an RBAC configuration establishing user permissions:

```
apiVersion: v1
kind: ConfigMap
metadata:
  name: argocd-rbac-cm
data:
  policy.csv: |
    p, role:reader, applications, get, *, *, allow
    g, tom, role:reader
  policy.default: role:readonly
```

In this policy, user 'tom' acquires read-only access, limiting application interactions to viewing activities only.

Securing Git Operations and Repositories

Repository operations are central in Argo CD, requiring secured access methods to interact with Git. Encryption, access tokens, and SSH key pairs are frequent methods for securing these connections to prevent unauthorized access and potentially malicious changes.

- **SSH Authentication**: Use SSH key pairs to secure communication channels.
- **GPG Verification**: Enforce cryptographic verification of commits, ensuring the authenticity and integrity of source code changes.

Secrets Management and Data Protection

Handling secrets is a pivotal aspect of securing deployments managed by Argo CD. It involves secure storage, retrieval, and usage of sensitive information like passwords, API keys, and service accounts.

- **Kubernetes Secrets**: By default, Kubernetes provides a mechanism to manage sensitive data, although concerns arise due to base64 encoding rather than encryption.
- **External Secret Management Tools**: Utilize tools such as Vault by HashiCorp, AWS Secrets Manager, or Azure Key Vault for more robust security capabilities, including encryption-at-rest, access control policies, and audit logging.

Example of secret creation in Kubernetes:

```
apiVersion: v1
kind: Secret
metadata:
  name: db-credentials
type: Opaque
data:
  username: bXllc2Vy # base64 encoded
  password: bXlwYXNz
```

- **Argo CD Plugins and Integrations**: Argo CD extends secret management capabilities with plugins like SealedSecrets, which encrypt secret manifests, ensuring they can only be decrypted by specific cluster controllers.

Auditing and Compliance

A comprehensive audit and compliance strategy is essential for maintaining adherence to regulatory requirements and ensuring system integrity. Argo CD logs provide vital telemetry data, capturing the full spectrum of user actions, synchronization events, and application state transitions.

- **Log Management**: Implement centralized logging solutions, such as ELK Stack or Grafana Loki, to collect, analyze, and visualize log data for actionable insights and compliance reporting.

- **Policy Enforcement and Tracking**: Use compliance as code tools to automatically enforce cloud resource policies and monitor drift from compliance standards, enhancing the audit-readiness of the deployment environment.

Data Encryption and Egress Security

Ensuring data protection in transit and at rest is an indispensable aspect of Argo CD's overall security strategy. Encryption ensures that sensitive data remains confidential and protected from potential intercepts.

- **TLS Communications**: Employ TLS for all external communication interfaces, including user interface interactions, Git repository access, and CLI operations, providing an encrypted channel to safeguard data integrity.

- **Egress Control**: Delineate strict egress rules, ensuring only necessary external communications are permitted to mitigate risks from external threats.

Example NetworkPolicy to control egress to trusted domains only:

```
apiVersion: networking.k8s.io/v1
kind: NetworkPolicy
metadata:
  name: restrict-egress
spec:
  podSelector:
    matchLabels:
      app: argocd
  egress:
  - to:
    - namespaceSelector:
```

```
      matchLabels:
            project: internal-systems
policyTypes:
- Egress
```

Implementing Best Practices for Networking and Security

The complex nature of network and security interplay within Argo CD necessitates strategic approaches and implementation of best practices tailored for safe and scalable deployments.

- **Isolation through Network Policies**: Delimit access to critical components and enable only necessary east-west and north-south communications.

- **Security Upgrades**: Regularly apply updates and patches to all interfacing modules, ensuring they remain resilient against emerging threats.

- **Regular Security Audits**: Conduct scheduled security audits to identify vulnerabilities and rebalance security controls.

- **Immutable Architectures**: Strive for immutability in deployment artifacts, offering zero-trust security layers that are resistant to unauthorized configurations and threats.

In concert, these practices reinforce a robust and resilient environment, aligning with decentralized orchestration paradigms prevalent in modern cloud-native infrastructures.

Conclusion

Networking and security within Argo CD intersect directly with the orchestration of application deployments in Kubernetes. By maintaining optimal security postures, configuring explicit network policies, and leveraging integrated authentication and authorization protocols, Argo CD ensures the integrity, confidentiality, and availability of applications. As network terrains and security threats evolve, continuous vigilance, integration of emerging technologies, and adherence to best practices remain essential for any enterprise leveraging Argo CD to achieve its deployment objectives.

3.7 Understanding Argo CD User Interface

Argo CD's User Interface (UI) serves as an invaluable tool for managing and visualizing continuous delivery workflows within Kubernetes environments. It provides a web-based graphical interface that extends the underlying capabilities of Argo CD, facilitating user-friendly interactions, operational insights, and intuitive management capabilities. This section explores the comprehensive features of Argo CD's UI, detailing its components and functionalities while illustrating how it supports collaborative DevOps practices and enhanced application lifecycle management.

Overview of the Argo CD User Interface

The Argo CD UI is designed to offer a seamless integration with the underlying GitOps workflows, providing an intuitive dashboard displaying application health, states, and deployment histories. Users can monitor application performance, conduct synchronized operations, and troubleshoot issues without the need to delve into command-line interface (CLI) interactions.

Upon accessing the Argo CD UI, users are greeted with a central dashboard that aggregates critical information about all managed applications. Key metrics, application statuses, and operational logs are made readily available, enabling holistic visibility across deployment environments.

Key Components and Features of the UI

Application Dashboard

The Application Dashboard is the main interface through which users interact with their applications. It presents a comprehensive view of all applications, detailing their overall health status, sync state, and history of commits and deployments.

- **Summary Panel**: A snapshot of each application, showing its current sync status (synced or out-of-sync), health status (healthy, progressing, degraded), and last sync activity. This summary offers an at-a-glance assessment of application integrity and performance.

- **Detailed View**: Users can click on individual applications to reveal a detailed view covering multiple sections including:
    - *Resource Tree:* A hierarchical depiction of Kubernetes resources associated with the application. It visually represents pods, services, deployments, and other configurations, delineating relationships and dependencies.
    - *Application Events:* A chronological list of events characterizing the application's lifecycle, including deployments, scaling actions, and failures, aiding in debugging efforts.
- **Sync Operations**: Manual synchronization operations can be initiated directly within the UI, facilitating deployment of new configurations or rolling back to previous states.

Health and Status Indicators

Argo CD UI employs health and status indicators to exhibit application conditions in real time, leveraging predefined metrics to assess deployment elements.

- **Health States**: Applications are categorized under states like Healthy, Progressing, Suspended, or Degraded, offering insights into potential issues.
- **Sync Status**: Shows whether resources are properly synchronized or if drift events have occurred, requiring remedial actions.
- **Examples of Status Icons**:
    - Healthy
    - Progressing
    - ☐ Degraded

Version Control and History

Part of the UI's capability rests in tracking the version history of application deployments.

- **Git Commits**: Users can view the commit history associated with each deployment or rollback, offering contextual insight into changes over time.

- **Rollback and Forwarding**: Intuitive controls allow for deployments to be rolled back to prior states or for successfully tested configurations to be forwarded to production environments.

Monitoring and Logging Facilities

The UI integrates with logging and monitoring frameworks, surfacing real-time metrics and logs. These aid operators in diagnosing issues, monitoring resource usage, and understanding the operational footprint of applications.

- **Embedded Log Viewer**: Facilitates real-time access to application logs directly from the dashboard, negating the need for external logging tools.

- **Metrics Visualization**: Essential metrics relating to deployments, synchronizations, and resource utilization are visualized graphically, supporting performance analyses and evolution dynamics.

Navigating the Argo CD UI: Step-by-Step Guidance

Successfully maneuvering through Argo CD's UI involves understanding how to initiate, manage, and troubleshoot applications using available features:

1. **Accessing the UI**: Users connect to the Argo CD server through a web browser, typically requiring authentication via integrated SSO or login credentials.

2. **Exploring the Dashboard**: Upon login, the dashboard provides a holistic perception of applications under management, detailing their current operational states.

3. **Managing Applications**: Navigation through the Application Dashboard allows users to delve into specific applications, viewing resource trees and status summaries, and executing synchronization tasks where required.

4. **Customization and Settings**: Configurable settings are accessible via the UI, enabling administrators to tailor visual and operational parameters in alignment with organizational needs. Permissions, UI themes, and interface language are among settings adjustable directly within the interface.

5. **Troubleshooting and Analysis**: Integrate insights gleaned from logs, metrics, and application events to identify root causes of failures or suboptimal behaviors. The UI facilitates streamlined access to all pertinent operational data.

Collaborative Features for Enhanced DevOps Practices

As an integral tool for DevOps workflows, the Argo CD UI supports collaborative practices through several specialized features:

- **Role-Based Access Controls (RBAC)**: Facilitates collaborative management of applications while maintaining security through access restrictions based on user roles.

- **Audit Trails and Change Logs**: Every action performed via the Argo CD UI is logged, providing comprehensive visibility into the change trail for auditing and retrospective analyses.

- **Notifications and Alerts**: Integration with notification services like Slack or Microsoft Teams ensures stakeholders receive timely notifications of application state changes or sync issues.

Extensibility and Customization of the UI

The user interface is highly customizable, facilitating extensibility through integration with additional plugins or external systems:

- **Custom Dashboards**: Organizations can compose personalized dashboards that highlight metrics or data most consequential to their operations.

- **Webhook Integrations**: Leveraging webhooks and APIs, the Argo CD UI can incorporate external event triggers, enabling reactions to environmental signals from third-party services or custom workflows.

Securing the User Interface

Given that the UI acts as the main point of interaction, securing it involves enforcing strict access controls, employing robust HTTPS configurations, and integrating advanced authentication methods.

- **HTTPS and TLS**: Ensure all communications between the UI and clients are encrypted using strong TLS protocols, expanding the security perimeter.

- **OIDC and Visual MFA**: Enforce OAuth or OIDC authentication for additional security layers, optionally incorporating multi-factor authentication (MFA) for sensitive environments.

Best Practices for Optimizing UI Usage

To fully exploit the user interface's capabilities, users should adopt best practices that ensure efficiency and security:

- **Regular Updates and Maintenance**: Keep the UI and its dependencies up-to-date to benefit from the latest features and security enhancements.

- **Training and Onboarding**: Equip users with comprehensive training to effectively navigate and utilize the UI's expansive feature set.

- **Feedback and Iteration**: Encourage user feedback on the UI's functionality, leading to iterative improvements aligned with user workflow preferences.

Argo CD's User Interface provides an invaluable toolset for managing and visualizing the complexities inherent in Kubernetes-based application delivery. Through an intuitive and coherent interface, users can efficiently deploy, monitor, and synchronize applications aligned with GitOps principles. As organizations continue to intensify their reliance on cloud-native technologies, Argo CD's UI will remain a crucial asset—supporting collaboration, enhancing visibility, and fortifying the security and efficiency of continuous delivery pipelines.

Chapter 4

Setting Up Argo CD for Continuous Delivery

This chapter provides a step-by-step guide to installing and configuring Argo CD for effective continuous delivery in a Kubernetes environment. It details the prerequisites necessary for deployment and offers comprehensive instructions for establishing Argo CD within a cluster. Readers will learn to configure access control mechanisms and link Argo CD to application repositories, facilitating seamless application management. By exploring the practical use of both the CLI and the web interface, this chapter ensures readers can verify their setup and deploy applications efficiently, laying the groundwork for automated and scalable delivery pipelines.

4.1 Prerequisites for Argo CD Installation

Argo CD, a Kubernetes-native continuous delivery tool, facilitates declarative GitOps-style application deployment and lifecycle management. To set up Argo CD effectively, a comprehensive understanding of its prerequisites is crucial. This section delineates the necessary tools and configuration settings required prior to the installation of Argo CD, emphasizing a robust infrastructure to ensure seamless deployment and operational efficiency.

- **Kubernetes Cluster**
  The primary requirement for deploying Argo CD is a functioning Kubernetes cluster. Kubernetes, an open-source container orchestration platform, enables the deployment, scaling, and management of containerized applications. For an optimal setup, the following aspects of the Kubernetes cluster configuration should be considered:

  - **Cluster Version**
    The Kubernetes cluster should be updated to a compatible version. Argo CD generally supports various stable releases, but adherence to the latest stable version is advantageous for accessing improved features and security patches. As compatibility may evolve, consulting the Argo CD documentation for authoritative version support is recommended.

    ```
    kubectl version --short
    ```

    ```
    Client Version: v1.21.0
    Server Version: v1.21.0
    ```

  - **Cluster Nodes and Networking**
    A capable Kubernetes environment should consist of multiple nodes, enhancing redundancy and resilience. Argo CD's resource requirements, although modest, can necessitate additional nodes based on concurrent applications being managed. Network configurations within the cluster need to support inter-node communication while allowing ingress to Argo CD services. CNI (Container Network Interface) plugins like Calico or Flannel can be utilized to configure networking.

- **kubectl Command-Line Tool**
  The 'kubectl' command-line tool enables interaction with Kubernetes clusters. It acts as a primary interface for cluster management, facilitating the execution of commands necessary for Argo

CD deployment and administration. Ensure 'kubectl' is installed and configured to communicate with the desired cluster context.

```
kubectl config current-context
```

This command should return the context aligned with the target cluster, validating proper linkage to Kubernetes.

- **Git Repository**
  A Git repository is integral to GitOps practices leveraged by Argo CD. The repository should host Application Manifests, which detail the desired state of the application. Key considerations for the Git repository include:

  – **Repository Structure**
  Properly structuring the Git repository enhances maintainability and traceability. A common structure might organize manifests by environment (e.g., staging, production) and applications. The use of directories or branches to delineate environments can facilitate efficient deployments.

  – **Access Control**
  Configuring appropriate access controls on the Git repository is critical. Implement read-only access for Argo CD's service account to protect against unauthorized changes while ensuring that the repository's credentials are stored securely, leveraging Kubernetes secrets for added security.

- **Technical Environment Preparation**
  Effective preparation of the technical environment predicates successful Argo CD installation. This includes ensuring all necessary packages are present along with establishing crucial configurations on both the server and cluster level.

  – **Resource Allocation**
  Allocate sufficient resources on the Kubernetes cluster to host Argo CD, accounting for CPU, memory, and storage requirements. While Argo CD is designed to be resource-efficient, the allocation should reflect the scale and scope of applications managed.

- **Security Configuration**
  Tested security configurations involve enabling TLS for Argo CD components. Incorporate HTTPS for communication security and authenticate connections via OAuth2 or SSO, aligning with organizational identity management and security policies.

  ```
  kubectl apply -f ingress.yaml
  ```

  An example ingress.yaml can be leveraged to set TLS configurations for UI access.

- **Container Registry and Image Specifications**
  An accessible container registry is mandatory where images of applications are stored for deployment. The chosen registry should comply with corporate policies for security and availability:

  - **Registry Access and Credentials**
    Argo CD requires appropriate permissions to pull images from the container registry. The use of credentials should be securely managed and integrated into the Kubernetes infrastructure using secrets.

    ```
    apiVersion: v1
    kind: Secret
    metadata:
      name: registry-secret
    data:
      .dockerconfigjson: <base64-encoded-json>
    type: kubernetes.io/dockerconfigjson
    ```

  - **Image Versioning and Management**
    Versioning of container images must be consistent and reflect application state changes. Use semantic versioning practices to maintain coherence across deployments, enhancing rollback and audit capabilities.

Argo CD utilizes openness and extensibility principles. Customizing its settings and parameters to fit unique deployment contexts is possible, making understanding the prerequisites essential to leveraging the full potential of Argo CD. This preparation framework provides the foundation, facilitating a streamlined installation and setup process. Implementing these prerequisites ensures that Argo CD can operate optimally, managing deployments across varied and complex environments.

4.2 Installing Argo CD on Kubernetes

The installation of Argo CD on a Kubernetes cluster marks a foundational step in implementing a continuous delivery solution. This section provides an exhaustive, step-by-step guide to installing Argo CD, ensuring an efficient and error-free deployment process. The guidance extends from accessing the necessary manifests to validating the installation and initial configuration. Throughout, this guide emphasizes key considerations for optimizing Argo CD performance.

Accessing Installation Manifests

Argo CD's installation begins with acquiring its deployment manifests. These manifests are pivotal in configuring the necessary Kubernetes resources. Two predominant methods exist: direct application of manifests from the official repository or customized deployment using Helm.

Direct Manifest Application

The simplest procedure involves applying manifests directly from the Argo CD GitHub repository. This method maintains greater alignment with the recommended defaults and ensures adherence to best practices.

```
kubectl apply -n argocd \
    -f https://raw.githubusercontent.com/argoproj/argo-cd/stable/manifests/install.yaml
```

Using Helm for Installation

Helm charts provide a flexible pathway for users preferring substantial customization. Helm encapsulates Argo CD parameters as values, offering granular control over the deployment.

```
helm repo add argo https://argoproj.github.io/argo-helm
helm install argocd argo/argo-cd --namespace argocd
```

Customize the Helm chart values as necessary to align Argo CD with organizational needs, enabling specific resource limits, persistence settings, and authentication methods.

Namespace Configuration

The recommended strategy for deploying Argo CD emphasizes the use of a dedicated namespace, promoting clear organization and resource management within the cluster.

```
kubectl create namespace argocd
```

A dedicated namespace isolates Argo CD components, streamlining monitoring and security management.

Verification of Deployment Components

Post installation, it is crucial to verify the deployment of Argo CD components. Checking the state of these components ensures that the installation is configured correctly and operationally sound.

Pod and Service Verification

Examine the pods and services within the argocd namespace to confirm their readiness. Each component—server, repo server, dex, and redis—must reach a 'Running' status for optimal functionality.

```
kubectl get pods -n argocd
```

```
NAME                          READY   STATUS    RESTARTS   AGE
argocd-application-controller 1/1     Running   0          5m
argocd-dex-server             1/1     Running   0          5m
argocd-redis                  1/1     Running   0          5m
argocd-repo-server            1/1     Running   0          5m
argocd-server                 1/1     Running   0          5m
```

Configuring Exposed Services

Select an appropriate method for exposing the Argo CD server to end-users and administrators. Common practices involve using an Ingress controller or employing a LoadBalancer.

```
kubectl describe svc argocd-server -n argocd
```

For environments supporting LoadBalancers, configure external access through an appropriate service type.

Configuring Authentication and Access

The security of the Argo CD installation hinges on robust authentica-

4.2. INSTALLING ARGO CD ON KUBERNETES

tion mechanisms. Out-of-the-box, Argo CD ships with a default set of credentials, which must be updated for production environments.

Changing Default Passwords

Immediately change the default admin password to thwart unauthorized access risks. Use the following command to reset credentials efficiently:

```
kubectl -n argocd \
  patch secret argocd-secret \
  -p '{"stringData": {
    "admin.password": "bcrypt-hash",
    "admin.passwordMtime": "'$(date +%FT%T%Z)'"}}'
```

Integrating External Authentication

Integrate OIDC or LDAP to manage authentication efficiently. Argo CD supports various identity providers, allowing seamless integration with existing corporate authentication protocols.

Configuring Ingress with TLS

To guarantee secure communication with the Argo CD UI, configure an Ingress resource equipped with TLS. This configuration enhances the security posture by encrypting data in transit.

```
apiVersion: networking.k8s.io/v1
kind: Ingress
metadata:
  name: argocd-server-ingress
  namespace: argocd
  annotations:
    cert-manager.io/cluster-issuer: "letsencrypt-prod"
spec:
  tls:
  - hosts:
    - <your-argocd-domain>
    secretName: argocd-tls
  rules:
  - host: <your-argocd-domain>
    http:
      paths:
      - path: /
        pathType: Prefix
        backend:
          service:
            name: argocd-server
            port:
              number: 443
```

Adjust the <your-argocd-domain> entries to align with the organizational domain structure.

Inicial Configuration and Usage Validation

Upon successful installation, the initial configuration of Argo CD involves adding and managing applications. This setup validates the deployment's effectiveness and expedites real-world usability.

Deploying a Sample Application

Start with a sample application deployment to validate the installation and check the orchestration process.

```
git clone https://github.com/argoproj/argocd-example-apps.git
```

Add this repository to Argo CD and deploy it through the UI for a hands-on validation.

Ensuring Synchronization and Health

Post-application deployment, monitor synchronization status and component health. Utilize the Argo CD dashboard or CLI to visualize application status, paying attention to any sync errors or health warnings.

```
argocd app list
```

The detailed inspection and tailored configuration steps ensure a robust Argo CD installation. With bent diligence towards understanding and implementing each section, any Kubernetes environment can enjoy continuous delivery improvements Argo CD offers, optimized for high performance and security.

4.3 Configuring Access and Authentication

The security architecture of Argo CD is pivotal to ensuring a balanced combination of accessibility and protection in managing continuous delivery workflows. This section explores the comprehensive configuration of access and authentication mechanisms within Argo CD, focusing on securing user access and integrating advanced authentication

4.3. CONFIGURING ACCESS AND AUTHENTICATION

methods, including role-based access control (RBAC) and external authentication providers.

User Authentication Mechanism

User authentication is the first line of defense against unauthorized access. Argo CD supports multiple authentication strategies, from the default local user database to federated identity providers, enabling flexible and secure access control suitable for diverse organizational requirements.

Local Authentication

Argo CD's default local authentication involves the creation of user accounts and passwords stored within the system. While simple to implement, local authentication can become cumbersome for large teams or organizations and is best used for smaller setups or development environments.

```
kubectl get secrets -n argocd -o name
kubectl edit secret argocd-secret -n argocd
```

This command sequence allows editing of the local user configuration directly within Kubernetes secrets, offering direct control over user credentials.

External Authentication Providers

For larger or enterprise-grade installations, integrating Argo CD with external identity providers (IdPs) enhances security and management flexibility. Commonly used protocols include LDAP, SAML, and OpenID Connect (OIDC).

OpenID Connect (OIDC): Allows integration with providers like Google, Okta, and Microsoft Azure AD, offering single sign-on (SSO) capabilities.

First, create a Kubernetes Secret to store the OIDC credentials:

```
apiVersion: v1
kind: Secret
metadata:
  name: argocd-oidc-config
  namespace: argocd
type: Opaque
stringData:
  client-id: your_client_id
  client-secret: your_client_secret
```

Then, update the Argo CD configuration with OIDC settings by modifying the 'argocd-cm' ConfigMap:

```
apiVersion: v1
kind: ConfigMap
metadata:
  name: argocd-cm
  namespace: argocd
data:
  oidc.config: |
    name: MyOIDCProvider
    issuer: https://your-oidc-provider.com
    clientID: your_client_id
    clientSecretName: argocd-oidc-config
    requestedScopes: [openid, profile, email]
```

This configuration allows Argo CD users to authenticate using the specified OIDC provider, simplifying user management and access control.

Role-Based Access Control (RBAC)

RBAC within Argo CD empowers administrators to define precise access controls, crucial for maintaining security and ensuring that users operate within their designated scopes. The RBAC model facilitates fine-grained permission control by defining roles and assigning them to users or groups.

Configuring Roles

Roles in Argo CD are sets of rules that define what actions users can perform. These roles are configured in the 'argocd-rbac-cm' ConfigMap.

```
apiVersion: v1
kind: ConfigMap
metadata:
  name: argocd-rbac-cm
  namespace: argocd
data:
  policy.csv: |
    p, role:admin, applications, *, */*, allow
    p, role:developer, applications, get, */*, allow
    p, role:developer, applications, sync, default/*, allow
    p, role:viewer, applications, get, */*, allow

  role:admin, data:
    description: Full access to all applications and settings.

  role:developer, data:
    description: Can view and sync applications but cannot alter settings.

  role:viewer, data:
    description: Read-only access to applications.
```

4.3. CONFIGURING ACCESS AND AUTHENTICATION

In this configuration, three roles are created: 'admin', 'developer', and 'viewer', each with distinct permission sets. This stratification ensures operational clarity and reduces the risk of privilege escalation.

Assigning Roles to Users

Roles can be assigned to specific users or groups based on OIDC claims or their username.

```
policy.default:
    g, username, role:developer
    g, oidc:sub, role:viewer
```

This snippet assigns the 'developer' role to a specific username and the 'viewer' role to users authenticated via an OIDC claim.

Securing the Argo CD API

The Argo CD API is integral for automation and scripting in CI/CD pipelines. Securing its access is vital to prevent abuse and ensure that only authenticated requests are processed.

API Tokens

API tokens offer programmatic access to Argo CD, typically used by automation scripts and CI/CD pipelines. Tokens can be generated using the 'argocd' command-line interface (CLI).

```
argocd login <argocd-server> --username <username> --password <password>
argocd account generate-token --account <account name>
```

The generated token should be treated as sensitive information and stored securely.

Transport Layer Security (TLS)

All communications with the Argo CD API should occur over HTTPS to prevent eavesdropping and man-in-the-middle attacks. Ensuring TLS is enforced entails configuring an Ingress with TLS certificates.

```
apiVersion: networking.k8s.io/v1
kind: Ingress
metadata:
  name: argocd-server-ingress
  namespace: argocd
  annotations:
    nginx.ingress.kubernetes.io/ssl-redirect: "true"
spec:
  tls:
  - hosts:
```

```
    - argocd.yourdomain.com
      secretName: argocd-tls
  rules:
  - host: argocd.yourdomain.com
    http:
      paths:
      - path: /
        pathType: ImplementationSpecific
        backend:
          service:
            name: argocd-server
            port:
              number: 443
```

This configuration illustrates enforcing HTTPS on the Argo CD server, securing all ingress points with TLS.

Auditing and Monitoring Access

Regular auditing and monitoring of access logs are fundamental practices in maintaining the integrity and security of Argo CD. These practices help in identifying any potential anomalies or unauthorized access attempts.

Enabling Audit Logs

Audit logging can be enabled by configuring Argo CD to write detailed logs of access and operations to a centralized logging service or persistent storage.

Using Monitoring Tools

Integrate with monitoring services like Prometheus and Grafana to visualize access patterns and alert on suspicious activities. Deploy exporters to collect and expose Argo CD metrics that can be consumed by these tools.

```
kubectl apply -f prometheus-exporter.yaml
```

This allows comprehensive visibility into Argo CD activities, facilitating preventive and responsive security strategies.

Access and authentication are critical components of securing any application lifecycle management tool. Argo CD provides a robust framework through local auth, OIDC support, RBAC, and secure API access, richening the process automation landscape. By instituting these security measures, administrators can ensure that Argo CD remains a reliable and secure centerpiece in the continuous delivery toolchain.

4.4 Connecting Argo CD to Application Repositories

Connecting Argo CD to application repositories is a crucial step that enables it to manage the desired state of applications via GitOps. This integration provides Argo CD with the necessary access to pull application manifests, configurations, and updates directly from version-controlled repositories. This section details the protocol for linking Argo CD to Git-based repositories, explores various repository types and configurations, and highlights best practices to ensure seamless connectivity and security.

Understanding Repository Types

Argo CD supports several repository types, which are primarily Git repositories, as they form the backbone of conventional GitOps workflows. It handles each type through a defined mechanism, ensuring scalability and efficiency in synchronization processes.

Self-Hosted Git Services

For self-hosted platforms like GitLab, Gitea, or an internal Git server, certain configurations need to be in place. Self-hosting provides enhanced control over the repositories but requires managing access, updates, and security internally.

- **Installation Setup:**
    - Install necessary Git clients on the server to enable Argo CD interaction with these repositories.
    - Set up SSH keys or HTTPS credentials for secure access.

```
ssh-keygen -t rsa -b 4096 -C "your_email@example.com"
```

This command generates SSH keys for secure repository access.

Cloud-Based Git Services

Popular cloud-based platforms like GitHub, Bitbucket, and GitLab.com offer integrated features making them attractive for Argo CD repositories. They handle scaling and security natively, reducing administrative overhead.

- **Auth Setup:** Authentication is typically managed through personal access tokens, OAuth tokens, or SSH keys, configured within the repository settings.

```
curl -u "username:password" \
  https://api.github.com/user/repos \
  -d '{"name":"new-repo"}'
```

This example showcases using GitHub's API to manage repositories, which can be integrated into Argo CD uses.

Repository Connection Configuration

Effectively linking Argo CD to these repositories requires precise configuration of repository credentials, leveraging Kubernetes secrets to maintain security and integrity.

Defining Repositories in Argo CD

Repositories are defined in the 'argocd-repo-server' environment by editing the 'argocd-cm' ConfigMap. Specify the repository URL and place its credentials securely within Kubernetes secrets.

```
apiVersion: v1
kind: ConfigMap
metadata:
  name: argocd-cm
  namespace: argocd
data:
  repositories: |
    - url: git@github.com:your-org/your-repo.git
      name: your-repo
    - url: https://bitbucket.org/your-org/another-repo.git
      name: another-repo
```

This snippet outlines configuring multiple repositories, allowing Argo CD to handle diverse applications.

Setting Up Kubernetes Secrets

Personal access tokens (PAT) or SSH keys should be stored as Kubernetes secrets for secure access management.

```
kubectl create secret generic repo-access \
  --from-literal=username='<username>' \
  --from-literal=password='<password>' \
  -n argocd
```

Integrate these secrets with Argo CD configurations, ensuring application deployment can occur without risk exposure.

Enhancing Security in Repository Connections

Secure repository connections form the cornerstone for safeguarding deployment integrity. By employing advanced security practices, organizations can ensure their applications remain resilient to unauthorized interventions.

SSH Access Configuration

SSH is preferred for secure communication over public networks, offering robust encryption for data transfer authenticity.

- Generate an SSH key pair, and deploy the public key to the Git repository host.
- Store the private key in Kubernetes using 'argocd-repo-server'.

```
kubectl create secret generic \
    my-ssh-key-secret \
    --from-file=ssh-privatekey=/home/user/.ssh/id_rsa \
    --from-file=ssh-publickey=/home/user/.ssh/id_rsa.pub \
    -n argocd
```

This configuration safeguards private key integrity, tightly controlling repository access.

Implementing Webhooks

Webhooks provide real-time synchronization between repositories and Argo CD.

- **Setup Process:**
    - Access repository settings and configure webhook URLs to point towards Argo CD's '/api/webhook' endpoint.
    - Define the payload content to ensure relevant events trigger the synchronization process.

Webhooks minimize latency in response to repository events such as code commits or merges, facilitating accelerated deployments.

Repository Health Checks and Validation

Continuous monitoring and validation are crucial to ensuring repository health and sync accuracy, mitigating potential issues before impacting deployments.

Repository Health Monitoring

Utilize health checks on repositories to detect and alert for anomalies such as downtime or unauthorized changes.

```
kubectl argo app sync <app-name> --manual
```

This command provides insights into application sync status, identifying potential repository misconfigurations.

Validation via Argo CD CLI

The Argo CD Command Line Interface (CLI) offers robust capabilities in managing and verifying the status of repository connections and applications.

```
argocd repo list
argocd repo add
argocd repo remove
```

These commands facilitate comprehensive repository management, offering potent tools for seamless operation.

Optimizing Performance for Large Repositories

Handling large repositories efficiently is essential. Features like shallow cloning and specific branch tracking often reduce bandwidth usage and synchronization time.

Shallow Cloning

Retrieve only the latest changes without complete repository history, enhancing performance, especially in CI/CD contexts.

```
git clone --depth 1 <repository_url>
```

Incorporate shallow clones selectively based on project requirements, balancing speed with historical access needs.

Branch-Based Deployments

Deploy applications from specific branches to reduce unnecessary synchronization overhead and deployment complexity.

```
apiVersion: argoproj.io/v1alpha1
kind: Application
metadata:
  name: my-app
  namespace: argocd
spec:
  source:
    repoURL: 'https://github.com/yourusername/my-app'
    targetRevision: master
```

Defining specific branches in application manifests ensures that Argo CD efficiently tracks upstream changes pertinent to the environment.

The connectivity framework between Argo CD and application repositories establishes a fundamental layer for GitOps automation. From leveraging secure credentials and incorporating best practices in SSH access to enabling real-time sync with webhooks, the approach described sustains an efficient, rapid, and secure deployment lifecycle. With these configurations, organizations can harness the full potential of Argo CD, deploying applications reliably and confidently.

4.5 Configuring Applications in Argo CD

Configuring applications in Argo CD is a strategic process that determines how efficiently and effectively you can manage application lifecycles using GitOps principles. This section explores the nuances of application configurations within Argo CD, encompassing application creation, management strategies, and the seamless deployment of applications using manifests and parameters. These instructions and insights provide a comprehensive understanding of how to optimize Argo CD for streamlined continuous delivery.

Creating Applications in Argo CD

The creation of applications within Argo CD begins with defining application manifests. These manifests describe the desired state of the application within the Kubernetes cluster, utilizing Kubernetes native resources, such as Deployments, Services, and ConfigMaps.

Defining an Argo CD Application

The core of an Argo CD application configuration resides in its Application manifest, a YAML file that delineates essential properties like source repository, target cluster, and synchronization policies. Here's a fundamental example:

```yaml
apiVersion: argoproj.io/v1alpha1
kind: Application
metadata:
  name: guestbook
  namespace: argocd
spec:
  project: default
  source:
    repoURL: 'https://github.com/argoproj/argocd-example-apps'
    targetRevision: HEAD
    path: guestbook
  destination:
    server: 'https://kubernetes.default.svc'
    namespace: default
  syncPolicy:
    automated:
      prune: true
      selfHeal: true
```

This manifest configures an application known as 'guestbook', sourced from a public GitHub repository, targeting the default namespace within the current Kubernetes cluster context.

Understanding Key Components

- **source:** Defines the source location for the application manifests. The 'repoURL' refers to the Git repository, 'targetRevision' can be a branch, tag, or commit SHA, and 'path' specifies the directory relative to the repository root.

- **destination:** Indicates where the application should be deployed. The 'server' is the Kubernetes API address, and 'namespace' specifies the deployment namespace.

- **syncPolicy:** Automates synchronization aspects. 'prune' removes resources no longer defined in Git, and 'selfHeal' ensures the cluster's state is consistent with the desired state in case of drifts.

Application Creation via CLI

While the manifest approach offers seamless version control, Argo CD's CLI can facilitate rapid application creation, ideal for interactive setups.

4.5. CONFIGURING APPLICATIONS IN ARGO CD

```
argocd app create guestbook --repo https://github.com/argoproj/argocd-example-apps \
    --path guestbook --dest-server https://kubernetes.default.svc --dest-namespace
        default
```

Managing Application Lifecycles

Proper lifecycle management equips teams to maintain applications, support updates, rollbacks, and troubleshoot inefficiencies or errors comprehensively.

Application Synchronization

Synchronization aligns the live state in the cluster with the versioned desired state in the repository, featuring two primary methods: manual sync and automatic sync. Manual sync offers direct control while automatic sync facilitates faster adaptation to upstream changes with less intervention.

Use the CLI to trigger manual sync:

```
argocd app sync guestbook
```

Verify synchronization results using:

```
argocd app get guestbook
```

Automated Rollbacks

Rollbacks are crucial in failure scenarios where recent changes must be undone. Argo CD stores past manifests, enabling swift restoration when needed.

Implement rollbacks via web UI or CLI:

```
argocd app rollback guestbook --revision HEAD~1
```

This command rolls back the application to its previous commit, ensuring stability after a regression.

Health Assessment and Troubleshooting

Health checks provide critical insights about application components' runtime state. They are categorized into Passenger and Kubernetes resources. Argo CD employs predefined health checks, visualizing states as Healthy, Degraded, or Missing within the user interface or CLI.

Inspect application health:

```
argocd app health guestbook
```

For troubleshooting, check application events and logs:

```
kubectl get events --namespace default
kubectl logs -l app=guestbook --namespace default
```

These commands provide event insights or specific pod logs relevant to the application.

Leveraging Parameters and Overlays

Argo CD's deployment flexibility is enhanced through the use of parameters and overlays, allowing the customization of application manifests dynamically.

Kustomize Overlays

Kustomize provides an overlay mechanism to modify base manifests in a structured and reusable manner. These overlays can encompass varied configurations across environments without altering the base manifest.

Define a 'kustomization.yml':

```
resources:
- ../../base

patchesStrategicMerge:
- replicas.yml

configMapGenerator:
- name: app-config
  literals:
    - GREETING=Hello
    - TARGET=World
```

The example above showcases adding a ConfigMap and altering replica values using strategic merge patches.

Helm Parameterization

When utilizing Helm charts, customize deployments by setting specific values through the 'values.yaml' file, enabling consistency and variability across environments.

```
service:
  type: ClusterIP
```

4.5. CONFIGURING APPLICATIONS IN ARGO CD

```
port: 8080
resources:
  limits:
    cpu: 200m
    memory: 256Mi
```

Apply these configurations during Helm-based deployment to embed environmental specificity in application settings.

Advanced Application Features

Delving into advanced features enhances the capability to manage large-scale deployments, improve resource efficiency, and support hybrid cloud architectures.

ApplicationSets

ApplicationSets in Argo CD can dynamically generate applications based on input criteria, often sourced from automatic discovery mechanisms within cloud providers or custom scripts. This enables flexible, automated application rollout across diverse environments or clusters.

Configuration can define a template with placeholders:

```
apiVersion: argoproj.io/v1alpha1
kind: ApplicationSet
metadata:
  name: simple-generator
spec:
  generators:
  - list:
      elements:
        - clusterName: cluster1
          url: https://1.1.1.1
        - clusterName: cluster2
          url: https://2.2.2.2
  template:
    metadata:
      name: '{{clusterName}}-guestbook'
    spec:
      project: default
      source:
        repoURL: 'https://github.com/argoproj/argocd-example-apps'
        targetRevision: HEAD
        path: guestbook
      destination:
        server: '{{url}}'
        namespace: default
```

Scaling and Performance Optimization

Managing the resource footprint and performance of Argo CD applications is a balancing act, particularly for extensive deployments. Optimize kustomize or Helm configurations to reduce CPU and memory overheads, monitor pod metrics, and dynamically scale to better manage throughput and latency.

Example of Horizontal Pod Autoscaling configuration:

```
apiVersion: autoscaling/v1
kind: HorizontalPodAutoscaler
metadata:
  name: guestbook
  namespace: default
spec:
  maxReplicas: 10
  minReplicas: 2
  scaleTargetRef:
    apiVersion: apps/v1
    kind: Deployment
    name: guestbook
  targetCPUUtilizationPercentage: 75
```

By integrating Argo CD into your Kubernetes workflows, establishing structured application configurations, and employing automated lifecycle controls, an organization enhances the scalability, robustness, and efficiency of its software delivery pipelines. This comprehensive configuration paradigm enables the realization of continuous delivery objectives, nurturing innovative development practices.

4.6 Using Argo CD CLI and User Interface

The Argo CD Command Line Interface (CLI) and User Interface (UI) are powerful tools facilitating operational efficiency and user-friendly management of application lifecycles. By leveraging the CLI, users can script and automate complex workflows, while the web-based UI provides a visual overview of application states and easy access for configuration. This comprehensive overview will guide you through advanced functionalities and best practices for using both interfaces to maximize productivity and streamline GitOps processes.

The Argo CD CLI is an essential tool for managing applications programmatically. Its installation and configuration require specific steps to ensure seamless interaction with the Argo CD server.

Installation and Configuration

Download the CLI binary for your system from the official Argo CD release page, or use a package manager where supported—for example, 'brew' for macOS.

```
brew install argocd
```

For Linux systems, set up the binary directly:

```
VERSION=$(curl --silent "https://api.github.com/repos/argoproj/argo-cd/releases/latest" | jq -r .tag_name)
curl -sSL -o /usr/local/bin/argocd https://github.com/argoproj/argo-cd/releases/download/${VERSION}/argocd-linux-amd64
chmod +x /usr/local/bin/argocd
```

Once installed, configure the CLI to connect to your Argo CD server. This involves logging in with valid credentials or tokens:

```
argocd login <ARGO_CD_SERVER>
# Use admin credentials or access token
argocd account get-user-info
```

Establish trust by using a server's URL. Confirm authentication by retrieving user info to ensure connectivity.

The Argo CD CLI provides comprehensive command sets, grouped into key functional areas such as application management, synchronization, and configuration.

Application Lifecycle Management

Managing the lifecycle of applications is a primary function of the CLI. It enables creation, update, and deletion of applications, along with monitoring their states.

Creating a new application:

```
argocd app create myapp \
    --repo https://github.com/argoproj/argocd-example-apps \
    --path guestbook \
    --dest-namespace default \
    --dest-server https://kubernetes.default.svc
```

To update an application's repository path or target revision:

```
argocd app set myapp --repo https://github.com/argoproj/new-repo
```

List all applications with their current status:

```
argocd app list
```

The 'list' command provides a quick overview of all managed applications and their respective states.

Synchronization and Rollback

Synchronization aligns the live state with repository manifests. Manual sync is often triggered via CLI, particularly after significant repository updates.

```
argocd app sync myapp
```

Rollback functionality is crucial when reverting to a known stable state:

```
argocd app rollback myapp --revision HEAD~2
```

This command restores the application to the state represented two commits ago, undoing recent changes.

Automate repetitive tasks by scripting CLI commands with shell scripts or complex workflows using CI/CD pipelines integrated within Argo CD, optimizing application delivery cycles.

```bash
#!/bin/bash

# Define application parameters
APP_NAME=myapp
REPO_URL=https://github.com/argoproj/new-repo
DEST_NAMESPACE=default

# Create application
argocd app create $APP_NAME --repo $REPO_URL --path guestbook --dest-
    namespace $DEST_NAMESPACE --dest-server https://kubernetes.default.svc

# Sync application
argocd app sync $APP_NAME
```

The Argo CD UI offers an interactive experience for application management, providing a visual representation of application deployments, histories, and states.

Navigating the UI Dashboard

Access via a web browser using the URL of the Argo CD server. The dashboard's intuitive layout structures information into actionable sections:

- **Applications**: Displays a list of all configured applications with status indicators.

- **Projects**: Group applications for management, policy enforcement, and access control.

- **Settings**: Administrative settings for configuring repositories and cluster connections.

Understanding Application Views

Each application entry expands to display detailed status, health checks, and synchronization history, with tabs like Overview, Parameters, Events, and Logs.

- **Overview**: Presents a summary and aggregated health and sync statistics.

- **Parameters & Values**: Expose configuration settings and values passed to a Helm deploy.

- **Events**: System-generated logs from Kubernetes, detailing recent activity and alerts.

- **Logs**: Access execution logs for deployed workloads, essential in debugging application problems.

The UI provides direct control for synchronization and rollback actions through intuitive functions:

- **Manual Sync**: Triggered via the SYNC button, aligns current state with declared manifests.

- **Rollback**: Executed by navigating through application history, restores previously stable states.

Advanced UI features extend management capabilities, supporting configuration changes, environment customization, and alert integration.

Interactive Configuration Editing

Modify live application configurations directly from the UI using built-in editing tools. This flexibility allows timely adjustments without requiring CLI interaction but requires caution with manual changes.

Editing manifests:

- Access an application's Parameters tab.
- Use built-in YAML editors for real-time modifications.

Custom Dashboards and Widgets

Extend dashboard functionalities with customized displays and monitoring widgets. Integrating Prometheus or Grafana allows embedding real-time graphs reflecting application metrics.

Define widgets tracking:

- Deployment successes/failures.
- Resource utilization and alert thresholds.
- Application runtime analytics and bottleneck watermarks.

Effective management of applications via Argo CD's CLI and UI enhances stability, scalability, and security in continuous delivery workflows.

Security Practices

- Secure API access via trusted authentication methods (SSH keys, OAuth).
- Regularly update and maintain CLI versions across all user environments to incorporate security patches.

Optimized Workflow Patterns

- Prioritize CLI automation scripts to reduce manual task overhead.
- Use webhooks for immediate synchronization on repository events.

- Schedule regular audits and rollbacks using saved version history.

User Interface Alignment

- Avoid directly editing manifests in production environments through the UI except for minor changes.
- Deploy applications into separate test environments via CLI or UI to ensure consistent behaviors pre-production.

Harnessing the full capability of both Argo CD's CLI and UI provides teams with the versatility to manage application lifecycles efficiently and effectively. By adopting these comprehensive management techniques, development and operations teams can create robust continuous delivery frameworks that support modern application deployment needs while ensuring agility and responsiveness across development pipelines.

4.7 Verifying the Setup

Ensuring that Argo CD is correctly installed and configured is essential for leveraging its capabilities in managing application deployments in Kubernetes. A comprehensive verification process encompasses functionality validation, configuration checks, and security assessments. This detailed guide outlines the steps and methodologies necessary to confirm the health and readiness of an Argo CD setup, ensuring operational confidence and system efficiency.

Initial Deployment Verification Begin by verifying the successful deployment of Argo CD components within your Kubernetes cluster. This involves checking the status of pods, services, and other Kubernetes resources essential for Argo CD's operation.

Pod Health and Status Checks Examine the Kubernetes pods within the 'argocd' namespace to ensure all are correctly running and initialized without errors or lingering restarts.

```
kubectl get pods -n argocd
```

An ideal 'get pods' output illustrates all components in 'Running' status with zero restarts, ensuring components like the application controller and repo-server are healthy.

NAME	READY	STATUS	RESTARTS	AGE
argocd-application-controller-0	1/1	Running	0	10m
argocd-dex-server-5995597f9c-8hrdp	1/1	Running	0	10m
argocd-redis-6cc947647d-s4k7g	1/1	Running	0	10m
argocd-repo-server-9494d4888-r4tvd	1/1	Running	0	10m
argocd-server-6849dbcb57-kcklj	1/1	Running	0	10m

Service Accessibility Testing Validate service endpoints ensuring 'argocd-server' and related services are accessible. Inspect service configuration for correct type (NodePort, LoadBalancer, Ingress).

```
kubectl get svc -n argocd
```

For LoadBalancer services, check for external IP assignment which indicates readiness for UI access:

NAME	TYPE	CLUSTER-IP	EXTERNAL-IP	PORT(S)
argocd-server	LoadBalancer	10.96.40.7	172.20.20.50	80:31747/TCP,443

Ensure you can reach Argo CD's UI through a browser by navigating to the 'EXTERNAL-IP' at the 'port' specified.

Functional and Application Verification Post deployment validation, focusing on Argo CD's ability to create and manage applications ensures complete operational verification.

Test Application Deployment Deploy a test application using Argo CD to evaluate system readiness and confirm pipeline workflow functionality. A simple example is deploying a known sample 'guestbook' application.

```
argocd app create guestbook \
  --repo https://github.com/argoproj/argocd-example-apps \
  --path guestbook \
```

4.7. VERIFYING THE SETUP

```
--dest-server 'https://kubernetes.default.svc' \
--dest-namespace default
```

Examine the application's sync status post-creation to ensure it reflects accurately within the Kubernetes environment.

```
argocd app sync guestbook
argocd app get guestbook
```

The sync operation should show the application state as 'Synced' and the health as 'Healthy' after a successful deployment.

Validation of Synchronization and Status Monitoring application synchronization and comparing live state vs. desired state checks for alignment discrepancies.

```
argocd app history guestbook
```

Inspect the synchronization history to validate correct deployment and rollback readiness, ensuring that recent updates reflect the Git history.

Network Connectivity and Security Verification Proper network configurations and security mechanisms safeguard operational integrity and protect sensitive deployments.

Network Policy and Connectivity Checks Ensure network policies do not unintentionally block Argo CD component communication. Use tools like 'kubectl' combined with network plugins for policy inspection.

Open visualization tools to map network relationships, revealing any misconfigured access between pods and services.

```
kubectl describe networkpolicy -n argocd
```

Ensure policies respect essential communications, such as those between components like 'argocd-dex-server' and OAuth providers.

TLS/SSL Encryption Validation Validate that all communications are encrypted using TLS/SSL, particularly where sensitive data flows through 'argocd-server' or between UI and browsers.

Review Ingress or LoadBalancer configurations for active TLS settings:

```
apiVersion: networking.k8s.io/v1
kind: Ingress
metadata:
```

```
  name: argocd-ingress
  namespace: argocd
  annotations:
    nginx.ingress.kubernetes.io/ssl-redirect: "true"
spec:
  tls:
  - hosts:
    - your-argo-domain.com
    secretName: argocd-tls
```

Verify that certificates are correctly setup and browsers reflect secure indicators when accessing the UI.

Configuration Integrity and Data Persistence Validation Confirm that configuration files are intact and data persists as expected across restarts, applying consistent state management.

ConfigMap and Secret Verification Check the integrity of ConfigMaps and Secrets by ensuring critical configurations are retrievable and readable by necessary Argo CD components.

```
kubectl get configmaps -n argocd
kubectl get secrets -n argocd
```

These commands cross-verify stored information matches intended configurations, as inceptioned during setup phases.

Database and Persistent Volume Verification For setups reliant on persistent volumes or databases for statekeeping, ensure proper connections and persistent data retention.

Use 'kubectl' to explore volume status:

```
kubectl get pvc -n argocd
```

Review entries for expected binding states, persistence duration, and correlated storage classes, guaranteeing data resilience.

Automation and Operations Monitoring Deploy monitoring and alert systems for comprehensive Argo CD visibility, supporting pre-emptive troubleshooting and operational awareness.

Metrics Integration and Monitoring Incorporate tool support like Prometheus and Grafana for dynamic metrics collection and visualization.

Set up metrics exporters and dashboards to track KPIs such as deployment latency, error rates, and resource utilization.

```
kubectl apply -f prometheus-argocd.yaml
```

Integrate Grafana dashboards to present readers with intuitive, actionable insights from exported data.

Log Aggregation and Alerting Establish log aggregation using services such as Elasticsearch, Fluentd, and Kibana (EFK stack), or native cloud logging services to centralize log data.

```
kubectl logs -f -l app=guestbook -n default
```

Define rules within alerting systems (e.g., PagerDuty, Slack) to receive immediate notifications on critical events recognized through logs or performance metrics.

Periodic Review and Improvement Strategy Adopt regular verification intervals aligned to organizational needs, adapting setup strategies based on insights from monitoring dashboards, deployment reports, and user feedback.

Expand verification processes to incorporate new technologies, methodologies, and integrated Argo CD extensions, emphasizing continuous improvement.

Success in Argo CD setup verification drives system reliability, secures applications, and underpins successful GitOps transformations across complex production landscapes. Engage cyclic assessments, benchmark standards, and boost configurative transparency, achieving optimal operational performance and reliability.

Chapter 5

Automating Kubernetes Deployments with Argo CD

This chapter focuses on leveraging Argo CD to automate deployments in Kubernetes environments, emphasizing the GitOps workflow. It explains the processes for defining and synchronizing applications, enabling automated rollouts and rollbacks. Readers will learn to manage multi-environment deployments and utilize Argo CD hooks for advanced automation. The chapter also covers monitoring deployment health and accessing logs, highlighting how Argo CD enhances operational efficiency. Real-world case studies illustrate the practical application of these concepts, providing a comprehensive understanding of deploying applications at scale with Argo CD.

5.1 Understanding GitOps Workflows with Argo CD

GitOps represents a methodology for continuous deployment centered around the concept of using Git as a single source of truth for the desired application state within Kubernetes clusters. Argo CD leverages GitOps principles to automate and streamline the entire Kubernetes deployment process by synchronizing the desired state defined in a Git repository with the actual state running in a Kubernetes cluster. This section delves into the details of how GitOps workflows are constructed and the automation capabilities facilitated by Argo CD.

At its core, GitOps encourages declarative infrastructure management, where the desired states of systems are defined in a format such as YAML, stored in a version control system like Git. This approach provides clear advantages such as observability, transparency, and the benefits of audit trails, versioning, and history inherent in version control systems.

Argo CD functions by continuously monitoring a targeted Git repository for configuration changes. Upon detection, it reconciles these changes to ensure that the live configuration of the Kubernetes cluster matches the state declared in the repository. This reconciliation loop is critical as it automates and enforces consistency across the deployment lifecycle.

The following pseudo-code outlines the high-level operations of the reconciliation loop:

```
def reconcile_desired_state():
    while True:
        desired_state = fetch_from_git_repository()
        current_state = fetch_from_kubernetes_cluster()

        if desired_state != current_state:
            apply_changes_to_cluster(desired_state)

        # Wait for a predefined interval before the next reconciliation
        sleep(interval)
```

Conceptually, this reconciliation loop is straightforward, yet implementing it in a robust, fault-tolerant manner involves intricate considerations such as error handling, rollback mechanisms, and network reliability.

GitOps Workflow Components

The GitOps workflow with Argo CD comprises several critical components:

- **1. Git Repository as the Source of Truth:** The Git repository is the foundation where all configuration files are defined, maintained, and versioned. This repository serves as the singular reference point for the desired state, facilitating a clear lineage and audit capability for all changes.

- **2. Argo CD Server and Its Components:** The Argo CD server is deployed within a Kubernetes cluster and is responsible for monitoring Git repositories, applying changes, and maintaining state. Key components include:
  - **API Server:** Handles communication between Argo CD and external clients via a REST API.
  - **Controller:** Orchestrates synchronization, health monitoring, and diffing processes between the Git repository and the Kubernetes cluster.
  - **Repository Server:** Manages Git repository interactions, performing tasks such as checking out code and rendering manifests.

- **3. Kubernetes Managed Environment:** This encapsulates the Kubernetes cluster where applications are deployed, managed, and monitored by Argo CD based on the configurations defined in the Git repository.

Synchronization Process

Synchronization within Argo CD ensures that the live state of a Kubernetes cluster matches the desired state defined in the Git repository. Argo CD enables a variety of synchronization strategies, either automatic or manual, offering flexibility to cater to different operational requirements.

- **Automatic Synchronization:** Configured to apply changes automatically whenever new commits are detected in the Git repository. This mode idealistically fits continuous delivery models, where any committed change translates to a deployment without requiring manual intervention.

```
apiVersion: argoproj.io/v1alpha1
kind: Application
metadata:
  name: example-app
spec:
  source:
    repoURL: 'https://github.com/example-org/config-repo'
    path: 'manifests'
    targetRevision: HEAD
  destination:
    server: 'https://kubernetes-default.svc'
    namespace: default
  syncPolicy:
    automated:
      prune: true
      selfHeal: true
```

In this example, 'prune' removes resources no longer defined in the latest Git repository state, and 'selfHeal' corrects any drift in the live state that diverges from the desired state.

- **Manual Synchronization:** Requires an explicit trigger to apply updates from a Git repository. This method provides control over when deployments occur, potentially aligning them with wider organizational schedules such as maintenance windows or approval processes.

Diffing and Drift Detection

Argo CD's ability to detect drifts — or discrepancies between the Git repository and the live state — is a fundamental aspect of the GitOps workflow. Drift detection is implemented through diffing operations that compare the current state of the cluster with the defined state in the Git configuration files.

Command-line tools or the Argo CD dashboard provide visibility into this process, allowing operators to review specific changes before synchronization, which plays a critical role in maintaining operational integrity and security.

```
argocd app diff example-app
```

Operational Advantages and Challenges

5.1. UNDERSTANDING GITOPS WORKFLOWS WITH ARGO CD

The operational advantages of adopting GitOps workflows with Argo CD are profound. This methodology provides a declarative, version-controlled, and reproducible infrastructure that is inherently auditable. CI/CD integrations become streamlined as infrastructure and application code changes are driven by pull requests, aligning with organizational best practices toward DevSecOps standards.

However, several operational challenges accompany the implementation of GitOps:

- **Complexity in Large-scale Deployments:** Managing numerous environments and applications can introduce challenges in repository organization and scalability.

- **Security Considerations:** Care must be taken to secure GitOps pipelines, especially concerning access controls to Git repositories and the information they contain.

- **Change Management:** With automation, ensuring that configuration changes are thoroughly reviewed and tested prior to deployment is imperative.

Advanced Concepts

Beyond basic synchronization and drift detection, Argo CD supports advanced configurations that extend its functionality and adaptability:

- **Multi-tenancy:** Allows multiple teams or projects to use a single Argo CD instance, applying Role-Based Access Control (RBAC) to ensure security and isolation.

    ```
    apiVersion: rbac.authorization.k8s.io/v1
    kind: Role
    metadata:
      namespace: argocd
      name: example-role
    rules:
    - apiGroups: [""]
      resources: ["applications"]
      verbs: ["get", "list", "watch"]
    ```

- **Resource Hooks:** Enables the execution of scripts or commands before and after synchronization processes, useful for complex deployment scenarios requiring additional customization.

Practical Application and Realization

Establishing a GitOps workflow using Argo CD requires initial strategic planning, particularly in determining how repositories are structured and managed. Best practices involve:

- Segregation of configuration files by environment and by application.

- Employing a modular, reusable structure, using templating tools such as Kustomize or Helm.

- Maintaining security through encrypted secret management and minimal access privileges.

Success in applying GitOps principles via Argo CD often hinges on establishing a culture of collaboration and continuous improvement. Teams should be encouraged to engage with version control regularly, partake in code review processes, and contribute to an evolving repository of knowledge captured in the form of pull requests and code comments. Furthermore, monitoring and analysis of how changes propagate through the system can result in refinements that improve deployment speed, reduce system downtime, and enhance overall reliability.

The seamless integration of GitOps practices with Kubernetes through Argo CD can lead to an acceleration of development velocity, provided that meticulous care is taken in its configuration, accompanied by a robust governance model that supports secure and stable operations.

5.2 Defining and Synchronizing Applications

In the GitOps methodology, defining and synchronizing applications are core activities that ensure a Kubernetes cluster's state aligns with the declared configuration. Argo CD facilitates this by providing a robust platform for defining how applications are represented within the Kubernetes ecosystem and ensuring synchronization with the Git repository that serves as the single source of truth. This section provides an in-depth exploration of methods to define applications in Argo CD and manage their synchronization effectively.

The process of defining an application in Argo CD involves specifying a repository that contains the infrastructure-as-code files (usually in YAML format) along with details about the targeted cluster and namespace. Synchronization encompasses aligning the live environment to the state expressed in the Git repository, enabling continuous delivery and deployment pipelines.

- An application in Argo CD is represented by an 'Application' custom resource definition (CRD) that specifies the source, destination, and other configurations necessary for deployment.

- The typical structure of an Argo CD 'Application' manifest includes several key sections:

```
apiVersion: argoproj.io/v1alpha1
kind: Application
metadata:
  name: example-app
  namespace: argocd
spec:
  project: default
  source:
    repoURL: 'https://github.com/example-org/config-repo'
    path: 'deployment-directory'
    targetRevision: HEAD
  destination:
    server: 'https://kubernetes.default.svc'
    namespace: production
  syncPolicy:
    automated:
      prune: false
      selfHeal: false
```

The 'Application' definition typically contains the following sections:

1. **Metadata**: This section includes attributes like 'name' and 'namespace' that uniquely identify the application within the Argo CD context.

2. **Spec**: The 'spec' section details several important sub-elements: - **Project**: Defines which Argo CD project the application belongs to, offering segmentation and management at a project level. - **Source**: Specifies the Git repository URL ('repoURL'), the path within the repository ('path'), and the branch, tag, or commit hash ('targetRevision') to

deploy. - **Destination**: Identifies the Kubernetes API server ('server') and namespace where the application will be deployed. - **SyncPolicy**: Describes whether synchronization should be automated and if 'prune' or 'selfHeal' mechanisms should be enabled to manage resources not in the defined state or to rectify out-of-state conditions automatically.

- Argo CD supports combining multiple sources for a single application using a 'Kustomize', 'Helm', or 'Jsonnet' approach. This capability allows developers to create complex applications that aggregate components defined in separate repositories or paths.

```
apiVersion: argoproj.io/v1alpha1
kind: Application
metadata:
  name: multi-source-app
  namespace: argocd
spec:
  project: multi-source
  source:
  - repoURL: 'https://github.com/example-org/component1'
    path: 'deployment-component1'
    targetRevision: HEAD
  - repoURL: 'https://github.com/example-org/component2'
    path: 'deployment-component2'
    targetRevision: HEAD
  destination:
    server: 'https://kubernetes.default.svc'
    namespace: multi-source
```

This advanced configuration design facilitates a microservices architecture where discrete components can be versioned and deployed individually or collectively.

- Synchronization in Argo CD can be initiated automatically or manually, depending on the operational model and policy defined in the application spec. The synchronization process involves several steps:

1. **Detection of Changes**: Argo CD monitors the specified Git repository for any changes in the branch, tag, or commit level defined in the application spec.

2. **Plan Phase (Dry Run):** Prior to applying changes, Argo CD performs a 'dry-run' of the prospective alterations to ensure that the anticipated state transition holds consistency and validity according to the current cluster state.

3. **Apply Phase**: During this phase, Argo CD translates and applies the Git repository state to the Kubernetes resources.

4. **Monitoring and Health Checks**: Continuous monitoring ensures the application is not only updated but also that its various components remain healthy and confirm to their intended operation post-deployment.

Manual Synchronization: Utilizing commands or accessing the user interface, operators can manually trigger synchronization when necessary. The CLI tool provides straightforward commands to achieve this:

```
argocd app sync example-app
```

This command instructs Argo CD to synchronize the specified application, ensuring the live state matches the declared state in the Git repository.

Automated Synchronization: Defined within the 'syncPolicy', automated synchronization continually ensures the Kubernetes cluster reflects the desired repository state without human intervention.

- A critical feature of the Argo CD system is its capability to detect and automatically remedy drift conditions. Drift occurs when the live configuration in the Kubernetes cluster diverges from the state versioned in the Git repository. Drift can arise due to manual changes or failed deployments that were not reconciled correctly.

Argo CD offers features, such as 'selfHeal' and 'prune', which, when enabled, automatically correct deviations:

- **SelfHeal**: When enabled, Argo CD continuously ensures resources match their declared definitions. If a resource deviates, Argo CD automatically realigns it with the desired configuration. - **Prune**: Facilitates the removal of leftover or unmanaged resources that are no longer defined in the current Git repository state. This feature helps maintain the deployment environment's cleanliness.

- To further enhance application definitions, several advanced techniques and configurations can be employed:

1. **Parameter Overrides**: Argo CD allows parameter overrides for environments using tools and templates like Kustomize and Helm.

2. **Environment Strategies**: Incorporating overlays can dynamically manage environment variances (e.g., development, staging, production) by defining distinct parameter files or templates for each environment.

3. **Resource Limitation**: Using Argo CD's 'resourcesSpec', users can fine-tune and restrict the kind of Kubernetes resources that an application can manage.

```
apiVersion: argoproj.io/v1alpha1
kind: Application
metadata:
  name: restricted-app
spec:
  source:
    repoURL: 'https://github.com/example-org/restricted-repo'
    path: 'restricted-path'
  destination:
    server: 'https://kubernetes.default.svc'
    namespace: restricted
  resources:
    ignoreDifferences:
    - group: apps
      kind: Deployment
      jsonPointers:
      - /spec/template/spec/containers
```

- In production environments, common optimization strategies may include adjusting the synchronization frequency, implementing resource quotas, and employing horizontal autoscaling for the Argo CD controller components to manage loads efficiently.

Ensuring that the Git repository is structured and partitioned effectively is key to promoting high performance. This entails organizing resources logically, leveraging modular patterns, and ensuring repositories are not overloaded with unrelated configurations.

The processes of defining and synchronizing applications with Argo CD, built upon GitOps principles, constitute powerful weapons for developers and operations teams managing Kubernetes deployments. By leveraging properly structured application definitions, implementing effective synchronization strategies, and using advanced configuration management, teams can reliably deliver consistent, secure, and scalable application environments. This results in systems that are not only well managed but also adhere to software development best practices, providing transparency and traceability throughout the deployment lifecycle.

5.3 Automated Rollbacks and Rollouts

In modern software deployment practices, achieving reliability and minimal downtime are paramount. Automated rollbacks and rollouts facilitated by Argo CD harness the power of GitOps to manage application lifecycle events effectively. These operations are crucial for maintaining system stability, especially within dynamic and ever-evolving Kubernetes environments. This section delves into the mechanisms, configurations, and considerations underpinning automated rollbacks and rollouts in Argo CD, elucidating their crucial role within continuous deployment pipelines.

Understanding Rollouts and Rollbacks

The concepts of rollouts and rollbacks are pivotal within DevOps methodologies:

- **Rollouts:** These consist of deploying new application versions to an environment systematically. This process can include sequentially replacing or upgrading components of an application, ensuring minimal interruption to service availability. The rollout process in a Kubernetes-managed environment leverages deployment strategies, such as blue-green deployments, canary releases, or rolling updates.

- **Rollbacks:** When issues arise with a newly deployed application version—such as bugs, performance degradation, or unintended side effects—rollback provisions allow a system to revert to the previous stable state. Automated rollbacks ensure rapid response and recovery, minimizing the impact on end-users.

Rollout Strategies in Argo CD

Argo CD facilitates various rollout strategies, each with distinct advantages depending on application requirements, risk tolerance, and infrastructure considerations.

Rolling Update: This is the default strategy where new application pods are gradually introduced, and old pods are proportionately scaled down. This ensures that the application remains functional during updates.

```
apiVersion: apps/v1
kind: Deployment
metadata:
  name: example-rolling-update
spec:
  strategy:
    type: RollingUpdate
    rollingUpdate:
      maxUnavailable: 1
      maxSurge: 1
```

The 'maxUnavailable' setting indicates the maximum number of pods that can be unavailable during the update, whereas 'maxSurge' specifies the maximum number of pods that can exceed the desired number during the process.

Blue-Green Deployment: This strategy involves running two environments simultaneously—blue (current version) and green (new version). Users are directed to the green environment upon successful verification, while the blue environment stands by as a fallback.

```
apiVersion: argoproj.io/v1alpha1
kind: Application
metadata:
  name: example-blue-green
spec:
  syncPolicy:
    blueGreen:
      autoPromotionEnabled: false
      previewReplicaCount: 2
```

By setting 'autoPromotionEnabled' to false, manual verification is required before shifting traffic, providing an additional assurance layer before full migration to the new version.

Canary Release: Canary releases incrementally introduce the new version to a subset of users, reducing risk by watching the performance and error metrics collected to make informed improvement decisions before a wider rollout.

5.3. AUTOMATED ROLLBACKS AND ROLLOUTS

```
apiVersion: argoproj.io/v1alpha1
kind: Rollout
metadata:
  name: example-canary-release
spec:
  progressDeadlineSeconds: 600
  canary:
    steps:
      - setWeight: 10
      - pause:
          duration: 5m
      - setWeight: 50
      - pause: {}
```

Steps within the canary strategy set traffic weights and introduce pauses to systematically validate each phase, thus incorporating robust checks.

Automated Rollbacks with Argo CD

Argo CD automates rollback processes, providing mechanisms to detect errors or deviations from healthy states during and following deployments. The automation flow is governed by health checks, status evaluations, and configurable thresholds.

Health Checks: Involves continuous monitoring of application metrics and health parameters. If predetermined criteria such as CPU utilization, error rate threshold, or specific metric levels are breached, an automated rollback is triggered.

```
apiVersion: argoproj.io/v1alpha1
kind: HealthCheck
metadata:
  name: cpu-utilization-check
spec:
  metricType: custom
  threshold: 85
  duration: 5m
  actionOnFailure: rollback
```

The above configuration triggers a rollback if CPU utilization surpasses 85% consistently for 5 minutes.

Status Evaluations: During deployment, Argo CD evaluates resource states—checking whether any fall into an unhealthy status (e.g., 'CrashLoopBackOff'). If so, these status changes can be configured to initiate rollbacks.

Configurator Thresholds: These define rules where any deviation from the baseline thresholds initiates rollbacks. Tailoring these to suit application criticality and operational environments significantly influences the reliability of the rollback mechanism.

Implementing Rollbacks in Practice

Practical implementations typically leverage rollback constructs integrated within CI/CD pipelines. This can involve utilizing annotated events or telemetry gathered from logging and monitoring systems to ensure rollbacks occur seamlessly and only when necessary.

Integration Example

Below is a synthesized approach combining CI/CD tools with Argo CD for holistic rollback handling:

- An integration tool such as Jenkins pushes a Helm chart update to a GitHub repository.

- Argo CD detects the change and applies the rollout in a Kubernetes environment using the configured strategy.

- During the deployment process, Prometheus monitors set metrics such as node usage and application performance.

- If triggered, Prometheus sends an alert to Grafana, which in turn executes an Argo CD API call to trigger a rollback.

```
import requests

def trigger_argo_cd_rollback(app_name, argocd_url, auth_token):
    url = f"{argocd_url}/api/v1/applications/{app_name}/rollback"
    headers = {
        'Authorization': f'Bearer {auth_token}'
    }
    response = requests.post(url, headers=headers)
    return response.status_code == 200

triggered = trigger_argo_cd_rollback("example-app", "https://argocd.example.com",
    "your-auth-token")
print("Rollback Triggered" if triggered else "Rollback Failed")
```

This automated flow ensures that all system layers contribute to maintaining seamless operations, with each playing a role in determining when rollbacks are warranted.

Challenges and Considerations for Automated Rollbacks and Rollouts

5.3. AUTOMATED ROLLBACKS AND ROLLOUTS

The implementation of automated rollbacks and rollouts entails several challenges:

- **State Management:** Maintaining exact state at rollback requires persistently capturing and storing the configuration and data states from prior versions.

- **API Stability:** Rollback processes can be hampered by changes in API structures between versions. Backwards compatibility must be carefully designed and tested.

- **Consistent Environment Setup:** Ensuring consistency between pre-production and production environments minimizes the risk of deployment failures that would necessitate rollbacks.

- **Configuration Drift:** Regular audits and reconciliation processes should be employed to mitigate deviations that may complicate accurate rollbacks.

Additional Benefits

Leveraging renowned cloud-native monitoring and instrumentation services such as *Prometheus*, *Grafana*, and *Istio* integrates improvements in observability and metrics-driven decisions, enhancing Argo CD's efficacy in executing rollbacks and rollouts.

The advancement of service mesh technologies underscores streamlined canary analyses, fostering more nuanced deployment strategies aligned to business priorities and risk modeling.

Automated rollbacks and rollouts in Argo CD form the backbone of resilient software delivery practices in Kubernetes environments, encapsulating both technical and operational insights intricate in nature. This empowers teams to embrace aggressive delivery cycles while adeptly managing risk, upholding system reliability, and accelerating time-to-market.

Implementing effective automated rollback and rollout strategies requires a comprehensive understanding of underlying infrastructure, strategic alignment to organizational goals, and a committed adherence to best practices. These capabilities, when combined with the

GitOps methodologies propagated through Argo CD, position organizations to achieve consistent and predictable deploy release cycles, maintaining a competitive edge in software delivery, and end-user satisfaction.

5.4 Handling Multi-environment Deployments

Managing deployments across multiple environments is a fundamental requirement for modern software engineering practices. Multi-environment deployments facilitate isolated environments for development, testing, staging, and production, each serving distinct purposes in the software delivery lifecycle. Argo CD addresses these needs by providing comprehensive strategies and tools to manage these deployments within Kubernetes clusters adhering to GitOps principles. This section explores the methodologies, best practices, and practical implementation strategies for handling multi-environment deployments using Argo CD.

Defining and Structuring Environments

Multi-environment deployment architecture typically involves multiple Kubernetes clusters or namespaces per environment. This segmentation allows differing configurations, data sets, and access controls suited to the unique requirements of each environment, promoting separation of concerns and operational safety.

- **Development Environment**: Acts as a sandbox for developers to build features and experiment with changes. Often less restrictive but frequently refreshed to mirror higher environments.

- **Testing/Quality Assurance Environment**: Used to run integration tests and verification processes, ensuring modifications perform as expected without impacting production data or services.

- **Staging Environment**: Closely mirrors the production environment to validate end-to-end processes under similar loads, configurations, and data-volume scenarios.

- **Production Environment**: The live application setup accessible to end-users, strictly controlled and monitored.

Configuration Management with Argo CD

Configuration management in Argo CD for multi-environment deployments often utilizes infrastructure-as-code (IaC) approaches and employs environment-specific overlays or templating techniques.

Kustomize Overlays: Kustomize is a templating solution natively supported by Argo CD, facilitating management through overlays where environment-specific configurations override base configurations.

```
apiVersion: v1
kind: ConfigMap
metadata:
  name: app-config
data:
  LOG_LEVEL: "info"
```

For environmental specificity, Kustomize configuration overlays can be applied:

```
apiVersion: kustomize.config.k8s.io/v1beta1
kind: Kustomization
bases:
- ../base
configMapGenerator:
- name: app-config
  literals:
  - LOG_LEVEL=debug
```

```
apiVersion: kustomize.config.k8s.io/v1beta1
kind: Kustomization
bases:
- ../base
configMapGenerator:
- name: app-config
  literals:
  - LOG_LEVEL=error
```

With these overlays, Argo CD automates generating and deploying environment-specific manifests.

Helm Charts: Helm is another packaging tool that provides constructs for managing application dependencies and versioning across environments using templates and value files.

```
image:
  repository: my-app-repo
  tag: 'staging'
resources:
  limits:
    cpu: 500m
    memory: 512Mi
persistence:
  storageClass: staging-storage
  size: 5Gi
```

Application Sets: Argo CD's ApplicationSets controller manages multiple Argo CD Applications based on a defined template, automatically synchronizing applications per environment configuration:

```
apiVersion: argoproj.io/v1alpha1
kind: ApplicationSet
metadata:
  name: my-applications
spec:
  generators:
    - list:
        elements:
          - cluster: dev
            url: https://kubernetes-dev.example.com
          - cluster: prod
            url: https://kubernetes-prod.example.com
  template:
    metadata:
      name: '{{cluster}}-app'
    spec:
      project: default
      source:
        repoURL: 'https://github.com/my-org/my-repo'
        targetRevision: HEAD
        path: '{{cluster}}/my-app'
      destination:
        server: '{{url}}'
        namespace: '{{cluster}}-namespace'
```

The 'ApplicationSet' configuration simplifies creation and synchronization across environments through automation.

Security and Access Control in Multi-environment Deployments

Securing multi-environment deployments is vital, with distinct controls applied contingent upon the specific environment's exposure and criticality. Argo CD incorporates robust security models such as Role-Based Access Control (RBAC) to define user rights and manage permissions with granularity.

5.4. HANDLING MULTI-ENVIRONMENT DEPLOYMENTS

```
kind: Role
apiVersion: rbac.authorization.k8s.io/v1
metadata:
  namespace: argocd
  name: dev-role
rules:
- apiGroups: [""]
  resources: ["pods", "configmaps"]
  verbs: ["get", "list", "watch"]
- apiGroups: ["argoproj.io"]
  resources: ["applications"]
  verbs: ["get", "create", "update", "delete"]
```

RBAC can be configured to limit deployments by environment, ensuring operations cannot inadvertently impact sensitive environments like production.

Continuous Integration and Continuous Deployment (CI/CD) Integration

Integrating CI/CD pipelines with Argo CD, especially for multi-environment deployments, propels automated validation, builds, deployments, and rollbacks. CI/CD enhancements streamline environment-specific testing and validation processes, ensuring quality assurance protocols are met.

Example Integration Workflow:

- Developers push changes to a feature branch in the Git repository.

- A CI system, such as Jenkins or GitLab CI, runs a suite of automated tests, including unit, integration, and UI tests.

- Successful tests trigger an update in a branch corresponding to a staging environment configuration.

- Argo CD detects the branch changes and performs automated synchronization to the staging Kubernetes cluster.

- On successful staging validation, code merges into the main branch, where Argo CD subsequently handles the gradual and secure rollout to the production environment.

```
pipeline {
  agent any
  stages {
```

```
stage('Build') {
  steps {
    script {
      // Build processes
    }
  }
}
stage('Test') {
  steps {
    script {
      // Integration & UI tests
    }
  }
}
stage('Deploy to Staging') {
  steps {
    script {
      withCredentials([usernamePassword(credentialsId: 'git-credentials',
          passwordVariable: 'GIT_PASSWORD', usernameVariable: '
          GIT_USERNAME')]) {
        sh 'git push origin feature-branch:staging'
      }
    }
  }
}
```

This example illustrates CI/CD components central to an automated multi-environment deployment lifecycle extending through Argo CD.

Monitoring and Observability

Ensuring visibility across environments is critical for diagnosing issues and tracking application health. Integrations with tools like Prometheus, Grafana, and ELK (Elasticsearch, Logstash, Kibana) stack elevate observability, with environment-specific dashboards delivering refined insights.

Real-time alerts and dashboards can alert appropriate teams to anomalies or performance degradation across any environment, providing opportunities for preemptive remediation actions before production is affected.

Challenges and Strategies for Multi-environment Management

Multi-environment deployments come with inherent challenges:

- **Configuration Drift**: Over time, environments tend to drift due to manual interventions or configuration sprawl, undermining deployment consistency.

- **Resource Contention**: Ensuring infrastructure and resource adequacy may entail cross-environment orchestration to optimize resource allocation.

- **Environment Reproduction**: Localizing issues replicated in production to lower environments requires upkeep to align configurations closely and maintain reproducibility.

Addressing these challenges frequently entails instituting disciplined infrastructure and configuration management practices, process automation, and real-time monitoring frameworks. Proactive planning and resource allocation cater to scaling environments in response to growing application demands, reflecting business evolutions and expansions.

The handling of multi-environment deployments through Argo CD provides a structured, scalable approach within Kubernetes frameworks, fortified by GitOps principles. By adequately segmenting environments, securing processes, and coordinating through CI/CD systems, teams can propel applications from development to production with assurance, accountability, and rapid adaptability.

This effective, streamlined management of deployments across multiple environments enables organizations to drive forward their delivery goals with confidence, ensuring that releases achieve intended outcomes while mitigating the risks inherent to production changes. Adopting these practices empowers robust software lifecycles conducive to strategic progress in an increasingly demanding technological landscape.

5.5 Using Argo CD Hooks for Automation

Argo CD provides a sophisticated mechanism to enhance automation by using hooks, which can extend and customize the deployment lifecycle, integrate complex workflows, and manage tasks involved in application deployment within a Kubernetes environment. Hooks allow users to define specific operations that run at distinct points during the application lifecycle, such as before and after synchronization actions. The flexibility of hooks contributes to fine-tuned control over deployment processes, enhancing the capabilities of continuous deployment pipelines.

Overview of Argo CD Hooks

Hooks in Argo CD are Kubernetes resources with defined annotations that signal Argo CD to execute them at predetermined stages in the application's lifecycle. These hooks can be used to manage dependencies, configure temporary resources, execute cleanup operations, and much more.

Types of Hooks

Argo CD supports several types of hooks, each designed to be triggered at specific moments relative to the main sync operation:

- **PreSync Hooks**: Executed before the main application manifests are applied. Often used for tasks such as performing pre-deployment checks, disabling ingress traffic, or setting up environmental prerequisites.

```
apiVersion: batch/v1
kind: Job
metadata:
  name: presync-hook
  annotations:
    argocd.argoproj.io/hook: PreSync
spec:
  template:
    spec:
      containers:
      - name: init
        image: busybox
        command: ['sh', '-c', 'echo Preparing deployment']
      restartPolicy: Never
```

- **Sync Hooks**: Executed concurrently with the main sync process. These hooks can modify ongoing deployment operations as needed.

- **PostSync Hooks**: Executed after the main application manifests have been successfully applied. Useful for re-enabling traffic routes, cleaning up pre-sync resources, or notifying external systems that deployment is complete.

5.5. USING ARGO CD HOOKS FOR AUTOMATION

```
apiVersion: batch/v1
kind: Job
metadata:
  name: postsync-hook
  annotations:
    argocd.argoproj.io/hook: PostSync
spec:
  template:
    spec:
      containers:
      - name: cleanup
        image: busybox
        command: ['sh', '-c', 'echo Cleaning up after deployment']
      restartPolicy: Never
```

- **SyncFail Hooks**: Triggered if the synchronization process fails, enabling rollback mechanisms or failure notification systems.

- **Skip Hooks**: Implements guardrails that facilitate conditional execution or skipping of particular parts of a deployment.

Integrating Hooks into Argo CD Deployments

Integrating hooks into Argo CD involves specifying Kubernetes resources with particular annotations, which signal Argo CD on how and when to execute these tasks. The flexibility of hooks allows integration with existing systems and workflows, enhancing deployment flexibility and robustness.

Example Scenario: Deploying a Complex Application

The deployment of a complex application may require both environment setup and cleanup operations. By leveraging PreSync and PostSync hooks, you can ensure all dependencies are handled before and after deployment:

```
apiVersion: argoproj.io/v1alpha1
kind: Application
metadata:
  name: complex-app
spec:
  source:
    repoURL: 'https://github.com/complex-org/app-config'
    targetRevision: HEAD
    path: manifests
  destination:
    server: 'https://kubernetes.default.svc'
    namespace: prod
  syncPolicy:
    automated:
```

```yaml
    selfHeal: true
---
apiVersion: batch/v1
kind: Job
metadata:
  name: prepare-env
  annotations:
    argocd.argoproj.io/hook: PreSync
spec:
  template:
    spec:
      containers:
      - name: prepare
        image: prepare-image:latest
        command: ['prepare-script']
      restartPolicy: OnFailure
---
apiVersion: batch/v1
kind: Job
metadata:
  name: cleanup-env
  annotations:
    argocd.argoproj.io/hook: PostSync
spec:
  template:
    spec:
      containers:
      - name: cleanup
        image: cleanup-image:latest
        command: ['cleanup-script']
      restartPolicy: OnFailure
```

In this example, the 'prepare-env' PreSync hook sets up necessary conditions, while the 'cleanup-env' PostSync hook ensures that the environment is left in a clean state. By encapsulating these tasks within Kubernetes Jobs, you can leverage native Kubernetes scheduling and lifecycle management.

Advanced Hook Patterns

Advanced use of hooks can include conditional logic, chaining hooks to create complex workflows, integrating third-party systems, and leveraging custom resource definitions for extended capabilities.

Conditional Execution with Skip Hooks

Skip Hooks provide a way to bypass certain operations based on conditions evaluated as part of the hook execution. For example, only executing certain actions if a specific condition within an environment is met, such as a feature flag or a particular date, can grant dynamic control over deployment operations.

```
apiVersion: batch/v1
kind: Job
metadata:
  name: conditional-hook
  annotations:
    argocd.argoproj.io/hook: PostSync
    argocd.argoproj.io/hook-delete-policy: HookSucceeded
    argocd.argoproj.io/skip: '"{{ (index . \"annotations\").\"deployment-date\" | date
        \"2006-01-02\" | eq (date \"2006-01-02\") }}'"
spec:
  template:
    spec:
      containers:
      - name: conditional
        image: conditional-image
        command: ['conditional-script']
      restartPolicy: OnFailure
```

Chaining Hooks and Tasks

By sequencing several hooks, you can achieve complex orchestration of tasks, akin to a workflow engine. This capability allows dividing sophisticated deployment logic into isolated tasks that are executed in predefined order, promoting modularity and reusability.

Security and Compliance in Hook Usage

Given its power, the use of hooks introduces certain security and compliance concerns, primarily related to executing code within application contexts. Key security practices include:

- **Ensuring Secure Image Sources**: Hooks often run as containers. Ensure images are from trusted sources, scanned for vulnerabilities, and signed.

- **Resource Limits and Quotas**: Apply resource constraints to avoid potential resource exhaustion attacks.

- **RBAC Configurations**: Restrict capabilities of hooks using Kubernetes RBAC policies to limit access to critical resources.

- **Audit Trails**: Enable logging and monitoring of hook activities to ensure transparency and traceability.

Troubleshooting and Optimization

Hooks should be monitored and maintained as part of the broader deployment strategy. Guard against common pitfalls and troubleshoot issues by:

- **Monitoring Execution**: Leverage Kubernetes native tools ('kubectl', metrics, logs) to observe hook execution status and diagnose failures.

- **Hook Timeout Management**: Define appropriate timeouts to avoid lambdas getting stuck, escalating issues if hooks run past their expected duration.

- **Mock Testing Hooks**: As part of the CI/CD process, mock test hook logic to ensure it functions correctly in controlled environments.

By using hooks, Argo CD extends GitOps automation beyond configuration management into full lifecycle orchestration, providing a powerful toolset for Kubernetes cluster operations. Properly implemented, hooks enhance deployment flexibility, safeguard against errors, and optimize operations, driving increased efficiency and reduced risk. The combination of hooks with Argo CD's declarative management framework significantly empowers teams to manage sophisticated deployment workflows that align with dynamic business objectives while maintaining adherence to compliance and security standards. This strategic extension of automation capabilities facilitates rapid innovation, responsive behavior adaptations, and resilient operations within modern cloud-native applications.

5.6 Monitoring Deployment Health and Logs

Monitoring the health of deployments and accessing logs are crucial practices in maintaining efficient and reliable Kubernetes operations. With Argo CD, these tasks are integrated into the GitOps workflow, enhancing continuous deployment by providing real-time insights into application health and detailed logging to facilitate troubleshooting

5.6. MONITORING DEPLOYMENT HEALTH AND LOGS

and performance analysis. In this section, we delve into techniques used to assess and improve deployment health, explore log management, and establish best practices for comprehensive observability within Argo CD-driven environments.

The health status of a deployment provides immediate feedback about the state of the application and its components. Effective monitoring involves not just watching applications during deployment but continuously observing them during their entire lifecycle to ensure they remain operational and perform as expected.

Argo CD utilizes health checks to indicate the status of resources managed within a deployment. This involves two primary levels:

- **Resource-Level Health**: Each Kubernetes resource (e.g., Pods, Deployments, Services) has an associated health status derived from its conditions and states. Argo CD visualizes this through its web UI, CLI, or API.

- **Application-Level Health**: Aggregates resource-level statuses to provide a holistic view of the entire application. Defined health statuses include:
    - **Healthy**: All defined resources are performing correctly.
    - **Progressing**: Deployment is mid-operation with pending updates or synchronization.
    - **Degraded**: Some resources are identified as unhealthy.
    - **Suspended**: Disabled resources require administrative attention.

Additional custom health assessments can be specified using health.lua scripts for more advanced evaluations:

```
apiVersion: argoproj.io/v1alpha1
kind: Application
metadata:
  name: custom-health-check
spec:
  source:
    healthChecks:
    - apiVersion: apps/v1
      kind: Deployment
      script: |
        hs = {}
```

```
    if obj.status.replicas ~= obj.status.availableReplicas then
        hs.status = "Progressing"
        hs.message = "Waiting for all replicas to be available."
    else
        hs.status = "Healthy"
        hs.message = "Deployment is healthy."
    end
    return hs
```

To automate the response to changes in deployment states, integration with alerting systems like Prometheus AlertManager or third-party services (e.g., PagerDuty, Slack) can be implemented. The following setup provides a basic configuration example for Prometheus integration:

```
groups:
- name: argo-cd-alerts
  rules:
  - alert: ArgoCDApplicationDegraded
    expr: argocd_app_health_status == 0
    for: 5m
    annotations:
      summary: "Application {{ $labels.application }} is degraded."
```

These alerts generate early warnings of potential issues, enabling rapid intervention and minimizing downtime or performance degradation.

Logs reveal a rich source of operational data, capturing events, errors, warnings, and informational messages produced by deployed applications. Collecting and analyzing logs is critical to understanding application behavior, troubleshooting issues, and supporting forensic investigations.

While Argo CD itself doesn't directly manage application logs, it provides access to deployment logs through integrations with logging services such as ELK Stack (Elasticsearch, Logstash, Kibana) or Fluentd/Fluentbit and predefined Grafana dashboards.

The following Fluentd configuration collects logs from Kubernetes nodes and transports them to an Elasticsearch cluster:

```
<source>
  @type tail
  path /var/log/containers/*.log
  pos_file /var/log/es-containers.log.pos
  tag kubernetes.*
  format json
</source>

<filter kubernetes.**>
  @type kubernetes_metadata
```

5.6. MONITORING DEPLOYMENT HEALTH AND LOGS

```
</filter>
<match kubernetes.**>
  @type elasticsearch
  host elasticsearch.example.com
  port 9200
  logstash_format true
  logstash_prefix kubernetes-logs
</match>
```

These logs can be searched, filtered, and visualized using Kibana, fostering informed decision-making and diagnostics.

- **Structured Logging**: Use structured formats (e.g., JSON) over unstructured text logs to simplify parsing and querying.

- **Log Rotation and Retention Policies**: Implement log rotation to manage storage efficiency and define retention policies aligned with compliance and operational needs.

- **Sensitive Data Management**: Ensure logs do not inadvertently capture sensitive data, encrypt sensitive fields if needed, and adhere to privacy regulations.

- **Dashboards for Visual Insights**: Employ Grafana or similar tools to create visual dashboards (bar charts, heatmaps) that offer an overview of log data, enabling operators to grasp insights quickly.

Beyond standard health checks and logging, advanced monitoring enriches observability:

- **Service Mesh Integration**: Tools like Istio provide fine-grained metrics and tracing between microservices, supporting more sophisticated analysis of inter-service communication performance.

- **Distributed Tracing**: OpenCensus or Jaeger provides end-to-end tracing across various infrastructure components, crucial for pinpointing bottlenecks or latency contributors.

- **Machine Learning for Anomaly Detection**: Utilize machine learning models integrated within observability stacks (such as Elasticsearch or supported AIOps platforms) to proactively detect anomalous behavior and anticipate potential issues.

```
import pandas as pd

# Example log data frame
log_data = pd.DataFrame({
    'timestamp': ['2023-10-01T12:00:00Z', '2023-10-01T12:05:00Z'],
    'latency': [200, 350]
})

# Identify anomalies using simple threshold
anomalies = log_data[log_data['latency'] > log_data['latency'].quantile(0.95)]
print(anomalies)
```

Such models require widespread training and data consumption but contribute significantly to predictive orchestration.

To maintain high availability and reliability:

- Use automated canary or blue-green deployments to test new changes under actual load conditions before full rollout.

- Enable resource constraints and pod quality of service (QoS) configurations to ensure resource availability under load variance.

- Schedule regular backups and snapshots to safeguard against data loss or corruption.

Real-world deployment monitoring in Kubernetes environments is fraught with challenges:

- **Data Overload**: Absorbing and processing high volumes of data from logs and metrics—establish buffers and filtering strategies.

- **Alert Fatigue**: Excessive alerts can obscure critical issues—employ deduplication and prioritization techniques in alerting paths.

- **False Positives in Anomalies**: Fine-tune detection models to minimize false positives, periodically reviewing alert definitions.

Integrating health and log monitoring into Argo CD workflows enables responsive, data-driven decision-making. Applying best practices and embracing advanced techniques not only assures stability and reliability across deployments but also contributes to optimizing service delivery and enhancing the user experience. By fostering a culture of observability and continuous feedback, organizations refine their ability to innovate within secure, performant, and resilient cloud-native architectures, propelling strategic evolution in alignment with technology and market dynamics.

5.7 Case Studies: Successful Automation with Argo CD

The application of Argo CD for automation in Kubernetes deployments has led to significant success in optimizing development workflows, easing infrastructure management, and enhancing deployment reliability. Real-world applications across diverse industries demonstrate Argo CD's flexibility and power in achieving continuous deployment objectives through GitOps practices. This section presents detailed case studies showcasing how different organizations implemented Argo CD, the challenges they overcame, and the resulting transformations in their software delivery pipelines.

Case Study 1: Transforming Healthcare Deployment Pipelines

Background: A leading healthcare provider was constrained by manual deployment procedures that resulted in slower release cycles, increased downtime, and a high risk of configuration drift. The organization aimed to automate its deployment processes to enhance reliability and speed up integration of critical features into their electronic health record system.

Argo CD Implementation: The healthcare provider adopted Argo CD to streamline its Kubernetes deployments across multiple environments, including development, staging, and production clusters. Each environment benefited from the following transformations:

- **GitOps Adoption:** All configuration files were migrated to a centralized Git repository. This repository served as the single source of truth, ensuring that all state changes were version-controlled and reviewable through pull request workflows.

- **Implementation of Hooks:** PreSync and PostSync hooks were strategically implemented to conduct data validation and backup operations and send notifications to operational teams, minimizing manual intervention.

- **Health and Compliance Monitoring:** Integrated Prometheus with Argo CD for real-time monitoring and alerting, while automated compliance audits ensured adherence to healthcare regulations and standards.

```
apiVersion: batch/v1
kind: Job
metadata:
  name: data-validation-hook
  annotations:
    argocd.argoproj.io/hook: PreSync
spec:
  template:
    spec:
      containers:
      - name: validate
        image: data-validator:latest
        command: ['sh', '-c', 'validate-data-script.sh']
      restartPolicy: OnFailure
```

Outcomes:

- **Reduction in Deployment Times:** Deployment times were reduced by 60%, with faster problem resolution thanks to automated rollbacks and robust health checks.

- **Increased Reliability and Traceability:** Traceability was enhanced with comprehensive audit trails linking every deployment action back to commit-specific changes.

- **Enhanced Developer Productivity:** Developers saw a 40% increase in productivity as automated processes alleviated manual configuration tasks and reduced error rates.

Case Study 2: Scaling an E-commerce Platform

5.7. CASE STUDIES: SUCCESSFUL AUTOMATION WITH ARGO CD

Background: A rapidly expanding e-commerce platform faced challenges in managing its microservices deployments due to increasing demand, global user base, and frequent feature rollouts. Achieving high availability and rapid deployment cycles was critical to maintaining a competitive advantage.

Argo CD Implementation: The e-commerce company integrated Argo CD to revolutionize its deployment processes by adopting continuous deployment supported by the following strategies:

- **Blue-Green Deployments:** Argo CD facilitated blue-green deployment strategies to ensure high system availability while deploying new services. Developers performed zero-downtime deployments by maintaining two parallel environments and performing manual cutovers post-validation.

- **Environment Segmentation:** Leveraged Argo CD's ApplicationSet and Kustomize overlays to efficiently handle environment-specific configurations and manage deployment across geographically distributed regions.

- **Advanced Rollouts with Canaries:** Implemented canary rollouts using Argo CD Rollouts for secure incremental feature rollouts, minimizing risk and enabling data-driven decisions.

```
apiVersion: argoproj.io/v1alpha1
kind: Rollout
metadata:
  name: e-commerce-canary
spec:
  strategy:
    canary:
      steps:
      - setWeight: 20
      - pause:
          duration: 10m
      - setWeight: 50
      - pause: {}
```

Outcomes:

- **Increased Flexibility and Speed:** Deployment frequency increased by 150% with reduced latency and improved system performance.

- **Operational Stability:** Achieved an uptime of 99.98%, reflecting enhanced reliability and confidence in deployment processes.

- **Improved Customer Satisfaction:** Faster feature delivery and reduced downtimes contributed directly to improved customer satisfaction scores and positive user feedback.

Case Study 3: Modernizing Financial Services Through Infrastructure as Code

Background: A financial services firm, grappling with legacy systems, aimed to modernize its software delivery by implementing infrastructure as code to reduce significant operational overhead and ensure compliance.

Argo CD Implementation: The firm adopted Argo CD as a part of an infrastructure modernization initiative that embedded the following innovations:

- **Declarative Infrastructure:** With every infrastructure component declaratively managed via Git, infrastructure modifications became versioned and reviewable alongside application code for increased transparency.

- **Policy Enforcement and Compliance:** Introduced strict Kubernetes RBAC policies comprising role limitations and hooks to enforce required security measures while also integrating compliance tests to ensure adherence to financial regulations.

- **Enhanced Observability:** Integrated with existing observability stacks (Prometheus/Grafana), enabling triggered rollbacks and delivering real-time insights into resource utilization.

```
kind: Role
apiVersion: rbac.authorization.k8s.io/v1
metadata:
  namespace: argocd
  name: finance-read-only-role
rules:
- apiGroups: [""]
  resources: ["pods", "deployments"]
  verbs: ["get", "list", "watch"]
```

Outcomes:

- **Compliance Assurance:** Achieved full compliance with financial regulations through controlled process automation and audit trails, eliminating manual corrective workflows.

- **Resource Optimization:** Reduced resource consumption by 30% through optimized infrastructure management and dynamic scaling components.

- **Highly Efficient Release Pipeline:** Release cycles saw a threefold acceleration which contributed to faster time-to-market for financial products and services, ultimately enhancing competitive positioning.

Lessons Learned from Implementations

Exploring these case studies highlights several important lessons applicable across various sectors considering similar transformations with Argo CD:

- **Start Small and Iterate:** Begin with non-critical services to build confidence and expertise before scaling automation efforts across the entire organization.

- **Cross-Functional Collaboration:** Foster collaboration between development, operations, and compliance teams to ensure smooth integration and alignment with company goals.

- **Continuous Improvement:** Leverage metrics and feedback from automated processes to iteratively enhance workflows and optimize deployment strategies for sustained benefits.

The deployment of Argo CD has enabled numerous organizations to revolutionize their infrastructure and software delivery, transcending the limitations imposed by traditional deployment paradigms. By adopting GitOps methodologies fortified with tools like Argo CD, enterprises are positioned to innovate rapidly, deploy consistently, and remain resilient amidst evolving technological and market landscapes. These case studies illustrate transformative journeys that underscore the potential of automation to elevate both operational efficiency and strategic objectives, delivering tangible benefits to organizations and their customers alike.

Chapter 6

Managing Application Lifecycles with Argo CD

This chapter explores how Argo CD facilitates comprehensive management of application lifecycles within Kubernetes environments. It details deployment strategies for various lifecycle stages, including updates and modifications. Techniques for implementing blue-green and canary deployments are examined, alongside practices for versioning and rollbacks. Additionally, the text addresses strategies for cleaning up and archiving applications while maintaining overall application health. By aligning Argo CD's capabilities with these lifecycle aspects, readers will gain the expertise necessary for efficient application management and operational consistency.

6.1 Overview of Application Lifecycles

Understanding the lifecycle of an application is pivotal for effectively managing and deploying it, particularly within Kubernetes-managed environments such as those coordinated by Argo CD. The application lifecycle encapsulates phases from conception through deployment and maintenance to eventual retirement. At each stage, specific activities, processes, and best practices come into play to facilitate seamless transitions and ensure optimal performance.

The first stage of the application lifecycle is the *Inception*. During this stage, requirements are gathered, feasibility is assessed, and initial planning occurs. This stage sets the foundation for all subsequent development and operational activities. Specification documents are generated to outline the objectives and functionalities, considering user requirements, technological feasibility, and budget constraints. At this juncture, the constraints and parameters within which the application will operate are defined, providing guidance for the next phases.

After inception, the *Design and Architecture* phase begins. This stage involves detailing the software architecture, selecting appropriate technologies, and designing the application components. Decoupling complex systems into manageable sub-systems and defining clear interfaces is critical. Within Kubernetes, this may include designing microservices architecture, which enables independent scaling and deployment of different application components. The architecture must consider idempotency, immutability, and declarative configurations, which are integral to implementations managed by Argo CD.

Subsequently, the *Development* stage is where actual coding takes place, following the set design. Version control systems, such as Git, are used to manage source code revisions, enabling multiple developers to collaborate efficiently. Continuous integration (CI) tools automatically build and test code changes, ensuring new code additions preserve existing system integrity. Ensuring code quality through rigorous testing is a focal point, with a particular emphasis on unit, integration, and end-to-end tests. An example of a continuous integration configuration using GitHub Actions might appear as follows.

```
name: CI

on:
  push:
    branches: [ main ]
  pull_request:
    branches: [ main ]

jobs:
  build:

    runs-on: ubuntu-latest
```

6.1. OVERVIEW OF APPLICATION LIFECYCLES

```
steps:
- uses: actions/checkout@v2
- name: Set up JDK 11
  uses: actions/setup-java@v1
  with:
    java-version: 11
- name: Build with Gradle
  run: ./gradlew build
```

With successful completion of development, the *Testing* phase intensifies in scope. Comprehensive testing, encompassing performance, security, and usability, verifies that the application meets all specified needs and performs well under anticipated operational loads. Test automation frameworks expedite this phase, providing consistency in test executions. Multiple environments mirroring production are used to simulate real-world usage.

The next phase, *Deployment*, becomes particularly crucial in Kubernetes environments orchestrated by tools like Argo CD. Deployment must ensure minimal disruption to existing services. Accordingly, strategies such as blue-green and canary deployments mentioned later in this chapter play a crucial role. Deployment configurations are meticulously defined in YAML manifests, which encapsulate the desired application state, thus enabling Argo CD to ensure environments remain consistent with these declarations.

```
apiVersion: apps/v1
kind: Deployment
metadata:
  name: nginx-deployment
spec:
  selector:
    matchLabels:
      app: nginx
  replicas: 3
  template:
    metadata:
      labels:
        app: nginx
    spec:
      containers:
      - name: nginx
        image: nginx:1.19.1
        ports:
        - containerPort: 80
```

Following deployment, the *Operation and Maintenance* phase ensures continuous performance and the refinement of user experiences. This operational phase involves monitoring, diagnostics, and patch management. Tools such as Prometheus and Grafana are often utilized within Kubernetes to provide real-time insights into system performance and resource utilization, maintaining service levels and preempting potential issues.

Security remains an important facet throughout the lifecycle. Implementing strong authentication, often by integrating identity providers with OAuth or OpenID Connect, hardening network boundaries, and ensuring encrypted communications protect applications from threats. Regular vulnerability assessments and patches safeguard the application against newly discovered security flaws.

Maintenance also involves gathering user feedback to inform future enhancements, and managing updates and scaling operations to accommodate growing demands. The use of Horizontal Pod Autoscalers in Kubernetes exemplifies a means of dynamically adjusting resources in response to an increase in load.

```
apiVersion: autoscaling/v1
kind: HorizontalPodAutoscaler
metadata:
  name: nginx-hpa
spec:
  scaleTargetRef:
    apiVersion: apps/v1
    kind: Deployment
    name: nginx-deployment
  minReplicas: 2
  maxReplicas: 10
  targetCPUUtilizationPercentage: 50
```

Ultimately, the application enters the *Retirement* phase, where it is decommissioned. This process involves archiving crucial data and safely removing application resources. Strategy is crucial to minimize disruptions, ensure data retention for compliance, and manage dependencies progressively over time.

For readers aiming to understand and engage deeply with this lifecycle, a key area of focus would be automating and optimizing each lifecycle stage for speed and reliability. Argo CD, an exemplary tool in this regard, allows for declarative configuration and automation, ensuring the desired application state is achieved across all environments. This approach significantly mitigates errors and manual effort, paving the way for robust application delivery pipelines. Understanding these stages enriches one's ability to manage complex applications effectively, optimize development practices, and most importantly, deliver consistent user experiences in dynamically evolving technological landscapes.

6.2 Deploying Applications with Argo CD

Deploying applications in a Kubernetes environment can be a complex endeavor without the right toolset. Argo CD comes forth as a powerful continuous delivery (CD) tool specifically designed to cater to Kubernetes by managing application deployments using GitOps principles. Argo CD ensures that a declared desired state in a Git repository is reconciled with the live state within a Kubernetes cluster, making the deployment process transparent, automated, and reliable.

Central to deploying applications with Argo CD is the concept of a *desired state*. In Argo CD, the desired state of an application is defined by Kubernetes manifests, Helm charts, or Kustomize configurations stored in a version-controlled repository. The system continuously monitors these manifests, automatically synchronizing the live state to reflect any changes, thus reducing the manual effort often associated with deployments.

When initiating application deployment with Argo CD, the system's configuration involves several key components that must be carefully defined. The first step involves setting up the Argo CD server, which acts as the control plane, interfacing between your Git repository and the Kubernetes clusters you wish to manage. Additionally, Argo CD's authentication and access controls are robustly designed to secure interactions with Kubernetes resources, often employing features like Single Sign-On (SSO) for user management and RBAC for granular permission settings.

To exemplify the deployment workflow in Argo CD, start by defining an *Application* resource. This CRD (Custom Resource Definition) dictates how Argo CD references and synchronizes an application with its version-controlled configuration.

```
apiVersion: argoproj.io/v1alpha1
kind: Application
```

```yaml
metadata:
  name: guestbook
  namespace: argocd
spec:
  project: default
  source:
    repoURL: 'https://github.com/argoproj/argocd-example-apps'
    targetRevision: HEAD
    path: guestbook
  destination:
    server: 'https://kubernetes.default.svc'
    namespace: default
  syncPolicy:
    automated:
      prune: true
      selfHeal: true
```

In this YAML definition:

- The source field specifies where the application manifests are located, the target branch, and the path within the repository.

- The destination field determines where in the Kubernetes cluster the application should be deployed, specifying the API server and namespace.

- A syncPolicy allows for automated synchronization, ensuring that any drift between the desired state and the live state is reconciled promptly.

Notably, Argo CD ensures that deployments remain non-intrusive by supporting automated rollback and progressive synchronization, which verifies the integrity of updates before completing the deployment. These procedures significantly enhance deployment stability.

An integral feature of Argo CD is its webhook integration capability, which aligns perfectly with a GitOps workflow. Webhooks automatically trigger application synchronization whenever a new commit is pushed to the configured Git repository. This immediate feedback loop is complemented by Argo CD's robust logging and monitoring infrastructure, which provides fine-grained observability into the deployment process.

```
{
  "ref": "refs/heads/main",
  "before": "a10867b14bb761a232cd80139fbd4c0d33264240",
  "after": "c5c4c3b5a48623aaaa52e454b6349233f1e518fc",
```

6.2. DEPLOYING APPLICATIONS WITH ARGO CD

```
"repository": {
  "id": 1296269,
  "name": "argocd-gitops",
  "owner": {
    "name": "octocat"
  }
},
"pusher": {
  "name": "octocat",
  "email": "octocat@github.com"
}
}
```

In practice, the benefits of deploying applications with Argo CD manifest through improved scalability, reduced outage times, and decreased human-driven error rates. For example, multi-cluster management, facilitated by Argo CD, allows a single source of truth to drive synchronized deployments across diverse environments, a crucial feature for organizations balancing development, staging, and production clusters.

Moreover, the inherent support for Helm Charts and Kustomize provides flexibility and power in defining application environments. Helm, being the package manager for Kubernetes, simplifies application deployment through predefined chart templates, making it easier to handle complex applications with parameterized configurations. Kustomize, on the other hand, allows practitioners to customize raw, template-free YAML files, enabling easier management of Kubernetes configurations by overlaying modifications atop base configurations.

```
apiVersion: v2
name: mysql
description: A basic MySQL helm chart for demonstration
version: 1.0.0
appVersion: 5.7
dependencies:
  - name: "percona"
    version: "1.0.0"
    repository: "https://percona-charts.storage.googleapis.com"
```

Argo CD's application dashboard furnishes real-time status updates, historical deployment logs, and detailed diffs between desired and live states, offering meaningful insights and enhancing users' ability to make informed decisions quickly.

From a security perspective, encrypting communication channels between Argo CD components and Kubernetes clusters is paramount. Utilizing TLS certificates for all communications ensures that data integrity and confidentiality are maintained. Additionally, setting up authenticating proxies or network policies can further safeguard access to Argo CD.

Deployments often require custom hooks or additional configurations which might not be covered by default application manifests. Argo CD supports customization through pre-sync and post-sync hooks, which provide an opportunity to define supplementary tasks that surround the synchronization process, thus increasing flexibility and adaptability for complex deployment requirements.

To sum up, deploying applications with Argo CD requires practitioners to leverage its comprehensive feature set to streamline deployment processes. By aligning with GitOps principles, embracing declarative configurations, and utilizing its robust synchronization and monitoring capabilities, organizations can achieve more stable, efficient, and secure Kubernetes application deployments, ultimately driving innovation and maintaining competitive advantage.

6.3 Updating and Modifying Applications

The dynamic nature of software development necessitates regular updates and modifications to deployed applications. These changes may range from minor bug fixes and feature enhancements to major architectural shifts and performance improvements. Within the Kubernetes ecosystem, especially when managed by tools like Argo CD, the efficiency and stability of application modifications become paramount.

Version Control and Change Management

Fundamentally, updating applications in a Kubernetes environment under a GitOps framework involves changing the version-controlled source of truth, typically YAML manifests or Helm charts stored in a Git repository. Every such update is meticulously tracked, ensuring a comprehensive history of changes. This approach not only facilitates auditability but also empowers teams with rollback capabilities if sub-

6.3. UPDATING AND MODIFYING APPLICATIONS

sequent issues arise.

An exemplary change in a Kubernetes Deployment manifest might look as follows:

```
apiVersion: apps/v1
kind: Deployment
metadata:
  name: webapp-deployment
  namespace: production
spec:
  replicas: 3
  template:
    spec:
      containers:
      - name: webapp
        image: webapp:1.0
        ports:
        - containerPort: 8080
        resources:
          requests:
            memory: "256Mi"
            cpu: "500m"
          limits:
            memory: "512Mi"
            cpu: "1"
```

In this diff output, resource requests and limits are modified, reflecting an increase in allocated memory and CPU for the application container—a common type of modification driven by traffic increases or performance optimization needs.

Automated Synchronization with Argo CD

Argo CD's automation engine can quickly synchronize these changes to the Kubernetes environment, minimizing downtime and human intervention. Through its continuous synchronization process, Argo CD observes the Git repository for new commits, signaling there has been a change to the manifests. This triggers a new deployment cycle to align the live state with the desired state.

The use of annotation-driven synchronization policies can further refine this process, enabling hooks or specific strategies that dictate how changes are propagated. For example, a team might want certain changes to necessitate manual approval, providing an additional layer of oversight.

```
metadata:
  annotations:
    argocd.argoproj.io/sync-wave: "0"
```

```
argocd.argoproj.io/sync-options: Prune=false
```

Configuring and Executing Updates with Helm

Helm, as a package manager for Kubernetes, simplifies updates through its chart-based approach. Modifications are executed by updating chart values or composing new chart templates. Helm automatically manages version increments, providing users with a seamless interface for conducting upgrades or rollbacks.

Example of upgrading an application using Helm:

```
$ helm upgrade --install webapp . -f values-production.yaml
```

This command updates the application with new configurations specified in the values-production.yaml file. Helm's inherent ability to diff new and existing deployments is invaluable for auditing purposes, offering insights into differences before the changes are applied.

Ensuring Stability with Canary Deployments

Incorporating canary deployments allows for precisely controlled rollouts of changes to a small subset of users before full deployment, using real-time feedback to guide further exposure. Argo CD's integration with rollouts facilitates canary-driven updates, making it easy to define and automate these processes.

Example of a canary strategy in an Argo CD rollouts specification:

```
apiVersion: argoproj.io/v1alpha1
kind: Rollout
metadata:
  name: webapp-rollout
spec:
  replicas: 10
  strategy:
    canary:
      steps:
        - setWeight: 10
        - pause: {duration: 10m}
        - setWeight: 50
  selector:
    matchLabels:
      app: webapp
  template:
    spec:
      containers:
        - name: webapp
          image: webapp:2.0
```

6.3. UPDATING AND MODIFYING APPLICATIONS

The above rollout gradually and cautiously transitions traffic to a new version, minimizing risk and allowing for real-time adjustments based on defined success criteria or performance monitoring.

Security and Compliance in Updates

Security, often a paramount concern during application updates, is addressed by integrating automated security checks within the CI/CD pipeline. Utilizing tools like Clair for container vulnerability scanning or Snyk for dependency analysis ensures that newly introduced changes do not compromise security postures, fostering trust and reliability.

Furthermore, Argo CD's RBAC model helps enforce policy compliance, managing who can make changes and under what conditions. This control mechanism ensures consistent security standards across all team operations, reducing the risk of breaches during updates.

Rolling Back Changes

In the event of significant issues introduced by an update, swift rollback capabilities are essential. GitOps inherently supports rollbacks, as reverting to a prior version simply entails re-applying YAML manifests from a previous commit, automatically prompting Argo CD to reconcile the changed desired state with the cluster's live state.

```
$ git revert HEAD
$ git push origin main
```

Executing the above commands reverts the last committed change and prompts Argo CD to execute a rollback operation within Kubernetes, preserving cluster stability.

Dealing with Configuration Management

Applications frequently undergo updates beyond just the codebase, often involving configuration changes such as environment variables or secrets. Kubernetes and Argo CD facilitate this through ConfigMaps and Secrets:

```
apiVersion: v1
kind: ConfigMap
metadata:
  name: webapp-config
  namespace: production
data:
  LOG_LEVEL: INFO
```

```
MAX_CONNECTIONS: "200"
```

When such ConfigMaps are updated in the Git repository, Argo CD automates synchronization, applying these changes to running applications without requiring full redeployments.

Post-Update Verification and Monitoring

Finally, any update process is incomplete without thorough validation and monitoring to ensure the changes achieve the intended effect without disrupting service performance. Implementing both health checks and service-level objectives (SLOs) can validate applications' endurance under new configurations.

The use of Prometheus and Grafana continues to be essential in this context, rendering performance metrics and logs that offer an analytical view into post-deployment activities. Real-time alerts inform DevOps teams of any anomalies, facilitating prompt response and mitigation.

In summary, the process of updating and modifying applications in environments governed by Kubernetes and Argo CD becomes a disciplined exercise in change management. By combining version control, continuous integration, deployment flexibility, and security best practices, development teams can efficiently implement updates while maintaining application stability and performance, underpinning consistent, robust service delivery. This strategic approach to updates not only prepares applications to handle the dynamic nature of modern workloads but also integrates them seamlessly into evolving enterprise goals and user expectations.

6.4 Implementing Blue-Green and Canary Deployments

In the multifaceted realm of application delivery, deploying updates can pose significant challenges if attempted without a structured mechanism to control risks and optimize the process. Two popular strategies—blue-green and canary deployments—address these challenges by facilitating safer, more efficient application rollouts in

6.4. IMPLEMENTING BLUE-GREEN AND CANARY DEPLOYMENTS

Kubernetes environments managed by Argo CD.

Blue-Green Deployments

The blue-green deployment model is characterized by the presence of two identically configured production environments: blue and green. At any given time, only one of these environments serves as the live environment ('blue' perhaps), receiving all user traffic. During an update, the new application version is deployed to the idle environment ('green'). Once the new version is fully vetted and deemed satisfactory, the router or load balancer is switched to direct user traffic to the green environment.

This zero-downtime strategy not only minimizes disruption but also offers a straightforward rollback mechanism. If issues arise during or after the switch, traffic can be redirected back to the original 'blue' environment with minimal downtime.

```
# Blue service pointing to version 1
apiVersion: v1
kind: Service
metadata:
  name: webapp-service
spec:
  selector:
    app: webapp
    version: v1
  ports:
  - protocol: TCP
    port: 80
    targetPort: 8080

# Green deployment pointing to version 2
apiVersion: apps/v1
kind: Deployment
metadata:
  name: webapp-v2
spec:
  replicas: 3
  selector:
    matchLabels:
      app: webapp
      version: v2
  template:
    metadata:
      labels:
        app: webapp
        version: v2
    spec:
      containers:
      - name: webapp
        image: webapp:v2
        ports:
```

```
        - containerPort: 8080
```

In a Kubernetes environment, services play a crucial role in orchestrating traffic flow. Transitioning between blue and green environments is effectuated by altering the service selector to target the alternate deployment version. The use of environment labels (e.g., 'version: v1' and 'version: v2') enables quick switching and version isolation.

Advantages of Blue-Green Deployments

This deployment strategy offers numerous benefits:

- **Reduced Downtime:** Switchover is instantaneous, ensuring users experience minimal disruption during deployment.

- **Instant Rollback:** Reverting changes is a matter of redirecting traffic back to the previously stable environment.

- **Easy Testing:** Prior to directing live traffic to the new version, teams can conduct thorough testing in the 'green' environment.

Limitations

Despite these advantages, blue-green deployments can demand significant resources, as maintaining two full production environments can be costly and complex. The requirement for duplicate resources may also not be feasible for applications with high data or computational needs.

Canary Deployments

Unlike blue-green deployments, canary deployments provide a more gradual update mechanism. This strategy involves rolling out the new version to a small subset of users first (the 'canary'), allowing teams to monitor the new version's performance and behavior before incrementally increasing its traffic share until it is fully deployed.

Such a phased rollout can identify any potential issues in a safe, controlled manner, drastically reducing the risk of widespread outages or performance degradation.

```
apiVersion: argoproj.io/v1alpha1
kind: Rollout
metadata:
  name: webapp-canary
```

6.4. IMPLEMENTING BLUE-GREEN AND CANARY DEPLOYMENTS

```
spec:
  replicas: 10
  strategy:
    canary:
      steps:
        - setWeight: 20
        - pause: {duration: 5m}
        - setWeight: 40
        - pause: {duration: 10m}
        - setWeight: 100
  selector:
    matchLabels:
      app: webapp
  template:
    metadata:
      labels:
        app: webapp
    spec:
      containers:
        - name: webapp
          image: webapp:v2
```

The preceding Argo CD Rollout configuration illustrates a canary deployment in which traffic is incrementally increased to version 2 of the 'webapp'. With each increase, specific criteria and performance metrics are evaluated to ensure the new version operates smoothly before further exposure. This sophisticated deployment strategy consequently minimizes risk while optimizing rollout outcomes.

Advantages of Canary Deployments

Canary deployments offer several benefits:

- **Incremental Risk Exposure:** Small initial usage minimizes broader impact in the event of a failure.

- **Real-World Testing:** The new version is subjected to actual production workloads, ensuring realistic performance evaluations.

- **Automated Adjustments:** With Argo CD, you can define automated rollback criteria based on predefined performance thresholds, quickly reverting to the prior stable state if necessary.

Technical Considerations

Implementing canary deployments effectively incorporates the use of feature flags, telemetry, and monitoring:

- **Feature Flags:** Enable or disable specific application functionality without deploying new code, facilitating real-time tweaks and adjustments.

- **Telemetry and Monitoring:** Leveraging platforms like Prometheus or Datadog provides real-time insights into application performance and user experience, enabling monitoring of metrics pertinent to business and technical goals.

- **Load Balancer Configuration:** Critical to canary deployments is the ability to control and dynamically reconfigure traffic allocations, often accomplished through Kubernetes' ecosystem components like Istio, which offers sophisticated traffic management.

Limitations

The complexity of tooling and configuration necessary to facilitate effective canary deployments can be daunting, requiring sophisticated automation and monitoring capabilities to execute successfully.

Choosing Between Blue-Green and Canary Deployments

The choice between blue-green and canary deployments often depends on business requirements, resource availability, and risk tolerance. Blue-green deployments might be more suitable for simpler, batch-oriented applications requiring quick switchovers, whereas canary deployments lend themselves well to complex, highly interactive systems that demand incremental adjustments and real-time feedback.

Ultimately, Argo CD's ability to integrate with Kubernetes and support customizable deployment strategies like these ensures that developers can leverage both to achieve effective, risk-mitigated application updates. By understanding the specific advantages and intricacies of each, organizations can craft a deployment strategy best aligned with their operational and technical goals, delivering enhanced value while maintaining system integrity.

6.5 Versioning and Rollback Practices

In the modern software development landscape, versioning and rollback practices are pivotal for maintaining stability and continuity within applications. Robust versioning allows clear identification and management of changes over time, while effective rollback strategies ensure quick recovery from disruptions. Within Kubernetes environments, managed by Argo CD, these practices gain heightened significance, providing structure and safety in dynamic, cloud-native applications.

Versioning Strategies

Versioning in software broadly refers to assigning unique identifiers to distinct states of software, typically encompassing both internal constructs and externally visible releases. This approach facilitates clear communication of changes, dependencies, and compatibilities across development and operations teams.

Common versioning schemes include:

- **Semantic Versioning (SemVer):** This method assigns a version string in the format MAJOR.MINOR.PATCH. Incrementing each segment conveys specific change significance (major structural changes, minor additional features, bug fixes). It helps consumers of the software understand the impact and nature of updates.

- **Git Commit Hashes:** Utilizing VCS-specific identifiers, such as commit hashes from Git, lends precision in referencing specific code states.

- **Date-based Versioning:** Often used in products with frequent releases, this method ties the version number to its release date, such as YYYY.MM.DD, ensuring straightforward temporal tracking.

Semantic versioning is commonly adopted within application development for its clarity and utility. Following the SemVer strategy, consider how a change within a Kubernetes deployment might be reflected:

```
apiVersion: apps/v1
kind: Deployment
metadata:
  name: webapp
spec:
  replicas: 3
  selector:
    matchLabels:
      app: webapp
      version: "1.2.3"
  template:
    metadata:
      labels:
        app: webapp
        version: "1.2.3"
    spec:
      containers:
      - name: webapp
        image: webapp:1.2.3
        ports:
        - containerPort: 8080
```

In this example, the deployment is explicitly versioned under 1.2.3. Conventional use of version tags in image specifications aligns container images effectively with their corresponding application deployments.

Incremental Versioning in Microservices

In microservices architectures, versioning complexities can expand, requiring careful tracking at both service and API levels. Backward compatibility becomes particularly crucial, demanding simultaneous support for multiple service versions when transitioning clients to new versions.

Strategies include incorporating version numbers into API routes and maintaining multiple deployment instances for different versions:

```
# Example route configuration
apiVersion: networking.k8s.io/v1
kind: Ingress
metadata:
  name: webapp-ingress
spec:
  rules:
  - host: webapp.example.com
    http:
      paths:
      - path: /v1/
        pathType: Prefix
        backend:
          service:
```

6.5. VERSIONING AND ROLLBACK PRACTICES

```
        name: webapp-v1-service
        port:
          number: 80
  - path: /v2/
    pathType: Prefix
    backend:
      service:
        name: webapp-v2-service
        port:
          number: 80
```

Defining API versioning in ingress manifests ensures routing fidelity, catering to multiple client versions and facilitating progressive migrations.

Rollback Mechanisms

Rollback procedures are an essential aspect of applying continuous delivery, enabling recovery from failures or undesirable operational states. Rollback practices might range in complexity from deployment rollbacks to database or configuration rollbacks, based on the nature and extent of the changes.

Argo CD Rollback Capabilities

Performing rollbacks in Argo CD typically involves:

- **Reverting Repository State:** A revert in the Git repository to a previous commit effectively triggers a rollback, as Argo CD aligns the cluster state with the reverted desired state.

- **Using Application Histories:** Argo CD also maintains an application history containing previous synchronized states, allowing users to select any of these states for rollback with a single command or interface action.

For example, a rollback command might look like:

```
$ argocd app rollback webapp --to-revision 1.2.2
```

By specifying a version, this command reverts the application webapp to the stated revision, achieved through Argo CD's GitOps-based synchronizing capabilities.

Database Rollback Considerations

Beyond application code and deployment configurations, rollbacks might affect associated databases. For transactional and consistent operations, databases often demand robust versioning strategies aligning with application versions. This may involve utilizing migrations with reversible actions, managed by tools like Flyway or Liquibase, ensuring schema changes can be undone cleanly.

```
liquibase --changeLogFile=changelog.xml rollbackCount 1
```

This rollback mechanism addresses database schema changes, aligning them with application code to maintain overall integrity during rollbacks.

Testing Rollback Scenarios

Thorough testing of rollback procedures ensures that emergency responses to incidents are effective and seamless. Underlying systems must support transactional consistency and idempotency, reducing ambiguity and ensuring deterministic rollback outcomes. Test environments should emulate production states, applying dry-run tests to validate rollback capabilities without affecting live systems.

Observability and Monitoring

Effective versioning and rollback practices include monitoring the application lifecycle through robust observability infrastructure. Monitoring tools such as Prometheus or ELK Stack ensure that all changes, rollbacks inclusive, are auditable, providing insights into the stability and performance impacts of these transitions.

Alerts can be configured to signal deviations in expected parameters, creating responsive, adaptive environments that promptly address potential issues.

Integrating with CI/CD Pipelines

Automating rollback procedures in the continuous integration and continuous delivery (CI/CD) pipelines ensures rapid, consistent responses to failures. Pipelines are configured to perform automated tests, ensuring application states meet the required criteria before deployment proceeds or executes rollbacks.

```
pipeline:
  stages:
    - name: Deploy
```

```
jobs:
  - name: Deploy to staging
    deploy:
      app: webapp
- name: Validate
  jobs:
    - name: Run tests
      test:
        script: ./run_tests.sh
      fail-criteria:
        any: [error, test-failure]
      actions:
        - rollback
```

This script structure represents a simplified depiction, articulating rollback actions for any failure detected during the validation stage, ensuring deployments remain resilient against unexpected conditions.

Overall, effective application of versioning and rollback practices is a cornerstone of resilient software delivery. By managing application state changes with precision and reliability, teams can build and deploy with confidence, embracing continuous adaptation while safeguarding system integrity. In articulating powerful GitOps contributions within Kubernetes ecosystems, Argo CD emerges as a central enabler of these crucial practices, enhancing both the predictability and agility of software releases.

6.6 Cleaning Up and Archiving Applications

As applications reach the end of their lifecycle, it is crucial to properly clean up and archive resources to maintain the efficiency, security, and cost-effectiveness of a Kubernetes environment. This process involves decommissioning unused or obsolete resources, retaining critical data for future reference, and ensuring that all cleanup operations adhere to compliance requirements and organizational policies. Within an Argo CD managed ecosystem, systematic methodologies for cleaning up and archiving applications ensure robust management, mitigate risks, and optimize resource utilization.

Resource Decommissioning

The first step in cleaning up applications is identifying and decommissioning resources that are no longer necessary. These resources can include unused deployment instances, outdated configuration maps, orphaned volumes, and any other persistent state left behind by old versions of applications.

Argo CD facilitates this process through automated pruning of Kubernetes resources. When an application is no longer required, Argo CD can prune associated resources that are no longer described in the source repository, guaranteeing environmental compliance with the declared state.

```
apiVersion: argoproj.io/v1alpha1
kind: Application
metadata:
  name: obsolete-app
spec:
  project: default
  source:
    repoURL: 'https://github.com/org/obsolete-app'
    targetRevision: HEAD
    path: obsolete-app
  destination:
    server: 'https://kubernetes.default.svc'
    namespace: default
  syncPolicy:
    automated:
      prune: true
```

In this example, the 'prune' option ensures that during synchronization, resources not described in the desired state are automatically removed, guaranteeing that obsolete components do not linger.

Data Retention and Archiving

While resource decommissioning focuses on eliminating unnecessary components, archiving is concerned with retaining important data and logs for compliance, reporting, or future analysis. Environments must implement strategies for data persistence, often relying on dedicated storage solutions.

Using Persistent Volumes and Snapshot Operations

Within Kubernetes, persistent volumes (PVs) offer a solution for maintaining application state, with support for snapshotting data before decommissioning. Automated snapshot tools, typically integrated with cloud provider APIs or storage plugins, enable regular data backups, allowing teams to effectively archive data points tied to specific time

6.6. CLEANING UP AND ARCHIVING APPLICATIONS

intervals.

```
apiVersion: snapshot.storage.k8s.io/v1beta1
kind: VolumeSnapshot
metadata:
  name: obsolete-app-snapshot
spec:
  source:
    persistentVolumeClaimName: obsolete-app-pvc
```

In this YAML configuration, the snapshot encapsulates the persistent volume claim (PVC) associated with an application, serving as a point-in-time copy of the data. These snapshots can be moved to long-term storage or re-applied to restore services if required.

Developing an Archival Strategy

For organizations handling sensitive data, articulated archival strategies encompass data encryption, access control, and compliance verification. Regulatory requirements such as GDPR or HIPAA define retention periods, encryption standards, and access restrictions, obligating organizations to align with these mandates while archiving data.

Configuration Management and Archival

Configuration management equally benefits from archiving processes, offering historical configurations for audits and troubleshooting. Version-controlled configurations in Git repositories inherently build an archival framework, ensuring that rollback or reference is facilitated as required.

Disaster Recovery Planning

While primarily focusing on cleanup, archiving also plays a crucial role in disaster recovery planning. By retaining critical application states and logs, systems are positioned to quickly recover from unexpected failures, minimizing business disruptions. Regular recovery drills and simulations enhance readiness, validating the effectiveness of archiving practices.

Compliance and Policy Adherence

Ensuring compliance with internal and external policies is a priority during cleanup and archiving processes. Organizations must establish clear policies delineating data retention, cleanup intervals, and employee roles and responsibilities in these procedures.

Automation tools, such as Argo CD in combination with other workflow engines, can enforce policy adherence by automatically triggering cleanup actions based on policy schedules or resource usage.

Cost Optimization and Resource Management

Unused resources impose an unnecessary burden on cloud expenditures. Cleaning up applications in a timely manner allows teams to optimize costs, redirecting financial resources to active projects and development efforts.

Instance and resource usage monitoring, often integrated into cloud vendor billing and monitoring platforms, empowers organizations to visualize usage patterns, identify inefficiencies, and enact cleanup interventions.

Operational and Security Implications

Security is integrally linked to resource cleanup. Unattended resources can become vulnerabilities, exposing systems to unauthorized access or information leaks. Effective cleanup practices remove these potential points of exploitation, enhancing the overall security posture.

Authentication and cleanup scripts or procedures often use credential-based access, necessitating strict audit trails and monitoring to prevent security breaches during cleanup operations.

Implementing Automated Cleanup and Archive Pipelines

Building automated pipelines for cleanup and archiving tasks integrate seamlessly with CI/CD workflows, fostering consistent, repeatable processes. These pipelines often execute scheduled operations, driven by scripts or Kubernetes cron jobs, ensuring cleanup occurs regularly without manual intervention.

```bash
#!/bin/bash

# List all deployments tagged as deprecated
DEPLOYMENTS=$(kubectl get deployments -l app=obsolete)

# Deleting outdated deployments
if [ -n "$DEPLOYMENTS" ]; then
    echo "Removing obsolete deployments..."
    kubectl delete deployment $DEPLOYMENTS
fi

# Cleanup unused persistent volume claims
PVCs=$(kubectl get pvc -l app=obsolete)
for pvc in $PVCs; do
```

```
    kubectl delete pvc $pvc
done

echo "Cleanup completed successfully!"
```

This sample Bash script identifies and deletes deprecated Kubernetes deployments, including associated persistent volume claims, executing a basic cleanup routine within a Kubernetes namespace.

In summary, the effective cleanup and archiving of applications underscore operational efficiency, cost management, security, and compliance adherence. By embracing automated systems like Argo CD for resource pruning, facilitating adequate data retention while adhering to archival policies, and sharpening disaster recovery readiness, organizations can ensure their Kubernetes environments remain optimized, robust, and aligned with longer-term business objectives. The strategic execution of these components serves as a critical foundation in the broader scope of application lifecycle management.

6.7 Monitoring and Maintaining Application Health

Monitoring and maintaining the health of applications is a cornerstone of modern software operations, ensuring that systems remain reliable, performant, and secure. In Kubernetes environments orchestrated by Argo CD, monitoring involves gathering and analyzing key metrics, logs, and alerts to detect anomalous behaviors and maintain desired operational states. A robust monitoring framework not only safeguards application performance but also guides capacity planning, optimization, and compliance, paving the way for proactive issue resolution.

- **Foundations of Observability**

Observability in software systems extends beyond simple monitoring. It encompasses a holistic view that includes metrics, logs, and traces, altogether providing insights into system behavior. The relationship between these elements builds a comprehensive context for maintaining application health:

- **Metrics:** Quantifiable data points typically captured over time, representing aspects like CPU utilization, request latencies, and error rates. These are often visualized in dashboards.

- **Logs:** Chronologically ordered, immutable records of discrete events that describe the system states at any point in time. Logs provide detailed context for errors or unusual activities.

- **Traces:** They capture requests' paths as they traverse through distributed systems, elucidating performance bottlenecks and dependencies.

Kubernetes-native tools, alongside open-source integrations, offer extensive observability capabilities crucial to successfully monitoring and maintaining application health.

- **Prometheus: Metrics Collection**

Prometheus is a leading monitoring system and time-series database widely adopted for collecting and analyzing application metrics within Kubernetes. Prometheus works by scraping targets for metrics data at specified intervals and applying defined expressions to generate alerts based on threshold breaches.

```
apiVersion: monitoring.coreos.com/v1
kind: PodMonitor
metadata:
  name: webapp-monitor
  labels:
    team: webapp-dev
spec:
  selector:
    matchLabels:
      app: webapp
  podMetricsEndpoints:
  - port: metrics
```

This example sets up a PodMonitor that registers a Prometheus monitoring target for all pods with matching labels under the 'webapp' application. The metrics are accessed through an exposed 'metrics' endpoint, adhering to Prometheus' scraping model.

- **Grafana: Interactive Dashboards**

6.7. MONITORING AND MAINTAINING APPLICATION HEALTH

Grafana complements Prometheus by offering rich, interactive visualization capabilities. It provides intuitive dashboards that help track key application performance metrics, generating actionable insights.

```
+------------------+
|                  |
| Grafana Dashboard |
| Visualizing      |
| Application      |
| Metrics          |
|                  |
+------------------+
```

Grafana allows for custom alerts, notifying teams when specific metrics deviate from acceptable ranges. Through integrations with communication platforms such as Slack, alerts are instantly shared with stakeholders, facilitating prompt interventions.

- **Kibana and Elastic Stack: Centralized Log Management**

Kibana, part of the Elastic Stack, pairs with Elasticsearch to offer a comprehensive solution for analyzing logs and discovering actionable insights. It empowers teams with powerful query capabilities, identifying patterns, outliers, and errors within log data.

```
{
  "_index": "webapp-logs",
  "_type": "_doc",
  "_id": "1",
  "_score": 1.0,
  "_source": {
    "timestamp": "2023-04-01T12:34:56Z",
    "level": "ERROR",
    "message": "Failed to connect to database",
    "app": "webapp",
    "environment": "production"
  }
}
```

This snippet illustrates a sample log entry stored in Elasticsearch - showing a timestamped error indicating a failed database connection. Log analytics locate problems swiftly, guiding troubleshooting efforts.

- **Tracing with OpenTelemetry**

OpenTelemetry has emerged as a standard in capturing distributed traces, collecting trace data that chronicles requests across distributed components, facilitating root cause analysis of performance bottlenecks or failures.

In Kubernetes, deployed applications can integrate OpenTelemetry SDKs, tracing data is sent to collectors, and visualized using compatible analysis tools, painting a holistic picture of inter-service interactions.

```go
import (
    "go.opentelemetry.io/otel"
    "go.opentelemetry.io/otel/exporters/stdout/stdouttrace"
    sdktrace "go.opentelemetry.io/otel/sdk/trace"
)

func initTracer() {
    exporter, err := stdouttrace.New(stdouttrace.WithPrettyPrint())
    if err != nil {
        log.Fatal(err)
    }
    traceProvider := sdktrace.NewTracerProvider(
        sdktrace.WithBatcher(exporter),
    )
    otel.SetTracerProvider(traceProvider)
}
```

The example above sets up an OpenTelemetry tracer within a Go application, enabling the capture and export of tracing data to a configurable exporter.

- **Health Checks and Probes**

Kubernetes natively supports readiness and liveness probes to ascertain the operational status of application components. Incorporating these probes guarantees self-healing capabilities, with Kubernetes automatically restarting unhealthy containers.

```yaml
readinessProbe:
  httpGet:
    path: /ready
    port: 8080
  initialDelaySeconds: 5
  periodSeconds: 10
livenessProbe:
  httpGet:
    path: /health
    port: 8080
  initialDelaySeconds: 15
  periodSeconds: 20
```

Here, readiness and liveness probes verify essential service endpoints within the application, ensuring the container is live and prepared to

6.7. MONITORING AND MAINTAINING APPLICATION HEALTH

handle traffic.

- **Automated Policy Enforcement with Policies**

Integrating tools such as Open Policy Agent (OPA) enables complex policy enforcement on Kubernetes resources, even during runtime. With defined policy constraints, applications adhere to targeted deployments ensuring reliability.

```
package kubernetes.admission

deny[msg] {
    input.request.kind.kind == "Pod"
    not input.request.object.spec.containers[_].resources.limits.cpu
    msg := "CPU limit is mandatory for all pods"
}
```

This sample policy mandates a CPU limit on all pods, blocking deployments that fail to specify necessary resource limitations via OPA integrations with Kubernetes admission controls.

- **Security Posture Management**

Monitoring involves safeguarding security by configuring alerts for violations such as unauthorized access, anomalous patterns associated with attacks (e.g., DDoS), or vulnerabilities using tools like Falco.

Implementing regular security posture validations reinforces compliant, resilient environments, mitigating potential disruption risks and upholding data protection practices.

- **Capacity Planning and Scaling**

Capacity monitoring and planning ensure that deployed applications scale appropriately, maintaining stability under varying loads. Kubernetes facilitates auto-scaling based on observed metrics, dynamically adjusting resource allocations.

```
apiVersion: autoscaling/v1
kind: HorizontalPodAutoscaler
metadata:
  name: webapp-hpa
spec:
```

```
scaleTargetRef:
  apiVersion: apps/v1
  kind: Deployment
  name: webapp-deployment
minReplicas: 2
maxReplicas: 10
targetCPUUtilizationPercentage: 70
```

This configuration establishes a Horizontal Pod Autoscaler, ensuring the application maintains optimal performance across fluctuating user loads. The autoscaler scales out additional replicas beyond the base to maintain desired CPU utilization.

Maintaining application health within Argo CD managed Kubernetes involves a synergy of observability practices, systematic monitoring, and proactive health checks. By leveraging comprehensive metrics, detailed logs, insightful traces, and cloud-native capabilities, organizations enforce robust application health standards that empower teams with the resilience needed to meet the demands of modern software deployments. Through concrete implementations of observability, applications sustain optimized operational states, driving successful, agile DevOps cultures in evolving technical landscapes.

Chapter 7

Integrating Argo CD with CI/CD Pipelines

This chapter outlines methods for integrating Argo CD into existing CI/CD pipelines to enhance efficiency and automation. Emphasizing the role of Argo CD within the broader CI/CD process, it provides guidelines for integration with commonly used tools such as Jenkins and GitLab CI/CD. Readers will learn to leverage Argo Workflows for complex orchestration and configure pipelines to trigger deployments automatically. Additionally, best practices for managing secrets and configurations securely within these pipelines are discussed, ensuring coherent and agile software delivery strategies.

7.1 Understanding CI/CD Pipelines

Continuous Integration and Continuous Delivery (CI/CD) pipelines are pivotal in modern software development, providing automated, reliable, and efficient paths from code development to deployment. This section delves into the architecture, components, and functions of CI/CD pipelines, illustrating their significance and operational benefits in the software development lifecycle (SDLC).

In contemporary software development environments, the complexity and velocity of projects demand robust solutions to streamline workflows. CI/CD pipelines address this need by automating the processes involved in integrating code changes and deploying applications, thus reducing human error, increasing development speed, and enhancing software quality.

Components of a CI/CD Pipeline

CI/CD pipelines consist of several interrelated components, each playing a crucial role in facilitating automated build, test, and deployment processes. Understanding these components is fundamental to grasping the operation of a CI/CD pipeline:

- **1. Source Control Management (SCM):** The pipeline begins with a Source Control Management system, such as Git, where code changes are versioned and managed. SCM systems are essential for tracking changes and managing collaboration among developers. Code changes committed to the repository trigger the CI/CD pipeline.

- **2. Continuous Integration Server:** A critical component, this server monitors the SCM for changes and orchestrates the build process. Tools like Jenkins, Travis CI, and CircleCI automate the tasks of fetching source code, executing automated tests, and preparing deployment artifacts.

- **3. Automated Testing:** Automated tests are integral to CI, ensuring new code does not break existing functionality. Tests can range from unit tests to integration and E2E (End-to-End) tests, executed automatically as part of the pipeline. These tests help in verifying code quality, functionality, and performance.

- **4. Build Automation:** Build automation tools compile code and package the software for deployment. Tools like Maven, Gradle, and Docker are commonly used, reducing time and effort required for manual builds and ensuring consistency across development environments.

- **5. Deployment Automation:** Deployment automation handles the deployment of applications to target environments. Har-

7.1. UNDERSTANDING CI/CD PIPELINES

nessing tools such as Kubernetes, Argo CD, and AWS CodeDeploy, the pipeline promotes efficient and error-free application releases.

- **6. Environment Management:** Managing different environments (development, testing, staging, production) requires infrastructure as code solutions like Terraform or AWS CloudFormation, helping maintain consistent environments across the SDLC.

The CI/CD Workflow

The CI/CD workflow encompasses distinct stages, each contributing to the seamless transition from code commit to application deployment.

- **1. Code Commit:** Developers make changes in the codebase, and these are committed to the repository. Feature branches may be used to isolate changes until they are ready to be merged into the main codebase.

- **2. Build Phase:** Once code changes are detected, the CI server initiates a build process. Build scripts compile code and package binaries, typically resulting in an artifact ready for testing.

```bash
#!/bin/bash
# Build the project
mvn clean install

# Run tests
mvn test
```

- **3. Test Phase:** Following a successful build, automated tests are executed. This can include various types of testing, from unit tests written in languages like Python or Java to integration tests verifying interactions among components.

```python
import unittest

class TestOperations(unittest.TestCase):

    def test_addition(self):
        self.assertEqual(add(2, 3), 5)

if __name__ == '__main__':
    unittest.main()
```

- **4. Deployment Phase:** If tests pass, the deployment process begins, where the build artifact is deployed to an environment. Typically, this involves deploying to a staging environment first for validation, before promoting it to production.

```
#!/bin/bash
# Deploy the application
echo "Deploying to staging environment..."
scp target/app.war user@staging-server:/path/to/deploy/
```

- **5. Monitoring and Feedback:** Post-deployment, monitoring tools provide feedback about the application's health and performance. Feedback loops are critical for promptly identifying and addressing issues.

Significance and Benefits of CI/CD Pipelines

CI/CD pipelines significantly enhance the agility and reliability of software delivery processes. Key advantages include:

- **1. Reduced Change Lead Time:** Automation shortens the time from code commit to deployment, enabling rapid response to business needs.

- **2. Improved Code Quality:** Continuous testing ensures code changes maintain the intended functionality and quality standards, minimizing defects in production.

- **3. Enhanced Collaboration:** By automating tedious manual processes, developers can focus on coding, fostering a collaborative and innovative environment.

- **4. Consistency and Reproducibility:** Automated pipelines eliminate variability, ensuring consistent and reproducible deployments across different environments.

Challenges in CI/CD Implementation

Despite the advantages, implementing CI/CD pipelines can present challenges:

- **1. Tool Selection:** Determining the appropriate tools and orchestrating them effectively requires careful consideration aligned with project needs and scalability.

- **2. Infrastructure Management:** Efficiently managing infrastructure for CI/CD can be complex, involving both on-premise and cloud resources.

- **3. Pipeline Maintenance:** Keeping the pipeline efficient and up-to-date with evolving software requirements necessitates continual monitoring and optimization.

- **4. Security:** Ensuring pipeline processes and outputs are secure against vulnerabilities demands vigilance and robust security practices.

Best Practices for Efficient CI/CD Pipeline Management

Adoption of CI/CD pipelines should be augmented by best practices to maximize efficacy:

- **1. Automate Everything:** Where possible, automate all aspects of the build, test, and deploy process to minimize manual intervention and errors.

- **2. Implement Robust Testing:** Broad test coverage is vital; employ unit, integration, and acceptance tests to validate new changes comprehensively.

- **3. Use Feature Toggles:** Allow new features to be released incrementally and tested in production by leveraging feature toggles.

- **4. Prioritize Security:** Embed security within the pipeline, applying principles of Shift-Left Testing to detect vulnerabilities early.

- **5. Continuous Monitoring:** Post-deployment, actively monitor application performance and system utilization, orchestrating dynamic adjustments as necessary.

- **6. Incremental Implementations:** Gradual adoption of CI/CD practices is advised, initially targeting essential processes before scaling comprehensively.

In many cases, CI/CD components can be managed via code, facilitating swift pipeline adjustments. Consider the following CI/CD configuration expressed in YAML for transparency and adaptability:

```yaml
version: '2.1'
executors:
  maven-executor:
    docker:
      - image: circleci/openjdk:11-jdk
jobs:
  build-and-test:
    executor: maven-executor
    steps:
      - checkout
      - run: mvn clean package --batch-mode
      - run: mvn test
workflows:
  version: 2
  dev_pipeline:
    jobs:
      - build-and-test
```

This configuration snippet outlines a basic CI/CD setup within a CircleCI context, illustrating the declarative nature of pipeline definitions, enabling transparent and maintainable process shifts. Additionally, adopting provisions such as code linting, static analysis, and tool integration can bolster pipeline efficacy, ultimately reflecting a comprehensive, cohesive SDLC.

7.2 Role of Argo CD in CI/CD

Argo CD is a Kubernetes-native continuous deployment (CD) tool that automates the deployment of applications and the management of application states in a Kubernetes ecosystem. It is designed to facilitate the declarative deployment of applications, leveraging Git repositories as the single source of truth, which is an integral part of modern CI/CD pipelines.

Understanding the role of Argo CD in CI/CD involves examining its contributions to streamlining deployment processes, promoting GitOps principles, and integrating with existing CI systems to create a cohesive DevOps workflow.

GitOps Paradigm and Argo CD

7.2. ROLE OF ARGO CD IN CI/CD

Argo CD is founded on the principles of GitOps, a paradigm that applies Git's version control mechanism to operational workflows, including application deployment. Key aspects of GitOps enable Argo CD to provide value within CI/CD pipelines:

- **1. Declarative Configuration:** Argo CD uses declarative configurations stored in Git repositories to define the desired state of applications in a Kubernetes environment. It ensures that the live state of applications always matches the declared state in Git.

- **2. Versioned Change History:** By storing configuration files in Git, Argo CD enables teams to leverage Git's powerful versioning capabilities, creating an auditable trail of changes and a rollback mechanism for applications.

- **3. Automated Synchronization:** Automatically synchronizing the Git-stored declarative configurations with the cluster, Argo CD ensures alignment between the desired and actual states of applications.

Integration of Argo CD in CI/CD Pipelines

Argo CD seamlessly integrates with various CI platforms to extend functionality beyond traditional CI practices, automating deployment workflows and enhancing system reliability. Here's how Argo CD fits into the broader CI/CD pipeline:

- **1. Continuous Deployment Engine:** While CI systems focus on building and testing applications, Argo CD complements them by tackling deployment tasks, allowing CI to trigger deployment flows via Git updates.

- **2. Environment Management:** Argo CD manages application environments directly within Kubernetes clusters, maintaining configuration consistency and operational reliability across different environments (e.g., development, staging, production).

- **3. Multi-Cluster Deployment:** Supporting deployment across multiple clusters, Argo CD provides scalability and reduces the complexity of managing multi-cluster operations within a unified control plane.

Configuration and integration with Argo CD typically involve defining applications declaratively and syncing them with Git repositories. Below is a YAML file that outlines a basic Argo CD Application configuration:

```
apiVersion: argoproj.io/v1alpha1
kind: Application
metadata:
  name: guestbook
  namespace: argocd
spec:
  destination:
    namespace: default
    server: https://kubernetes.default.svc
  project: default
  source:
    path: guestbook
    repoURL: 'https://github.com/argoproj/argocd-example-apps'
    targetRevision: HEAD
  syncPolicy:
    automated:
      prune: true
      selfHeal: true
```

In this configuration, Argo CD is instructed to deploy the "guestbook" application by fetching the desired state from a specified Git repository. The 'syncPolicy.automated' field signifies that Argo CD automatically syncs the application's live state to match the repository's declared state, maintaining consistency and self-healing capabilities.

Benefits of Using Argo CD in CI/CD Workflows

Incorporating Argo CD within CI/CD workflows delivers several operational advantages:

- **1. Enhanced Deployment Automation:** Argo CD's automation capabilities reduce manual intervention in deployment processes, allowing engineering teams to focus on development and innovation.

- **2. Increased Consistency and Reliability:** By enforcing the desired state via GitOps, Argo CD ensures application environments are consistently managed, reducing configuration drift and increasing system reliability.

- **3. Rapid and Secure Rollbacks:** Version-controlled configurations facilitate the rapid rollback of changes, enhancing recovery strategies in the event of deployment issues.

- **4. Improved Observability and Control:** Argo CD's intuitive dashboard provides visibility into the state of applications, enabling teams to monitor and manage deployments efficiently.

- **5. Scalability and Flexibility:** Argo CD scales across large numbers of applications and teams, accommodating diverse deployment scenarios and complex application topologies.

Challenges of Implementing Argo CD

Despite its strengths, implementing Argo CD presents challenges that organizations may encounter:

- **1. Complexity of Configuration Management:** Defining and managing complex configurations declaratively can be challenging, requiring meticulous version control and configuration management practices.

- **2. Infrastructure Dependencies:** Argo CD depends on Kubernetes, necessitating robust Kubernetes infrastructure and operational expertise to maximize its potential.

- **3. Security Concerns:** Securing Git repositories and access credentials is paramount, as repository contents define the live state of applications.

Addressing these challenges involves employing best practices such as maintaining clean repository structures, implementing stringent access controls, and leveraging Kubernetes' native security features to safeguard deployments.

Argo CD Use Cases in CI/CD Pipelines

Argo CD can be harnessed for a multitude of use cases within CI/CD pipelines, demonstrating its versatility across various deployment strategies:

- **1. Microservices Deployments:** Argo CD's application-centric approach benefits microservices architectures, allowing independent deployment, scaling, and rollback of services contained within a larger ecosystem.

- **2. Infrastructure as Code (IaC):** Integrating Argo CD with IaC tools like Terraform enhances infrastructure management, enabling automated infrastructure deployment and updates alongside application deployments.

- **3. Blue/Green and Canary Deployments:** Deploying applications via blue/green or canary release strategies is streamlined with Argo CD's deployment policies, ensuring seamless transition and minimal downtime.

- **4. Edge and IoT Applications:** With its support for multi-cluster setups, Argo CD is well-suited to deploy IoT and edge computing applications across distributed environments.

Implementing Effective Argo CD Deployments

Implementing Argo CD effectively within a CI/CD context involves following a structured approach that maximizes deployment efficiency and operational impact:

- **1. Define Clear Application Specifications:** Initiate by detailing comprehensive application specifications within YAML files, representing every component's desired state and operational parameters.

- **2. Establish Robust Repository Structures:** Organize Git repositories with coherent directory structures, ensuring easy traceability and modularization of configurations.

- **3. Integrate with CI Tools:** Configure CI tools to manage application builds and synchronize results with Argo CD for deployment intelligence and automation.

- **4. Monitor and Observe:** Utilize available monitoring and logging capabilities to scrutinize deployments, track application performance, and ensure prompt detection of anomalies.

- **5. Iteratively Optimize Pipelines:** Regularly review and refine Argo CD pipelines, reflecting on performance metrics and deployment feedback to enhance efficiency and robustness.

7.2. ROLE OF ARGO CD IN CI/CD

Below is an adapted CI/CD pipeline configuration that illustrates how Argo CD integrates with Jenkins, another popular CI tool, to automate deployment tasks:

```
pipeline {
    agent any
    stages {
        stage('Build') {
            steps {
                checkout scm
                run {
                    sh 'mvn clean install'
                }
            }
        }
        stage('Test') {
            steps {
                run {
                    sh 'mvn test'
                }
            }
        }
        stage('Deploy') {
            environment {
                ARGOCD_SERVER = 'https://argocd.example.com'
            }
            steps {
                script {
                    def result = sh(script: """
                        argocd app sync guestbook --server $ARGOCD_SERVER --insecure
                    """, returnStatus: true)
                    if (result != 0) {
                        error "Argo CD deploy failed!"
                    }
                }
            }
        }
    }
}
```

The Jenkins pipeline depicted here builds, tests, and subsequently deploys an application utilizing Argo CD, illustrating how CI and CD tools can conjointly orchestrate full lifecycle management of applications, benefitting from the strengths of both paradigms.

Argo CD emerges as a formidable toolset within CI/CD architectures, offering transformative capabilities for application deployment and lifecycle management. Its successful integration hinges upon understanding its underlying principles, deploying systematic implementation strategies, and leveraging its strengths to assure resilient and agile software delivery processes.

7.3 Integrating Argo CD with Jenkins

The synergy between Argo CD and Jenkins provides a powerful combination for implementing a sophisticated Continuous Integration (CI) and Continuous Deployment (CD) strategy. Both tools, highly regarded in their domains, allow organizations to automate the entire software development lifecycle effectively, making it essential to understand how to integrate them to achieve seamless automation across codebuild, test, and deployment phases.

Overview of Jenkins

Jenkins is a widely used open-source automation server capable of orchestrating a series of actions to achieve the CI part of CI/CD. It provides an extensive set of plugins to support building, deploying, and automating any project. Jenkins excels in automating tasks required to build code, execute tests, and deliver applications to production or other environments.

Integrating Jenkins and Argo CD: Key Considerations

The integration of Jenkins with Argo CD revolves primarily around utilizing Jenkins as the CI server to produce build artifacts and trigger deployment processes via Argo CD. This integration benefits from the declarative nature of Argo CD and Jenkins' orchestrative capabilities, enhancing deployment consistency and enabling real-time monitoring.

Here are the key considerations for integrating Jenkins with Argo CD:

- **Communication Between Jenkins and Argo CD:** The primary mechanism for communication between Jenkins and Argo CD involves Jenkins triggering synchronizations or deployments in Argo CD through API calls.

- **Securing API Interactions:** Jenkins needs permission to interact with Argo CD's API. Ensure API tokens or credentials are securely stored and managed within Jenkins to prevent unauthorized access.

- **Version Control Repository:** Argo CD operates on a GitOps model, thus the source of truth (i.e., the Git repository) for deployment configurations must be appropriately structured and accessible.

- **Pipeline Scripts:** Jenkins can utilize pipeline scripts in Groovy (or other declarative formats) to outline the build, test, and deployment process, calling Argo CD as needed.

- **Feedback Loops:** Incorporate feedback loops to manage application health checks and deployment statistics post-deployment to monitor application performance and initiate rollbacks if necessary.

Setting Up the Jenkins-Argo CD Integration

To establish an operative Jenkins-Argo CD integration, follow the outlined steps:

- **Install the Argo CD Command Line Interface (CLI) on the Jenkins Server:** This CLI tool interacts with the Argo CD server, making it vital for triggering deployments. Install it using the official package repository:

```
# Download the latest version
curl -sSL -o argocd-linux-amd64 https://github.com/argoproj/argo-cd/releases/download/v2.1.6/argocd-linux-amd64
# Make it executable
chmod +x argocd-linux-amd64
# Move to binary location
sudo mv argocd-linux-amd64 /usr/local/bin/argocd
```

- **Configure API Access:** Direct Jenkins to authenticate and access the Argo CD API by setting up a service account in Argo CD associated with a token stored securely in Jenkins.

- **Define Jenkins Pipeline:** Author the Jenkins pipeline script to incorporate Argo CD commands. The pipeline should reflect build, test, and deployment stages integrated with Argo CD. An example is provided below:

```
pipeline {
    agent any
    environment {
        ARGOCD_SERVER = 'argocd.company.com'
        ARGOCD_AUTH_TOKEN = credentials('argocd-token')
    }
```

```
stages {
    stage('Checkout') {
        steps {
            checkout scm
        }
    }
    stage('Build') {
        steps {
            sh 'mvn clean install'
        }
    }
    stage('Test') {
        steps {
            sh 'mvn test'
        }
    }
    stage('ArgoCD Deployment') {
        steps {
            script {
                def syncCommand = "argocd app sync my-application --
                    server $ARGOCD_SERVER --auth-token
                    $ARGOCD_AUTH_TOKEN"
                sh script: syncCommand, returnStatus: true
            }
        }
    }
}
post {
    always {
        script {
            archiveArtifacts artifacts: '**/target/*.jar', fingerprint: true
        }
        cleanWs()
    }
}
}
```

This example script illustrates Jenkins using the Argo CD CLI to synchronize and subsequently trigger deployments determined by the state defined in a Git repository.

Monitoring and Handling Deployments

After configuring Jenkins to leverage Argo CD for deployment orchestration, monitoring and feedback post-deployment become critical components of the CI/CD workflow. Effective practices include:

- **Real-time Monitoring and Alerts:** Monitoring tools like Prometheus or Grafana can be integrated with Argo CD and Jenkins to offer real-time insight into deployment progress and application performance indicators.

- **Logs and Reporting:** Maintain comprehensive logs to provide diagnostics about the build, test, and deployment operations. These records aid in troubleshooting unforeseen deployment issues.

- **Automated Rollbacks:** Implement rollback strategies within pipeline scripts to revert applications to a previous stable state upon detection of a fault in the deployment process.

- **Failure Notifications:** Configure email or Slack notifications to alert developers and operations teams instantly upon build failures or deployment irregularities, enabling swift corrective actions.

Benefits of Using Jenkins and Argo CD in Tandem

The combination of Jenkins and Argo CD yields significant advantages in CI/CD workflows:

- **Separation of Concerns:** Jenkins handles CI processes efficiently (code compilation, testing), while Argo CD specializes in CD processes (deployment, environment synchronization), allowing each tool to excel in its domain.

- **Flexibility:** The integration supports multiple environments (development, QA, production), efficiently managing distinct deployment strategies such as canary deployments, blue/green deployments, and rolling updates.

- **Enhanced Deployment Control:** Argo CD's declarative model introduces predictability and visibility, capable of providing detailed insights into Kubernetes application states, which complement Jenkins' CI insights.

- **Efficiency and Speed:** Automation minimizes human error, reducing cycle time from code commit to deployment and fostering an agile development environment.

Considerations for Security and Compliance

Security is a paramount consideration when integrating Jenkins and Argo CD. Key security measures include:

- **API Security:** Protect Jenkins-Argo CD interactions by restricting API token permissions to only necessary operations, employing SSL/TLS for data transport encryption.

- **Credential Management:** Store sensitive credentials and tokens securely using Jenkins' Credentials Plugin, and employ environment isolation principles to restrict access further.

- **Access Control:** Enforce role-based access control (RBAC) in both Jenkins and Argo CD, preventing unauthorized access and restricting operations to legitimate users.

- **SLA and Compliance Documentation:** Maintain compliance with organizational policies and external regulations through logging and audit trails, leveraging Jenkins and Argo CD's logging capabilities.

Extending Capabilities: Plugins and Integrations

The Jenkins-Argo CD integration can be further enhanced through additional plugins and integrations that expand pipeline capabilities:

- **Notifications and Alerts Plugins:** Utilize Jenkins plugins for sending Slack/Mattermost messages or emails to keep teams informed about pipeline statuses and Argo CD deployments.

- **IaC Integration:** Integrate Infrastructure as Code (IaC) tools like Terraform or Ansible within Jenkins pipelines for infrastructure configuration, aligning infrastructure updates with application deployments.

- **Docker and Kubernetes Plugins:** Jenkins plugins dedicated to Docker and Kubernetes operations can extend Jenkins capabilities, improving Docker image creation and Kubernetes resource management.

- **Advanced Environment Management:** Leverage feature toggles and dark launches managed through Jenkins along with Argo CD for progressive delivery and controlled feature releases.

By comprehensively understanding the integration process, configuration details, and potential benefits, organizations can harness the combined strengths of Jenkins and Argo CD to create a highly efficient, automated, and scalable CI/CD pipeline, ensuring rapid and consistent application delivery. The collaboration between CI engines and CD orchestrators exemplifies a harmonious balance within DevOps practices, aligning development and operational objectives towards achieving optimal business outcomes.

7.4 Using Argo CD with GitLab CI/CD

Integrating Argo CD with GitLab CI/CD creates a robust framework for managing the end-to-end automation required in modern DevOps practices. GitLab CI/CD offers a seamless platform for code integration and automated testing, while Argo CD injects powerful deployment automation capabilities into the pipeline. This integration streamlines application deployment and ensures continuous delivery directly from the version control system.

Overview of GitLab CI/CD

GitLab CI/CD is a potent continuous integration and delivery toolset integrated into the GitLab platform. It provides automation capabilities to build, test, and deploy code, leveraging GitLab's omnipresent version control, issue tracking, and pipeline monitoring functionalities. The declarative nature of GitLab CI/CD allows for concise, readable YAML-based pipeline definitions, akin to Argo CD's configuration approach.

Integrating GitLab CI/CD and Argo CD: Key Considerations

Effective integration between GitLab CI/CD and Argo CD involves aligning the CI/CD processes to leverage the strengths of each tool, employing Git as the versioned source of truth. Considerations for successful integration include:

- **Pipeline Orchestration:** Use GitLab CI/CD to orchestrate the execution order of various tasks, triggering Argo CD as a deployment orchestrator for reaching desired application states based on committed code.

- **Secure API Interactions:** Authorize GitLab CI/CD interactions with Argo CD through bearer tokens, ensuring secure API access for deployment tasks.

- **Repository Structure:** Structure repositories to facilitate clear separation of application code and configuration management, maximizing Argo CD's GitOps model.

- **YAML Configuration:** Employ YAML syntax to define tasks and configure both GitLab CI/CD pipelines and Argo CD applications, ensuring clarity and maintainability.

Setting Up GitLab CI/CD and Argo CD Integration

To establish integration between GitLab CI/CD and Argo CD, follow these systematic steps:

- **Set Up Argo CD:** Install and configure Argo CD on the Kubernetes cluster where applications will be deployed. This involves ensuring Argo CD has access to a Git repository with the desired state configuration:

    ```
    kubectl create namespace argocd
    kubectl apply -n argocd -f https://raw.githubusercontent.com/argoproj/argo
        -cd/stable/manifests/install.yaml
    ```

- **Configure Argo CD API Access:** Generate a token for Argo CD API access and store it securely within GitLab's secret management settings. The token ensures secure communication between GitLab CI/CD and Argo CD.

    ```
    # Log in to Argo CD CLI
    argocd login <ARGOCD_SERVER_URL> --username admin --password <
        PASSWORD>

    # Create token
    argocd account generate-token --account <account-name>
    ```

- **Define GitLab CI/CD Pipeline:** Create a '.gitlab-ci.yml' file at the root of your Git repo. Define stages that compile, test, and utilize Argo CD for deployment. Sample configuration is as follows:

```
stages:
  - build
  - test
  - deploy

variables:
  ARGOCD_SERVER: argocd.example.com
  ARGOCD_AUTH_TOKEN: $CI_JOB_TOKEN

build:
  stage: build
  script:
    - echo "Building application..."
    - ./gradlew build

test:
  stage: test
  script:
    - echo "Running tests..."
    - ./gradlew test

deploy:
  stage: deploy
  script:
    - echo "Starting Argo CD deployment..."
    - argocd app sync my-application --server $ARGOCD_SERVER --auth-token $ARGOCD_AUTH_TOKEN
```

In this example, the pipeline is divided into three stages: build, test, and deploy. The deploy stage uses the Argo CD CLI to synchronize the application, effectively implementing continuous delivery.

Monitoring Deployments and Handling Feedback

Effective monitoring practices are crucial for managing applications once GitLab CI/CD and Argo CD deploy them. Consider:

- **Continuous Monitoring:** Implement continuous monitoring for applications using tools like Grafana and Prometheus to gather real-time metrics and visualize application performance and infrastructure health.

- **Feedback Mechanisms:** Utilize GitLab CI/CD to output logs and results immediately, providing critical feedback about the success or failure of builds, tests, and deployments.

- **Robust Logging:** Ensure logging is comprehensive to capture essential details of deployment operations, useful for diagnostics in case of failure.

- **Issue Tracking and Rollback Strategies:** GitLab's issue tracking and merge request pages should be integrated within the workflow to correlate issues arising from commits. Rollback can be automated by adding steps in pipelines to revert to previously known stable states upon deployment failures.

Benefits of Argo CD and GitLab CI/CD Integration

Integrating Argo CD with GitLab CI/CD provides multiple benefits supporting both development and operations teams:

- **Unified Workflows:** Developers operate within a singular GitLab platform, from commit through deployment, reducing task-switching and enhancing productivity.

- **Simplified GitOps Execution:** Argo CD powerfully extends GitLab CI/CD with GitOps capabilities, maintaining uniform application environments and providing clear, auditable trails of application state changes.

- **Agility and Automation:** Combined use of these tools accelerates development cycles through effective automation, ensuring rapid release uptake with negligible lapses in quality assurance.

- **Enhanced Observability:** Seamlessly integrating monitoring tools and dashboards facilitates comprehensive insights into release processes, supporting informed decision-making and operational resilience.

Security Considerations for Integration

Security is paramount when orchestrating the interplay between GitLab CI/CD and Argo CD:

- **Token Security:** Securely manage Argo CD API tokens using GitLab's secret variables, ensuring they are encrypted and accessible only within appropriate pipeline contexts.

- **Role-Based Access Control:** Leverage Kubernetes' RBAC settings and GitLab's access control policies to limit permissions, safeguarding sensitive operations and maintaining the principle of least privilege.

- **Repository Access Control:** Properly configure Git repository permissions, permitting access control mechanisms to guard against unauthorized repository modifications.

- **Audit Trails and Compliance:** Implement and maintain audit trails through Git history, annotated deployments, and event logging to ensure comprehensive tracking for compliance and incident review.

Extending Integration Capabilities

Extending this integration to enhance DevOps functionality could involve:

- **Multi-Environment Deployments:** Configure GitLab CI/CD pipelines to manage deployments across multiple environments, utilizing Argo CD's project and policy configuration for seamless transitions between, e.g., testing and production stages.

- **Advanced Testing Strategies:** Implement Canary Deployment or Blue/Green Deployments directly through pipelines to roll out new features incrementally, rewarding rapid feature validation without compromising stability.

- **Infrastructure-as-Code (IaC) Alignment:** Pair GitLab CI/CD with Argo CD and IaC tools such as Terraform for holistic infrastructure and application lifecycle management allowing for dynamically created and destroyed ephemeral environments.

- **Integrations with Notification Services:** Further enhance operational feedback loops by integrating with Slack, Mattermost, or email systems to provide real-time notifications about deployment status or performance issues.

By understanding the operational dynamics and potential benefits derived from integrating Argo CD with GitLab CI/CD, organizations can craft robust CI/CD pipelines capable of delivering agile, efficient, and reliable deployment processes. The complementary capabilities of GitLab and Argo CD combine to create an environment conducive to continuous innovation and operational excellence, where infrastructure and applications are harmoniously managed to the stringent demands of modern-day software delivery expectations.

7.5 Leveraging Argo Workflows with Argo CD

Argo Workflows and Argo CD, both developed by the Argo Project, offer complementary solutions for orchestrating container-native workflows and managing application deployments within Kubernetes environments. Integrating these tools provides a cohesive framework for enhancing Continuous Integration (CI) and Continuous Deployment (CD) processes, fostering advanced orchestration capabilities essential in modern, cloud-native software ecosystems.

Overview of Argo Workflows

Argo Workflows is a powerful, Kubernetes-native workflow engine designed for orchestrating parallel tasks and complex workflows. It allows users to define workflows using a YAML-based configuration to describe directed acyclic graphs (DAGs) of tasks, which are executed as Kubernetes pods. This capability is valuable for automating CI/CD pipelines, data processing scripts, or any computational tasks deployable in containerized environments.

- **Key Features of Argo Workflows:**

    - 1. **DAG and Step Workflow Support:** Provides flexible constructs for defining both DAGs, which can represent tasks executed in parallel or conditionally, and step-by-step workflow sequences.

    - 2. **Scalability:** Able to manage thousands of workflows simultaneously across Kubernetes clusters, leveraging Kubernetes' inherent scalability.

- **3. High Availability:** Supports highly-available configurations suitable for production-grade environments, ensuring resilience and fault tolerance.
- **4. Workflow Templates:** Facilitates reuse through workflow templates, simplifying complex workflows and easing their management.
- **5. Rich Ecosystem:** Integrates with external tools such as Prometheus, and offers plugins for outputs, artifacts, and parameters, boosting functionality.

Integrating Argo Workflows and Argo CD

Integrating Argo Workflows with Argo CD offers a seamless orchestration solution for automating multi-step processes that culminate in complex deployments. This integration aligns workflow execution with application delivery, enhancing efficiency and synchronizing CI/CD operations.

- **1. Use Case Overlap:** Engaging Argo Workflows for task orchestration complements Argo CD's deployment capabilities, facilitating automation cycles that begin with data processing or model training workflows, culminating in artifact deployment via Argo CD.
- **2. Workflow to Deployment Hand-Off:** Workflows calculated or rendered using Argo Workflows may output as application components deployable by Argo CD—this clear hand-off accelerates build and deployment rhythms.

```
apiVersion: argoproj.io/v1alpha1
kind: Workflow
metadata:
  generateName: build-and-deploy-
spec:
  entrypoint: build-and-deploy
  templates:
  - name: build-and-deploy
    steps:
    - - name: build
        template: build-app
    - - name: deploy
        template: deploy-to-cluster

  - name: build-app
```

```
      container:
        image: golang:1.15
        command: ["/bin/sh", "-c"]
        args: ["echo Building... && sleep 5 && echo Build complete"]
    - name: deploy-to-cluster
      container:
        image: google/cloud-sdk:alpine
        command: ["/bin/sh", "-c"]
        args: ["echo Deploying... && sleep 5 && echo Deploy complete"]
```

This simplified Argo Workflow example illustrates how tasks execute sequentially, culminating in a deployment phase that could integrate with Argo CD for transitioning built artifacts into real Kubernetes environments.

Benefits of Leveraging Argo Workflows alongside Argo CD

Advancing with an integrated approach comprising both Argo Workflows and Argo CD yields substantial benefits encompassing operational efficiency and system agility:

- **1. Unified CI/CD Management:** Pumping workflow outputs directly into the deployment pipeline streamlines operations, creating a seamless CI/CD process capable of accommodating various workloads and heterogeneously configured service applications.

- **2. Enhanced Automation:** Argo Workflows automate intricate task dependencies, freeing operations teams to focus on strategic enhancements rather than manual task overrides, while Argo CD ensures these outputs are expediently deployed.

- **3. Focused Role Specialization:** Argo Workflows specializes as an engine for task orchestration, aligning task provisioning with deployment operations handed over to Argo CD, thereby encapsulating DevOps roles within clean delineations.

- **4. Improved Resource Utilization:** Utilizing Kubernetes' compute efficiency ensures optimal resource management by dynamically provisioning and reclaiming nodes, efficiently managing task execution across available cluster resources.

- **5. Scalability and Fault Tolerance:** Collaboration between these components, each endowed with intrinsic Kubernetes traits, supports scaling application deployments alongside multi-task orchestrative demands without compromising system reliability.

Integration Challenges and Considerations

Integrating Argo Workflows with Argo CD requires addressing potential challenges, ensuring cohesive inter-operation:

- **1. Configuration Complexity:** While providing powerful functionality, properly configuring both components demands understanding application architecture and resource availability factors, vigilant YAML management is crucial for accurate task definitions.

- **2. Network Overheads:** As workflows execute via Kubernetes-managed pods, inter-pod communications and external service access may incur network overhead, accentuated by expansive workflow sizes or geographically dispersed clusters.

- **3. Security Practices:** Secure API interactions and tightly controlled access roles are pivotal, bound by principles of least privilege and secure credential management practices within cluster environments.

To alleviate configuration intricacies, employing templating strategies, standardization practices, and leveraging Argo's ecosystem capabilities could significantly optimize operational workflows.

Argo Workflows Use Cases in Argo CD-Integrated CI/CD Pipelines

Key use cases emerge when leveraging Argo Workflows in concert with Argo CD, advancing complex automation pipelines across diverse domains:

- **1. Data Processing and ETL Tasks:** Automating Extract, Transform, Load (ETL) processes using Argo Workflows improves efficiency, delivering prepared data directly to Argo CD-provisioned environments.

- **2. Machine Learning Model Deployment:** Triggered model training, testing, and validation pipelines within Argo Workflows ease continuous model delivery, deploying validated models with rigorous testing, facilitated by ensuing Argo CD deployments.

- **3. Microservices Chaining:** Orchestrate complex inter-service communications and processing chains through workflows, deploying microservices using Argo CD, effectively managing dependency lifecycle within microservice environments.

- **4. Multi-Phase Planning:** Situations demanding multi-phase build-test-deploy cycles across multidisciplinary teams benefit from workflow-managed orchestration ensuring cohesive sequence execution before transitioning to Argo CD deployments.

Advancing Capabilities through Enhancements and Extensibility

Balancing Argo Workflows and Argo CD enhancements could further enrich CI/CD pipeline capabilities beyond ordinary paradigms:

- **1. Enhanced Integration Layers:** Employing REST APIs, webhooks, and external triggers integrates external systems seamlessly, building complex logic chains firing from workflow completion across domain-specific extensions.

- **2. Continuous Monitoring and Logs:** Integrate Prometheus metrics and Grafana dashboards to maintain real-time insights into workflow progress and process effectiveness, associating events with deployment outcomes.

- **3. Resource Management Adapters:** Coupling with Helm for repeated state management, or adopting custom Kubernetes operators, could align additional orchestration layers across dependent task/resource alignments.

- **4. Collaboration and Visualization:** Rendering workflow representations using Argo's web UI or enriched graphical visualizers span the complete workflow-to-deployment journey, aiding comprehension across multi-disciplinary teams.

This synergy between Argo Workflows and Argo CD exemplifies the power of Kubernetes-native solutions automating CI/CD pipelines. Organizations capturing this integration achieve sophisticated orchestration capabilities required for agile, stable, and highly competitive software development cycles. Through coherent task delegation and deployment specialization, enhanced pipeline throughput and system observability become achievable, bolstering organizational commitment towards seamless, scalable, and robust production paths responsive to the evolving needs of modern business landscapes.

7.6 Triggering Deployments from CI Pipelines

Efficient automation of deployment processes has become a fundamental requirement in Continuous Integration (CI) systems, where the integration of delivery and deployment tasks within pipelines accelerates the time-to-market and enhances software development workflows. Triggering deployments directly from CI pipelines enables seamless continuity between code integration and delivery, ensuring rapid application readiness for production environments with minimal manual intervention.

Understanding Deployment Triggers in CI Pipelines

Deployment triggers in CI pipelines represent automated mechanisms designed to initiate application delivery processes following successful code integration stages. Triggers ensure that artifacts resulting from build and integration phases undergo systematic deployment procedures, resulting in up-to-date applications reaching the designated environments efficiently.

Key components and factors when considering deployment triggers include:

- **Source Control Integration:** Pipeline triggers often hinge upon code changes pushed to a version control system (VCS), such as commits, merges, or tags in a Git repository.

- **Conditional Staging:** Successful builds and satisfactory test results function as prerequisites for triggering deployment processes, introducing safeguard checks and conditional pathways within pipelines.

- **Environment Targeting:** Deployments may be directed towards several environments (development, staging, production), managed via environment-specific trigger configurations ensuring suitability.

- **Feedback Mechanisms:** Frameworks for capturing results from deployment processes through notifications or monitoring ensure that deployment health is observable and situational awareness is maintained.

Implementing Deployment Triggers: A Strategic Blueprint

Effective implementation of deployment triggers within CI pipelines prohibits unnecessary complexity, leveraging efficient practices purposefully designed to align with strategic goals. A structured approach entails:

- **Define Event Triggers:** Determine which events or conditions within the pipeline will initiate deployment tasks. Common examples include new commits, successful integration testing, tagging practices, and manual approvals. Usage of Git hooks to automate trigger invocations based on code repository events forms a critical part of this strategy.

```sh
#!/bin/sh
# Pre-push hook to trigger deployment
curl -X POST -H "Authorization: Bearer YOUR_API_KEY" \
https://ci.example.com/deployments/trigger \
-d "ref=$GIT_BRANCH"
# Ensure this script is executable: chmod +x .git/hooks/pre-push
```

- **Build Comprehensive Pipelines:** Construct CI pipelines in languages native to the chosen CI/CD platform, enabling systematic progress through stages. Platforms like Jenkins, CircleCI,

7.6. TRIGGERING DEPLOYMENTS FROM CI PIPELINES

GitLab CI/CD, or Travis CI offer pipelines as code structures conducive to representing complex workflows.

```
stages:
  - build
  - test
  - deploy

build:
  stage: build
  script:
    - mvn clean install

test:
  stage: test
  script:
    - mvn test

deploy:
  stage: deploy
  when: manual
  script:
    - curl -X POST https://deployment.api/trigger
```

- **Utilize CD Tools:** Employ Continuous Deployment (CD) tools like Argo CD, Spinnaker, or AWS CodeDeploy within pipelines, managing environment state transitions and supporting auto-synchronization of application deployments thereof:

```
#!/bin/bash
argocd app sync my-application --server argocd.mycompany.com --auth-token $ARGOCD_TOKEN
```

- **Identify Environment Variables:** Establish environment variables containing sensitive credentials, deployment parameters, and configuration details, leveraging CI/CD innate security and secret management provisions to protect sensitive information.

Advantages of Triggering Deployments from CI Pipelines

Integrating deployment triggers within CI pipelines overshoots traditional boundaries of automation, offering unbounded advantages including:

- **Speed and Consistency:** Automated pipelines ensure that deployments are executed predictably, avoiding human errors and inconsistencies resulting from manual processes, leading to accelerated and reliable pipeline flows.

- **Disaster Recovery and Rollbacks:** The structured nature of CI pipelines permits well-defined, automated rollback procedures by maintaining previous stable states, thereby reducing downtime during catastrophic deployments or failures.

- **Alignment with DevOps Principles:** Enhancing delivery and deployment automation aligns with modern DevOps principles, promoting a culture of collaboration, rapid iteration, and minimized friction within software development teams.

- **Comprehensive DevSecOps Integration:** Security measures such as vulnerability scans, compliance verification, and risk assessment may be integrated directly into pipelines, providing a complete picture of application delivery quality and security.

Challenges and Considerations in Deployment Automation

Despite significant advantages, challenges lurk when triggering deployments from CI pipelines, chiefly:

- **Complex Dependency Management:** Aligning dependent services, databases, and configurations, especially in microservice architectures, necessitates methodical management operations to assure service cohesion and dependency satisfaction.

- **Infrastructure Scalability:** Architecting pipelines to scale in concert with applications requires discerning architectural insights, specifically resource allocation and task distribution within CI/CD frameworks commensurate with pipeline demands.

- **Multi-Environment Deliverability:** Strategies for managing complex, multi-environment deployments within overlapping development, QA, staging, and production environments inherently increase configuration complexity.

- **Networking Constraints:** Managing internal pipeline networking, especially across different cloud or on-premises resources, poses potential bottlenecks and network latency challenges.

Strategic application of templating, modular pipeline practices, and sophisticated infrastructure provisioning could militate against these challenges, ensuring that deployment processes remain nimble and enduringly scalable.

Example Use Cases and Real-World Scenarios

Armed with deployment triggers within CI pipelines, use cases and practical scenarios reveal significant real-world impact:

- **Continuous Feature Deployment:** Employing deployment triggers allows continual release of incremental features under feature toggles, validated by Canary Releases or A/B Testing, providing instantaneous user feedback loops.

- **Infrastructure Upgrades and Patches:** Automated triggers that re-deploy updated or patched infrastructure as code (IaC) configurations across cloud-native environments alleviate lengthy downtime risks.

- **Automated Schema Evolutions:** Aligning CI pipeline stages with database schema updates or version enhancements, orchestrating deployments with zero-downtime migrations and rollback-ready sequences.

- **Blue-Green Deployment Strategy:** Automated swap between actively served versions using deployment triggers articulates seamless version transitions leveraging distinct environments without user interruption.

Enhancements and Extensions in Deployment Trigger Practices

Optimizing deployment triggers involves adopting state-of-the-art practices, facilitating advanced capabilities and extensibility:

- **Trigger Customization and Conditional Logic:** In-depth customization and conditions injected into deploy stages based on metrics, results, or predefined rules enhance precision.

- **Real-Time Monitoring Integration:** Link real-time data visualizations or dashboards reflecting deployment health and status, enabled through Prometheus, Grafana, or DataDog integrations to preemptively detect anomalies.

- **Cross-Service Coordination:** Extend orchestration across interdependent services, ensuring coherent configurations and state management using service mesh technologies (e.g., Istio) or orchestration frameworks (e.g., Kubernetes).

- **Collaborative Deployment Governance:** Leverage feedback-driven, collaborative deployment decisions involving broader teams using notification hooks to Slack, Microsoft Teams, or JIRA for transparent deployment status updates.

Incorporating deployment triggers within CI pipelines exemplifies a leap toward maximized automation and continuous deployment achievements, fortifying the bridge between developers and operators toward unified objectives. A robust blend of comprehensive organizational alignment and technological enablement transforms automated pipelines into powerful tools, optimized for agile responses to evolving requirements, solidifying process consistency, performance, and stability. Ultimately, strategic deployment integration fosters an environment where innovation thrives at the pace of business, within reliable, repeatable, and transparent operational frameworks.

7.7 Managing Secrets and Configurations

Modern software deployment environments necessitate robust management of secrets and configurations to maintain security, ensure seamless application performance, and reduce risk of sensitive data exposure. This requirement amplifies within the context of continuous

7.7. MANAGING SECRETS AND CONFIGURATIONS

integration and deployment (CI/CD) pipelines, which automate the stages of software development, testing, and deployment. Managing secrets effectively, such as API keys, database credentials, and configuration settings, is critical to safeguarding applications from potential vulnerabilities and unauthorized access.

Secrets and configurations in a CI/CD pipeline context refer to sensitive information and parameters that control application behavior within diverse environments. Effective handling of these elements is crucial in maintaining the pipeline's integrity while aligning with best security and operational practices.

- **1. Secrets Management:** Ensures controlled access to sensitive information, preventing unauthorized access while allowing applications and services to function correctly within various environments.

- **2. Configuration Management:** Involves defining and applying the correct set of parameters that dictate application settings, enabling consistent deployment processes across different environments.

- **3. Dependency Control:** Managing interdependencies between configurations and secrets ensures updates occur without disrupting application stability or functionality across all phases of the pipeline.

- **4. Versioning and Auditing:** A diligent version control and auditing system allows tracking, rollback, and accountability for secret and configuration modifications.

Several strategies have evolved to manage secrets and configurations effectively within CI/CD pipelines, each befitting different deployment contexts and compliance requirements.

- **1. Environment-Specific Configuration:** Separate configuration files and secrets for each environment (development, staging, production) safeguard against accidental cross-environment contamination. Container orchestration platforms like Kubernetes facilitate this through insightful APIs and tooling.

```
apiVersion: v1
kind: ConfigMap
metadata:
  name: myapp-config
  namespace: development
data:
  DATABASE_URL: "jdbc:postgresql://dev-db.mycompany.com/database"
```

- **2. Leveraging Configuration Management Tools:** Tools like Ansible, Chef, or Puppet automate the process of managing and deploying configurations across diverse systems, ensuring adherence to best practices and repeatability.

- **3. Secret Management Tools:** Employ secret management solutions such as HashiCorp Vault, AWS Secrets Manager, or Azure Key Vault to centralize storage, access control, and lifecycle management for secrets.

```
# Ensure you're authenticated
vault login <auth-method>

# Retrieve secret
vault kv get secret/mycredentials
```

- **4. Encryption and Secure Transmission:** Encrypt configurations and secrets both at rest and in transit using established protocols and algorithms to protect against interception and unauthorized access. Use TLS for pipeline interactions to safeguard data flow.

An effective strategy for implementing secrets and configurations within CI/CD pipelines involves:

- **1. Integration with CI/CD Systems:** Seamlessly integrate secret and configuration management tools with pipeline systems like GitLab CI/CD, Jenkins, or Travis CI, ensuring secure retrieval and subsequent functionality in tasks. This includes using plugins or direct interfaces supported by CI/CD systems.

```
pipeline {
    agent any
    environment {
        DB_PASS = credentials('db-password')
    }
```

7.7. MANAGING SECRETS AND CONFIGURATIONS

```
stages {
    stage('Build') {
        steps {
            sh 'echo "Building application"'
        }
    }
    stage('Deploy') {
        steps {
            sh """
            ansible-playbook -i inventory.yaml deploy.yml --extra-vars "
                db_password=${DB_PASS}"
            """
        }
    }
}
```

- **2. Secure Access Policies:** Set fine-grained access controls, employing role-based access control (RBAC) to restrict who can access secrets and modify configurations, thereby enforcing least privilege principles.

- **3. Automate Rotation and Expiry:** Incorporate automated secrets rotation mechanisms and define TTL (Time to Live) for configurations, minimizing exposure time in case of unauthorized access.

- **4. Use of Immutable Infrastructure Principles:** Immutable infrastructure, where servers are replaced rather than modified, decreases the likelihood of configuration drift, helping maintain consistent application states.

Proper management of secrets and configurations significantly improves application and pipeline security, enhancing control and efficiency throughout development workflows:

- **1. Security Enhancement:** Protecting sensitive information against unauthorized disclosure or modification decreases potential vectors for cyber attacks and data breaches.

- **2. Consistency Across Environments:** Structured approaches ensure consistency, reliability, and predictability for deployments across different environments, resulting in traceable configurations and expedited troubleshooting processes.

- **3. Compliance and Governance:** Many industries require strict adherence to data protection and compliance standards—maintaining log trails and managed access policies satisfy such mandates and build organizational trust.

- **4. Risk Mitigation:** Minimize human error by automating and abstracting the management of secrets and configurations, ensuring proper application states across infrastructures.

Encountering and overcoming challenges such as misconfigurations, scalability, and coordination is crucial to perpetuating effective security and operational balances:

- **1. Misconfiguration Risks:** If not managed appropriately, misconfigurations may inadvertently expose sensitive information or impact application functionality. Emphasizing the "Check Early" mindset employing static analysis tools can abate these risks.

- **2. Scalability Concerns:** As applications scale, the volume of secrets and configuration data increases; relying on dated practices often leads to management difficulties.

- **3. Coordination Challenges:** Particularly in microservices architectures, coordinating secrets and configurations across independent services necessitates sophisticated management and monitoring solutions.

- **4. Organizational Perception:** Emphasizing the value of good secret management practices and workflow automation to the entire organization ensures security efforts are well-supported and maintained.

Enhancing secret and configuration management practices may involve several advanced considerations:

- **1. Dynamic Secrets Generation:** Employ dynamic secret generation techniques, especially for database credentials, to ensure short-lived, highly secure temporary secrets using tools like Vault's database secrets engine.

- **2. Use of Service Meshes:** Integrate with service meshes such as Istio, to manage encryption, authentication, and access security across microservices securely without substantial network interference.

- **3. Policy as Code (PaC):** Adopting PaC approaches establishes configurations and policies declaratively, easily version-controlled, and are manually and automatically verifiable.

- **4. Secure Service Discovery:** Implement secure service discovery methods ensuring configurations remain tight and service access restricted to authorized endpoints by combining proxies like Envoy with management systems.

Bridging the gap between security and continuous delivery demands precision, forethought, and the capitalisation of contemporary technologies; managing secrets and configurations incorporates fundamental practices toward maintaining a sustainable and compliant digital infrastructure. The ever-evolving landscape of cloud-native applications continuously emphasizes protection, accountability, and coordination reactive to threats, ensuring technology unceasingly facilitates organizational growth and innovation within protected frameworks.

Chapter 8

Best Practices for Scaling Argo CD Implementations

This chapter offers insights into effective strategies for scaling Argo CD implementations within large Kubernetes environments. It discusses performance optimization and resource management, ensuring Argo CD operates efficiently at scale. Techniques for managing multi-cluster deployments and implementing role-based access control for large teams are covered. The chapter also explores architectural patterns that promote high availability and uses automation to facilitate scaling operations. By emphasizing robust monitoring and observability practices, it provides a well-rounded approach to maintaining operational excellence in expansive deployments.

8.1 Scaling Argo CD Deployments

In large Kubernetes environments, effectively scaling services such as Argo CD presents numerous technical challenges and considerations. Argo CD, as a declarative, GitOps continuous delivery tool for Kubernetes, requires particular strategies to ensure its efficacy at scale, particularly when deploying complex applications or managing numerous clusters. This section delves into the strategies required to scale Argo CD deployments, analyzing both the technical configurations and the operational tactics that facilitate scalability.

The primary objective when scaling Argo CD is to maintain operational effectiveness while managing increased loads. This involves optimizing for resource usage, ensuring high availability, and enhancing performance. Let's explore these elements in more detail.

- **Technical Configurations**

One of the initial steps in scaling Argo CD is to ensure that the underlying infrastructure is suitably provisioned. This involves configuring Argo CD's components to manage an increased number of requests and operations. Argo CD consists of multiple components, all of which need tuning: the API server, the repository server, the application controller, and other Helm-based charts.

```
helm upgrade --install argo-cd argo/argo-cd --namespace argocd \
  --set server.replicas=3 \
  --set controller.replicas=3 \
  --set repoServer.replicas=3 \
  --set dex.replicas=3
```

The above command exemplifies scaling Argo CD components using the Helm package manager. By increasing the number of replicas across critical components (API server, repository server, etc.), you ensure that the workload is efficiently distributed, accommodating higher demand without compromising performance.

The API server, responsible for exposing the Argo CD user interface and GitOps engine, is crucial for orchestrating interactions between Kubernetes clusters and Git repositories. Implementing load balancing strategies, such as using service meshes or network layers, can op-

8.1. SCALING ARGO CD DEPLOYMENTS

timize these interactions by distributing incoming requests across multiple service instances.

- **Resource Management**

Managing the resource footprint of each Argo CD component is critical. As deployments scale, the efficient use of CPU and memory resources becomes pivotal. Proper configuration of requests and limits on these resources ensures that Kubernetes efficiently schedules pods without overprovisioning. Presenting an example:

```
resources:
  requests:
    memory: "512Mi"
    cpu: "250m"
  limits:
    memory: "1024Mi"
    cpu: "500m"
```

Configuring appropriate resource requests and limits for Argo CD components can prevent overutilization scenarios that can lead to node exhaustion. Monitoring tools like Prometheus can be integrated for real-time resource usage insights, allowing for proactive management and adjustment of resource allocations based on observed trends.

- **Database Considerations**

Argo CD's performance largely hinges on its backing databases. Deployments at scale often necessitate high-performance databases with robust capabilities. Configuring Argo CD to work with a highly available and scaled-out database solution like PostgreSQL ensures data consistency and availability during high throughput scenarios. Implementing database replicas can also offload read operations from the primary instance, thereby enhancing performance.

```
postgresql:
  enabled: true
  replication:
    enabled: true
    replicas: 3
```

The reinforcement of the database layer is crucial. Enabling and configuring PostgreSQL replication ensures that the database layer does not become a bottleneck during times of elevated activity. This setup promotes data redundancy and enhances read scalability. Additionally, database backups and regular consistency checks are imperative practices to safeguard against potential data loss and ensure operational continuity.

- **Versioning and Upgrade Strategies**

Another key aspect of scaling involves managing the versioning and upgrading of Argo CD and its dependencies. In large environments, the ability to roll out updates without disrupting ongoing operations is of utmost importance. Canary deployments, and if feasible, blue-green deployments, can be leveraged to implement gradual version rollouts within a cluster or across clusters.

Utilizing an automated pipeline for version upgrades ensures systematic and reliable deployment processes. Incorporating strategies such as running automated tests against the new versions prior to full deployment mitigates risks associated with new releases.

- **Network Policies and Security**

Scaling requires robust security postures, particularly in managing communications between the components of Argo CD and between different clusters. Implementing network policies that regulate traffic flow, and securing communications with TLS for data-in-transit protection, is imperative.

```
apiVersion: networking.k8s.io/v1
kind: NetworkPolicy
metadata:
  name: allow-argo-cd-traffic
spec:
  podSelector:
    matchLabels:
      app: argocd
  policyTypes:
  - Ingress
  - Egress
  ingress:
  - from:
    - podSelector:
        matchLabels:
          app: argocd
  egress:
```

8.1. SCALING ARGO CD DEPLOYMENTS

```
- to:
  - podSelector:
      matchLabels:
        app: argocd
```

This Kubernetes network policy ensures that only necessary traffic within the context of Argo CD operations is allowed, securing application communication channels and reducing potential exposure to malicious attacks.

- **Operational Tactics**

Large-scale deployments also require operational strategies to manage the complexity and scale effectively. This includes maintaining operational efficiency with automation, implementing strategies such as Infrastructure as Code (IaC) and leveraging GitOps principles to ensure that configurations are consistent and standardized across environments.

Moreover, adequate training and knowledge dissemination are essential for teams managing scaled-out environments. Ensuring that team members are well-versed in the principles of scaled Argo CD deployments can mitigate human errors and boost overall system reliability.

- **Monitoring and Troubleshooting**

Finally, every scaled deployment must be underpinned by a robust monitoring and troubleshooting framework. Deploying Argo CD with integrated logging and monitoring solutions (e.g., Grafana and Prometheus) aids in tracking performance metrics and alerting on threshold breaches. Such solutions should be configured to report on various aspects of the deployment, such as API response times, database query performance, resource consumption, and error rates.

In-depth logging facilitates quick diagnosis of issues and potential bottlenecks. Implementing structured logging (using tools like the Elastic stack) can enhance the ability of DevOps teams to identify, trace, and rectify system issues expeditiously.

By adopting these extensive scaling strategies, Kubernetes environments using Argo CD stand resilient to growth challenges, ensuring robust and flexible application deployments across expansive infrastructures.

8.2 Optimizing Performance and Resource Usage

The effectiveness of Argo CD in a Kubernetes environment is closely linked to how well its performance and resource usage are optimized. As we delve into techniques for optimizing Argo CD deployments, it is essential to consider both the computational resources it utilizes and the application's overall execution efficiency. This section explores configurations, best practices, and tools designed to enhance the performance and resource utilization of Argo CD, thereby ensuring smooth operations even as deployments scale up.

At its core, optimizing Argo CD involves configuring its components to minimize delays and maximize throughput, as well as managing the resources (CPU, memory, I/O) efficiently so as not to underutilize or exhaust system capabilities. The following are considered to achieve optimization objectives.

Efficient Component Configurations

Argo CD comprises various components, such as the API server, application controller, and repository server. Each of these requires careful configuration tailored to the specific workload characteristics of the deployment.

- **API Server Optimization:**

    The API server, which handles user requests and web interactions, operates as a gateway to other components. Optimizing the API server involves reducing response times and handling large volumes of concurrent requests effectively. Implementing horizontal pod autoscaling helps in dynamically adjusting the number of running pods based on observed latency or CPU utilization metrics.

8.2. OPTIMIZING PERFORMANCE AND RESOURCE USAGE

```
apiVersion: autoscaling/v2beta2
kind: HorizontalPodAutoscaler
metadata:
  name: argo-cd-api-server
  namespace: argocd
spec:
  scaleTargetRef:
    apiVersion: apps/v1
    kind: Deployment
    name: argo-cd-api-server
  minReplicas: 2
  maxReplicas: 10
  metrics:
  - type: Resource
    resource:
      name: cpu
      target:
        type: Utilization
        averageUtilization: 70
```

The HorizontalPodAutoscaler, as defined above, automatically manages and scales the number of pods for the API server, balancing CPU utilization and reducing latency issues by ensuring adequate capacity during peak loads.

- **Application Controller Configuration:**

  The application controller orchestrates the state reconciliation of Argo CD applications with their source repositories. Tuning synchronization policies and leveraging optimized reconciliation loops reduce lag times and unnecessary operations.

  To further minimize resource use, you might configure the app controller not to sync changes to applications on every commit but based on an optimized schedule that reflects the enterprise's actual needs.

```
spec:
  source:
    repoURL: git@github.com:example/repo.git
    targetRevision: HEAD
    path: app/config
  syncPolicy:
    automated:
      prune: true
      selfHeal: true
    syncOptions:
    - CreateNamespace=true
    - PrunePropagationPolicy=foreground
    retry:
      limit: 5
```

By setting sync options, such as 'PrunePropagationPolicy', the application controller is instructed to remove any obsolete Kubernetes resources, thereby keeping the environment clean and reducing unnecessary strain on resources.

Resource Allocation and Monitoring

Optimization is inherently tied to resource management. Properly allocated CPU, memory, and I/O resources ensure that each component operates within its limits while maintaining high efficiency.

- **Resource Reservations:**

    Establishing resource requests and limits for Argo CD's components allows Kubernetes to manage and optimize node allocations effectively. These configurations help in maintaining the right balance—neither starving a component of resources nor provisioning excess, which can degrade performance through inefficient utilization.

    ```
    resources:
      requests:
        cpu: "250m"
        memory: "512Mi"
      limits:
        cpu: "500m"
        memory: "1024Mi"
    ```

    These resource limits ensure that critical processes receive the necessary resources to run smoothly, while at the same time ensuring that Argo CD's usage doesn't monopolize cluster resources, allowing for other workloads to perform optimally.

- **Performance Monitoring:**

    Implementing comprehensive monitoring setups using tools such as Prometheus and Grafana is indispensable in detecting bottlenecks and understanding resource consumption patterns. For example, utilizing Prometheus can yield valuable insights into CPU, memory usage, and custom metrics, which can be configured to trigger alarms or autoscaling events.

    ```
    apiVersion: monitoring.coreos.com/v1
    kind: ServiceMonitor
    ```

8.2. OPTIMIZING PERFORMANCE AND RESOURCE USAGE

```
metadata:
  name: argocd-service-monitor
  labels:
    release: prometheus-operator
spec:
  selector:
    matchLabels:
      app: argocd
  endpoints:
  - port: web
    interval: 30s
```

Through the instantiation of such a 'ServiceMonitor', relevant metrics on resource availability and health can be readily enforced. This setup allows for reactive steps when trends indicate rising resource demand or potential resource exhaustion.

Performance-Enhancing Techniques

Beyond configuration and monitoring, numerous performance-enhancing techniques can be implemented to augment the efficiency of Argo CD operations.

- **Git Repository Performance:**

  Optimizing interactions with Git repositories is often overlooked but is key to the performance of Argo CD. Techniques such as shallow cloning ('depth=1') reduce data transfer and repository processing load, especially advantageous in large repositories.

- **Cache Usage:**

  Utilizing caching mechanisms like Redis to store intermediate states or frequently accessed information can offload the direct API and database query load, allowing the application controller and server to handle requests more efficiently.

- **Load Balancing:**

  In a multi-node setup, deploying load balancers facilitates optimal distribution of incoming network traffic across multiple Argo CD servers. This distribution helps maintain low response times and ensures high availability.

```yaml
apiVersion: v1
kind: Service
metadata:
  name: argo-cd-server
  namespace: argocd
spec:
  type: LoadBalancer
  ports:
  - port: 80
    targetPort: 8080
  selector:
    app: argo-cd
```

The defined YAML snippet configures a LoadBalancer service type to ensure efficient request distribution across available Argo CD server pods.

The optimization of Argo CD for performance and resource usage is a multi-faceted challenge, encompassing configuration, resource management, and advanced performance techniques. By strategically choosing how resources are managed, how applications sync, and monitoring the ecosystem effectively, enterprises can maximize the productivity of Argo CD deployments. These optimizations will lead to a robust and efficient environment capable of scaling alongside organizational needs without compromising on performance or reliability.

8.3 Managing Multiple Clusters with Argo CD

As organizations expand their use of Kubernetes, the need to manage applications across multiple clusters becomes increasingly common. Argo CD, with its comprehensive toolset, provides robust capabilities to handle such multi-cluster environments efficiently. Managing applications across numerous Kubernetes clusters introduces complex challenges, including configuration management, security, scalability, and consistency. This section examines the strategies and best practices for using Argo CD to achieve effective multi-cluster management, ensuring applications are deployed consistently and securely across diverse environments.

Argo CD's GitOps methodology provides a systematic approach to managing desired states of various clusters via Git repositories. By codifying and storing the configurations declaratively, it facilitates automated synchronization across clusters, ensuring that deployments remain consistent.

Cluster Management and Configuration

Successfully integrating and managing multiple clusters with Argo CD begins with properly configuring cluster access and ensuring secure network communication.

- Cluster Registration:

Each target cluster must be individually registered with Argo CD. This process involves setting up a Service Account on the target Kubernetes cluster and configuring Access Control to manage permissions effectively.

```
kubectl config use-context my-target-cluster
kubectl create namespace argocd
kubectl create serviceaccount argocd-manager --namespace argocd
```

Next, create a ClusterRoleBinding to bind the service account with necessary roles:

```
kubectl create clusterrolebinding argocd-manager-role-binding \
--clusterrole=cluster-admin \
--serviceaccount=argocd:argocd-manager \
--namespace=argocd
```

Once the setup on the individual clusters is complete, integrate these clusters with the Argo CD server for management. The following command uses 'argocd' CLI for adding a cluster:

```
argocd cluster add my-target-cluster
```

This process repeats for each cluster intended to be under Argo CD's management.

- Namespace Isolation:

For large organizations, it's wise to implement namespace isolation across clusters. This approach ensures logical separation of resources and enforces context boundaries. By organizing applications in distinct namespaces, you reduce cross-interference and provide a more secure multi-tenant environment.

Here's how you can define an application with a namespace allocated:

```
apiVersion: argoproj.io/v1alpha1
kind: Application
metadata:
  name: my-app
  namespace: argocd
spec:
  destination:
    server: https://kubernetes.default.svc
    namespace: my-app-namespace
  source:
    repoURL: git@github.com:example/repo.git
    path: my-app-chart
    targetRevision: HEAD
```

The 'destination' field specifies precisely which cluster and namespace to deploy the application, allowing for explicit control over its deployment targets.

Security and Access Control

With applications deployed over multiple clusters, defining secure access and clear policies is crucial. Role-based access control (RBAC) becomes an essential aspect of maintaining secure multi-cluster operations.

- RBAC Configuration:

Enforce RBAC policies both within Argo CD and across each managed cluster. This ensures users and services have authorization only for the intended actions or resources. Configure roles and bindings to align with the principle of the least privilege.

```
kind: Role
apiVersion: rbac.authorization.k8s.io/v1
metadata:
  namespace: my-app-namespace
  name: my-app-role
rules:
- apiGroups: [""]
  resources: ["pods", "services"]
  verbs: ["get", "list", "watch"]
```

8.3. MANAGING MULTIPLE CLUSTERS WITH ARGO CD

This YAML snippet outlines a sample Role within Kubernetes. RoleBindings or ClusterRoleBindings should be applied to associate these policies with appropriate user groups or service accounts.

- Secure Git Integration:

Implement secure practices for Git repository access, employing SSH keys or environment-based Git credentials to protect repository interactions. Validate that GitOps accounts or bots have restricted, audit-traced access to only relevant segments of the Git repository pertinent to deployments.

Cross-Cluster Synchronization and Governance

Synchronization across multiple clusters should be consistent and governed by an overarching policy structure.

- Ensuring Consistent Configuration:

GitOps provides a mechanism to enforce configuration consistency across numerous clusters. By adopting declarative configurations stored in version control systems (VCS), you can maintain a single source of truth enabling uniform configuration application.

```
project: default
source:
  repoURL: git@github.com:example/repo.git
  path: app-config
  targetRevision: HEAD
destination:
  server: https://04281c309b9601f3.gr7.us-east-1.eks.amazonaws.com
  namespace: default
```

This configuration file exemplifies an application deployment specification that ensures consistent state application to a specific cluster within a given namespace based on the repository's configurations.

- Policy Enforcement:

Implement tools like Open Policy Agent (OPA) to enforce compliance policies across clusters. OPA, integrated with Argo CD, helps define organization-wide policies that automatically validate application configurations for security and compliance before being applied.

Incorporating automated security scanning tools as part of the CI/CD process complements this approach, ensuring configurations are validated for potential vulnerabilities before deployment.

Performance and Scalability Considerations

With scalability requirements, it becomes crucial to monitor cluster communications, application health, and sync status efficiently.

- Monitoring and Observability:

Deploy comprehensive monitoring solutions using Prometheus or Grafana for visualizing metrics across clusters. Set up alerting for key indicators, such as pod lifecycle events, resource usage anomalies, sync errors, or network latency issues.

```
apiVersion: monitoring.coreos.com/v1
kind: Prometheus
metadata:
  name: argocd-prometheus
spec:
  serviceMonitorSelector:
    matchLabels:
      team: argocd
```

- Scaling Strategies:

Implement autoscaling based on workloads. Define policies for dynamic infrastructure scaling wherein cluster sizes automatically adapt to handle varying loads either through horizontal or vertical scaling mechanisms.

- Log Management:

Centralized logging solutions, such as ELK stack (Elastic, Logstash, Kibana), allow for effective management and querying of logs from multiple clusters. Consistent log schema and structured logging practices ease troubleshooting and maintain comprehensive logs for forensics.

Conclusion and Best Practices

Managing multiple clusters with Argo CD requires robust configurations, strong governance frameworks, and scalable monitoring setups. By ensuring secure, consistent, and compliant processes, it provides a streamlined approach to deploying applications across complex, multi-cluster environments. The application of GitOps principles, coupled with proper access controls and observability practices, allows organizations to effectively manage their sprawling Kubernetes infrastructures, achieving operational excellence and strategic agility.

8.4 Role-based Access Control for Large Teams

Managing access control in Kubernetes environments, particularly when scaling for large teams, necessitates a robust and adaptable mechanism to ensure security and operational efficiency. Role-based Access Control (RBAC) is a powerful method employed within Kubernetes and Argo CD to manage permissions and define what actions users, groups, or service accounts can perform within a cluster. This section details the implementation and best practices of RBAC tailored for large teams, ensuring that system access is both secure and aligned with organizational policies.

The fundamental concept of RBAC involves binding user-level actions to roles which are then associated with specific resources within the cluster. By structuring access through role and role-binding configurations, organizations achieve a more scalable and maintainable access control paradigm.

RBAC Foundations

Understanding the core components of RBAC within Kubernetes is crucial in effectively managing access controls. RBAC is built on four principal component constructs: Roles, ClusterRoles, RoleBindings, and ClusterRoleBindings. These elements form the foundation upon which granular permission sets are defined and allocated.

- **Role and ClusterRole:** Roles define a set of permissions within a namespace, while ClusterRoles confer permissions cluster-wide. It is important to articulate the scope of actions required, whether they pertain to a specific namespace or the entire cluster.

    Here's an example of a Role that grants read-only access to pods within a particular namespace:

```
kind: Role
apiVersion: rbac.authorization.k8s.io/v1
metadata:
  namespace: development
  name: pod-reader
rules:
- apiGroups: [""]
  resources: ["pods"]
  verbs: ["get", "list", "watch"]
```

- In contrast, a ClusterRole is applied when the scope necessitates access spanning multiple namespaces or involves sensitive cluster-wide resources:

```
kind: ClusterRole
apiVersion: rbac.authorization.k8s.io/v1
metadata:
  name: cluster-admin
rules:
- apiGroups: ["*"]
  resources: ["*"]
  verbs: ["*"]
```

- **RoleBinding and ClusterRoleBinding:** Once roles are defined, RoleBindings associate these roles with specific users, groups, or service accounts within a namespace. ClusterRoleBindings expand this association beyond a single namespace, facilitating cluster-wide access permissions.

```
kind: RoleBinding
apiVersion: rbac.authorization.k8s.io/v1
metadata:
  name: read-pods
  namespace: development
subjects:
- kind: User
```

8.4. ROLE-BASED ACCESS CONTROL FOR LARGE TEAMS

```
  name: johndoe
  apiGroup: rbac.authorization.k8s.io
roleRef:
  kind: Role
  name: pod-reader
  apiGroup: rbac.authorization.k8s.io
```

- For broader access requirements across namespaces or cluster scope:

```
kind: ClusterRoleBinding
apiVersion: rbac.authorization.k8s.io/v1
metadata:
  name: johndoe-cluster-admin
subjects:
- kind: User
  name: johndoe
  apiGroup: rbac.authorization.k8s.io
roleRef:
  kind: ClusterRole
  name: cluster-admin
  apiGroup: rbac.authorization.k8s.io
```

Best Practices for Implementing RBAC in Large Teams

For larger teams, implementing RBAC effectively requires more than just defining roles and bindings. It involves strategic planning and adherence to best practices to maintain a secure and efficient environment.

- **Principle of Least Privilege:** Assign permissions strictly based on necessity to minimize potential security risks. The principle of least privilege dictates that users and processes should only have the minimum levels of access—or permissions—necessary to perform their job functions.

- **Segmentation of Duties:** Segregate responsibilities among team members to prevent access combinations that may lead to security breaches. Define distinct roles based on operational needs, such as developers, DevOps engineers, and administrators.

```
kind: Role
apiVersion: rbac.authorization.k8s.io/v1
metadata:
  namespace: development
  name: dev-access
rules:
- apiGroups: ["apps"]
  resources: ["deployments", "services"]
  verbs: ["create", "update"]
```

The above role could be designated to development teams responsible for managing and updating application deployments but without access to potentially destructive operations like deletions.

- **Auditing and Regular Review:** In rapidly evolving environments, access configurations can quickly become outdated or excessive as team roles evolve. Periodic audits should be conducted to examine and refine granted permissions. Kubernetes provides audit logging features which can be configured to track access and actions, offering visibility into cluster activities.

Argo CD Integration with RBAC

Argo CD extends RBAC to manage access controls specific to its interface and operations. RBAC in Argo CD governs how users interact with applications, projects, and other resources within the platform.

- **Application and Project Level RBAC:** In Argo CD, applications and projects can have specific RBAC policies which provide fine-grained access controls.

```
apiVersion: v1alpha1
kind: AppProject
metadata:
  name: example-project
  namespace: argocd
spec:
  roles:
    - name: team-dev
      policies:
        - p, team-dev, applications, get, example-project/*, allow
        - p, team-dev, applications, create, example-project/*, allow
```

Define policies within a project that grant specific capabilities to team members assigned to that project. The use of wildcards can help simplify policy management while retaining flexibility.

- **SSO and External Authentication:** Integrating Argo CD with single sign-on (SSO) solutions such as LDAP, SAML, or OAuth provides centralized identity management, facilitating consistent policy enforcement across tools and reducing the complexity of maintaining separate user databases.

```
server:
  config:
    url: https://argocd.example.com
  dex:
    config: |
      connectors:
      - type: oidc
        id: google
        name: Google
        config:
          clientID: YOUR_CLIENT_ID
          clientSecret: YOUR_CLIENT_SECRET
          issuer: https://accounts.google.com
```

This integration not only simplifies user experience but strengthens security by authenticating users through a trusted provider.

Advanced RBAC Strategies and Tips

For teams scaling beyond the conventional structure, advanced RBAC strategies may be employed to tailor to complex organizational needs.

- **Custom Resources and Operations:** Define custom roles with specific verbs for unique resources, extending RBAC capabilities to include sophisticated operations. This requires a deep understanding of the Kubernetes API and potential extensions the systems leverage.

- **Dynamic Policy Generation:** For environments undergoing continuous changes, dynamically generating RBAC policies using Infrastructure as Code tools such as Terraform or Helm helps automate and synchronize policy changes with infrastructure updates.

RBAC plays a critical role in managing Kubernetes environments, particularly at scale with large teams. By understanding and implementing effective RBAC practices—from the foundational elements to advanced integration with Argo CD—organizations can safeguard their infrastructure against unauthorized access while enabling efficient team collaboration. Proper configuration of RBAC, ongoing audits, and alignment with organizational policies ensure a secure yet flexible permission model that adapts as teams and technical landscapes evolve.

8.5 Architectural Patterns for High Availability

Ensuring high availability in Argo CD deployments is paramount for maintaining uninterrupted operations, especially when handling mission-critical workloads on Kubernetes clusters. High availability (HA) architectures aim to minimize downtime and ensure that applications remain accessible, even in the face of failures. This section explores architectural patterns that support high availability in Argo CD, detailing the principles, components, and practices that foster resilience across deployments.

To achieve high availability, deployments must effectively manage redundancy, scalability, and fault tolerance throughout infrastructure components. Argo CD itself becomes a critical part of the pipeline, requiring particular attention to its service-level and infrastructure-level integrations.

Core Principles of High Availability

High availability is supported by architecture designed to meet specific non-functional requirements that ensure resilient operations. The core principles include redundancy, failover, load balancing, and health monitoring.

- **Redundancy:** Critical components should not present a single point of failure. By introducing redundancy at both the software and hardware levels, systems become more robust against individual failures. In the context of Argo CD, redundancy might involve deploying multiple replicas of essential components.

- **Failover Mechanisms:** Systems must detect and recover from failures swiftly. Mechanisms that enable automated failovers—such as service restarts, traffic rerouting, and stateful recovery—are central to maintaining availability.

- **Load Balancing:** By spreading workloads evenly across available resources, systems can maintain performance standards while preventing any single component from becoming overwhelmed.

- **Health Monitoring and Alerts:** Comprehensive monitoring ensures that system health is visible and issues can be promptly addressed. Automated alerts and diagnostic tools help in quickly tracking anomalies that might affect service availability.

Architectural Components and Patterns

Building a highly available Argo CD architecture involves specific design choices at various levels, from infrastructure deployment to service configuration. Each component of the system plays a role in achieving and maintaining availability.

- **Distributed Infrastructure Deployment:** Utilizing a distributed deployment pattern implies spreading components and services across multiple geographical regions or availability zones. This setup mitigates the risks associated with localized failures.

    - **Multi-Region Deployments:** By distributing instances of applications across regions, failovers can be made automatic, thus maintaining accessibility even if one region becomes unavailable.
    ```
    kubectl apply -f argo-cd-ha.yaml --context=region-cluster1
    kubectl apply -f argo-cd-ha.yaml --context=region-cluster2
    ```

Here, deploying Argo CD across multiple Kubernetes clusters in distinct geographical regions will enhance resilience against localized failures.

- **Cross-Availability Zone Replication:** Within a single cloud region, deploy Argo CD components such as the API server or repository server across multiple availability zones, ensuring that resources remain accessible even amidst zone-specific outages.

• **Resilience in Service Architecture:** Architecture resiliency is reinforced by the design and deployment strategies adopted within the service boundaries of Argo CD.

- **Stateless Service Design:** Statelessness allows easy scaling and failover, as services do not rely on local state continuity. Services like the Argo CD API server, when deployed statelessly, can leverage dynamic load balancing across replicas.

```
apiVersion: apps/v1
kind: Deployment
metadata:
  name: argo-cd-api-server
spec:
  replicas: 3
  selector:
    matchLabels:
      app: argo-cd
  template:
    metadata:
      labels:
        app: argo-cd
    spec:
      containers:
      - name: argocd-server
        image: argoproj/argocd:v2.1.2
```

Multiple replicas of a stateless service such as this API server guarantee its availability even if individual instances fail.

- **Service Mesh Implementations:** Leveraging service meshes like Istio or Linkerd introduces advanced control over traffic management, retries, and failovers, improving HA by abstracting complex networking topologies.

• **Data Storage Strategies:** Handling stateful applications, such

8.5. ARCHITECTURAL PATTERNS FOR HIGH AVAILABILITY

as the database backends that Argo CD depends on, requires particular strategies to ensure data consistency and availability.

- **Database Replication and Sharding:** Deploy clustered databases with replication mechanisms. Using a primary-replica configuration, where the primary handles writes and replicas handle reads, ensures continuity and scalability.

```
postgresql:
  primary:
    replicaCount: 3
streaming_seconds: 60
```

By configuring replication and automatic failover, systems can minimize downtime when transitioning control to the replica database.

- **Backup Protocols:** Regularly scheduled backups with consistent verification provide a fallback mechanism by which data can be retrieved in the event of corruption or loss.

• **Component Isolation:** Separating critical components in isolated environments—such as distinct namespaces or VPCs—reduces the risk of cascading failures and ensures security and control.

Ensuring Operational Continuity

High availability is not solely about components but also involves the practices and processes that keep systems operational under adverse conditions. Operational continuity encompasses fault detection, automated healing, and comprehensive testing.

• **Automated Fault Detection and Remediation:** Define health checks and readiness probes within Kubernetes to automatically detect issues and trigger corrective actions, such as restarting pods or diverting traffic.

```
readinessProbe:
  httpGet:
    path: /healthz
    port: 8080
  initialDelaySeconds: 5
  periodSeconds: 10
```

Implement readiness probes that periodically check service health and ensure that unhealthy instances do not serve traffic.

- **Chaos Testing:** Introduce controlled disruptions within the environment using tools like Chaos Monkey or LitmusChaos to measure system responses and validate failover strategies.

- **Capacity Planning and Autoscaling:** Implement Horizontal Pod Autoscalers or Cluster Autoscalers to dynamically adjust resource allocation, ensuring systems can cope with varying demand levels.

```
apiVersion: autoscaling/v2beta2
kind: HorizontalPodAutoscaler
metadata:
  name: argo-cd-application-controller
spec:
  scaleTargetRef:
    apiVersion: apps/v1
    kind: Deployment
    name: argo-cd-application-controller
  minReplicas: 2
  maxReplicas: 5
  metrics:
  - type: Resource
    resource:
      name: cpu
      target:
        type: Utilization
        averageUtilization: 60
```

Architecting for high availability requires diligent attention to redundancy, failover, and operational robustness. By implementing these strategies within an Argo CD-managed Kubernetes environment, organizations can ensure that their workloads remain accessible and reliable amidst potential disruptions. High availability is not an afterthought but a foundational design principle that, when effectively realized, can drive significant value and trust in an organization's technical capabilities.

8.6 Automating Scaling Strategies

As the demand for applications fluctuates in modernized environments, dynamic scaling becomes a pivotal capability in maintaining

8.6. AUTOMATING SCALING STRATEGIES

both performance and cost-efficiency. Automating scaling within Kubernetes clusters using tools like Argo CD allows organizations to rapidly adjust resources in response to changing loads. This section explores comprehensive strategies for implementing automated scaling, ensuring systems remain agile and responsive without manual intervention.

Achieving effective scaling begins by understanding the types and scopes of scaling available in a Kubernetes ecosystem. Scaling strategies fall into vertical scaling (scaling up or down the resources allocated to a pod) and horizontal scaling (adjusting the number of pod replicas).

Horizontal Pod Autoscaling (HPA)

Horizontal scaling manages fluctuations in application demand by altering the number of pod replicas. Kubernetes accomplishes this via Horizontal Pod Autoscalers (HPA), which monitor metrics such as CPU utilization or custom metrics to determine when to scale.

- **Configuration of HPA:**

Here's an example configuration for auto-scaling a deployment based on CPU utilization:

```
apiVersion: autoscaling/v2beta2
kind: HorizontalPodAutoscaler
metadata:
  name: web-app-hpa
spec:
  scaleTargetRef:
    apiVersion: apps/v1
    kind: Deployment
    name: web-app
  minReplicas: 2
  maxReplicas: 10
  metrics:
  - type: Resource
    resource:
      name: cpu
      target:
        type: Utilization
        averageUtilization: 70
```

This HPA monitors the average CPU utilization, scaling the number of replicas between the defined minimum and maximum thresholds to achieve the target CPU utilization.

CHAPTER 8. BEST PRACTICES FOR SCALING ARGO CD IMPLEMENTATIONS

- **Custom Metrics:**

Beyond CPU and memory, HPA supports custom metrics, enabling more granular control over the scaling triggers. Utilizing adapter layers such as Prometheus Adapter allows integration of Prometheus metrics into Kubernetes scaling decisions.

```
apiVersion: autoscaling/v2beta2
kind: HorizontalPodAutoscaler
metadata:
  name: transaction-hpa
spec:
  scaleTargetRef:
    apiVersion: apps/v1
    kind: Deployment
    name: transaction-service
  minReplicas: 3
  maxReplicas: 10
  metrics:
  - type: Pods
    pods:
      metric:
        name: transactions
      target:
        type: AverageValue
        averageValue: 500
```

The above configuration scales pods based on the number of transactions handled, utilizing a custom metric for more relevant scaling.

Vertical Pod Autoscaling (VPA)

Vertical scaling focuses on adjusting the resource requests and limits for existing pods, ideally suited for applications where workload variability is high but the scale unit shouldn't change.

- **VPA Components:**

Components like the VPA Recommender, Updater, and Admission Controller manage vertical resource allocation:

- **Recommender:** Suggests changes to the pod resource requests based on historical usage.
- **Updater:** Applies recommended changes, but might evict pods to do so.

8.6. AUTOMATING SCALING STRATEGIES

- **Admission Controller:** Allocates resources for newly created pods.

- **VPA Example:**

To configure a VPA that adjusts CPU and memory utilization dynamically:

```
apiVersion: autoscaling.k8s.io/v1
kind: VerticalPodAutoscaler
metadata:
  name: my-app-vpa
spec:
  targetRef:
    apiVersion: "apps/v1"
    kind: Deployment
    name: my-app
  updatePolicy:
    updateMode: "Auto"
```

The automatic mode allows Kubernetes to modify resource requests directly, ensuring smooth handling of workload variations.

Cluster Autoscaler

To complement pod-level scaling (HPA/VPA), the Cluster Autoscaler can adjust the size of the Kubernetes node pool itself, adding or removing nodes based on unscheduled pod requirements.

- **Purpose and Functionality:**

Cluster Autoscaler increases the node pool when pods cannot be scheduled due to resource constraints and reduces the pool when excess capacity is detected.

- **Configuration Example:**

Running in cloud environments like AWS, GCP, or Azure, the typical Cluster Autoscaler configuration includes auto-discovery of node groups:

```
./cluster-autoscaler \
  --cloud-provider=aws \
  --nodes=1:10:k8s-node-group \
  --balancing-ignore-label=spot-instance
```

This configuration sets a range for the node count in the specified node group, allowing for flexibility in scaling up and down as dictated by workload demands.

Advanced Scaling Considerations

Effective scaling automation also considers application-specific factors and system-wide impacts. The following advanced strategies ensure more responsive and efficient scaling.

- **Scaling Policies:**

Define scaling policies with cooldown periods to prevent flapping, where oscillating load triggers excessive scaling actions. Policies help maintain cluster stability by smoothing out transient load variations.

- **Predictive Scaling:**

Augment reactive systems with predictive algorithms (e.g., machine learning models) to anticipate future demands based on historical trends. This enables proactive scaling decisions, aligning resources ahead of anticipated peaks.

- **Multi-Metric Autoscaling:**

Combine several metrics in HPA configurations to incorporate simultaneous considerations—CPU usage, request latency, or throughput can collectively inform more accurate scaling.

```
metrics:
- type: Resource
  resource:
    name: cpu
    target:
      type: Utilization
      averageUtilization: 80
- type: Object
  object:
    metric:
      name: requests-per-second
    describedObject:
      apiVersion: apps/v1
```

8.6. AUTOMATING SCALING STRATEGIES

```
kind: Service
name: my-service
target:
  type: Value
  value: 200
```

This multi-metric approach allows balancing between resource usage and application performance KPIs.

Integration and Monitoring

Automation's efficacy in scaling is intertwined with monitoring—visibility into system behavior is vital for validation and ongoing refinement of scaling strategies.

- **Observability Frameworks:**

Integrate monitoring solutions—Prometheus, Grafana, or Datadog—to visualize resource usage and scaling actions, and correlate these with application performance.

- **Alerting Systems:**

Set alerts for metric anomalies or scaling failures, ensuring rapid response to potential issues. Automated alerts facilitate proactive operations maintenance by notifying operational teams of deviations in expected patterns.

```
alerting:
  alertmanagers:
    - static_configs:
        - targets: ['localhost:9093']
rule_files:
  - 'scaling_rules.yml'
```

- **Continuous Feedback:**

Evaluate scaling strategies via continuous integration pipelines that incorporate feedback loops for dynamic tuning based on observed efficacy and operational metrics.

Automating scaling within Kubernetes ecosystems using Argo CD and allied tools is a strategically empowering initiative. By harnessing the combined power of HPA, VPA, and Cluster Autoscaler, organizations can adeptly handle fluctuating loads, ensuring robust performance while optimizing resource utilization. With sophisticated scaling configurations and comprehensive monitoring, systems can be tuned to align precisely with business and technical goals, delivering adaptability and cost-effectiveness at scale.

8.7 Monitoring and Observability at Scale

Monitoring and observability are essential components of managing applications at scale, providing visibility into system health, performance, and security. As Kubernetes environments grow more complex with the scaling of Argo CD deployments, establishing a robust monitoring and observability framework becomes critical. This section delves into the strategies, tools, and best practices for achieving comprehensive observability, enabling organizations to effectively monitor large-scale deployments and maintain operational excellence.

Monitoring and observability, while often used interchangeably, address different aspects of understanding system behavior. Monitoring focuses on collecting and analyzing predefined metrics to track system health. Observability, on the other hand, provides insights into the internal state of a system based on the outputs it generates, such as logs, metrics, and traces, allowing for in-depth troubleshooting and performance optimization.

Key Components of Observability

To ensure complete observability of Argo CD in large Kubernetes environments, three main pillars need to be addressed: metrics, logs, and distributed tracing.

- **Metrics:** Metrics provide quantitative data points that can be used to understand the system's performance and resource usage.

Common metrics include CPU and memory usage, request rates, error rates, and latency.

- **Logs:** Logs contain detailed records of discrete events that happen over time. They provide context for understanding how individual requests or processes are handled within the system.

- **Distributed Tracing:** Tracing enables end-to-end tracking of requests as they traverse through distributed systems. It helps identify bottlenecks and latency issues by providing visibility into the path and duration of requests across services.

Building a Monitoring and Observability Stack

To efficiently monitor large-scale Argo CD deployments, an effective observability stack is required. Popular open-source tools include Prometheus for metrics, Grafana for visualization, Loki and Fluentd for logging, and Jaeger for tracing.

- **Metrics Collection with Prometheus:** Prometheus is a widely used monitoring tool in Kubernetes environments, known for its powerful query language and efficient time-series database. It collects metrics from instrumented applications and Kubernetes itself, providing a central repository for metric data.

  Deploying Prometheus in a Kubernetes cluster involves setting up Prometheus servers, exporters, and alert managers.

  ```
  apiVersion: monitoring.coreos.com/v1
  kind: Prometheus
  metadata:
    name: argo-prometheus
  spec:
    replicas: 1
    serviceAccountName: prometheus
    serviceMonitorSelector:
      matchLabels:
        app: argocd
  ```

  Prometheus can be configured to scrape metrics from Argo CD and other applications using service monitors, allowing centralized collection and analysis of metrics data.

- **Visualization with Grafana:** Grafana is a visualization tool that integrates seamlessly with Prometheus to create rich dashboards for real-time analysis. It supports a wide array of data sources and visualizes complex metric data through graphs, charts, and alerts.

  Creating dashboards in Grafana allows operations teams to visualize the health and performance of Argo CD:

    - **Setup and Configuration:** Once Grafana is installed and configured, it can connect to Prometheus as a data source. Dashboards can then be constructed to contain panels mapping specific metrics to graphical representations.

      ```
      apiVersion: v1
      kind: ConfigMap
      metadata:
        name: grafana-dashboards
      data:
        argo-dashboard.json: |
          {
            "title": "Argo CD Overview",
            "panels": [
              {
                "type": "graph",
                "metrics": "argo_cd_resource_usage",
                "title": "Resource Usage"
              }
            ]
          }
      ```

  These dashboards consolidate key metrics into a coherent interface, enabling real-time monitoring and rapid anomaly detection.

- **Logging with Loki and Fluentd:** Loki is a log aggregation system that pairs well with Prometheus and Grafana. It permits the storage and indexing of logs generated by Kubernetes pods without complex setups or log transformations.

    - **Setting Up Logs Collection:** Deploy Fluentd as a log collector to forward Kubernetes logs to Loki:

      ```
      apiVersion: apps/v1
      kind: DaemonSet
      metadata:
        name: fluentd
      spec:
      ```

8.7. MONITORING AND OBSERVABILITY AT SCALE

```
    selector:
      matchLabels:
        app: fluentd
    template:
      metadata:
        labels:
          app: fluentd
      spec:
        containers:
        - name: fluentd
          image: fluent/fluentd
```

Logs collected by Fluentd from various sources can be indexed in Loki, making them searchable and enabling correlation with metrics in Grafana.

- **Distributed Tracing with Jaeger:** Jaeger provides end-to-end distributed tracing, crucial for understanding request flows through complex microservices architectures. It assists operations teams in pinpointing latency issues and optimizing service interactions.

Set up Jaeger within Kubernetes to trace application requests managed by Argo CD:

```
apiVersion: v1
kind: Deployment
metadata:
  name: jaeger
spec:
  replicas: 1
  containers:
    - name: jaeger
      image: jaegertracing/all-in-one:1.21
```

Jaeger can collect trace data from instrumented applications, providing deep insights into the transactions within distributed systems.

Advanced Observability Strategies

For large-scale Argo CD deployments, basic observability might not be enough. Advanced techniques ensure more comprehensive system visibility:

- **Alerts and Anomaly Detection:** Prometheus alert rules can be configured alongside Alertmanager to trigger alerts on threshold breaches, facilitating proactive issue resolution before degradation affects users.

```
apiVersion: monitoring.coreos.com/v1
kind: PrometheusRule
metadata:
  name: alert-rule
spec:
  groups:
  - name: example
    rules:
    - alert: HighErrorRate
      expr: rate(errors[5m]) > 0.05
      for: 10m
      labels:
        severity: critical
      annotations:
        summary: "High request error rate"
        description: "High error rate detected on service {{ $labels.service }}"
```

- **Capacity Planning:** By leveraging historical data and trend analysis, capacity planning becomes more accurate, ensuring resources are provisioned efficiently to meet future demands without overprovisioning.

- **Integration with CI/CD Pipelines:** Integrate observability tooling within the CI/CD lifecycle, ensuring that performance and reliability metrics guide the deployment process, preventing regressions in production environments.

Ensuring Observability Scalability

Scaling observability operations requires strategic data management, fortified systems, and strategic resource allocation:

- **Data Retention and Management:** Control data retention policies to ensure observability storage systems don't become bottlenecks. Define retention limits within Prometheus and employ long-term storage solutions like Thanos for metrics archiving:

```
retention: 15d
storage.tsdb.path: "/prometheus/data"
```

- **Dedicated Observability Resources:** Allocate sufficient computing resources to observability stacks ensuring they don't compete with application workloads for system resources. Consider deploying observability tools across separate nodes or infrastructure.

- **Continuous Improvement and Feedback Loop:** Regular audits and refinements to observability practices ensure tools and strategies remain aligned with scale and complexity. Leverage insights gained from monitoring platforms to drive iterative improvements.

Monitoring and observability are critical for maintaining performance and reliability in scaled Argo CD deployments. These practices empower organizations to maintain visibility into their systems, effectively manage large-scale operations, and ensure that applications remain performant and robust under varying conditions. With the right strategies and tools in place, organizations can ensure that their Kubernetes environments are transparent, predictable, and agile.

Chapter 9

Security and Compliance in Argo CD Deployments

This chapter addresses critical aspects of ensuring security and compliance in Argo CD deployments. It outlines best practices for securing installations, including implementing role-based access control and managing secrets effectively. Strategies to meet industry compliance standards are discussed, alongside methods for monitoring and auditing Argo CD operations to maintain security integrity. Additionally, the chapter examines network security considerations and how to integrate security tools within CI/CD pipelines, fostering a secure and compliant deployment framework.

9.1 Securing Argo CD Installations

Securing Argo CD installations is a foundational element in ensuring not only the safeguarding of application deployments but also the broader infrastructure they occupy. This section elaborates on the critical aspects, configurations, and best practices needed to secure Argo CD installations effectively. These best practices, while focused on Argo CD, naturally extend implications into Kubernetes environments, offering a holistic approach to security.

Argo CD operates as a tool that automates Kubernetes deployments, offering continuous delivery with a declarative GitOps approach. As an extension of Kubernetes, it inherits many of its security features and challenges. Securely configuring Argo CD requires an understanding of both these aspects: securing the hosted environment and the Argo CD application itself.

Namespace Isolation. One fundamental security practice is to ensure namespace isolation. Kubernetes namespaces can be utilized to create boundaries within the cluster which helps limit access to resources and workloads. Argo CD should be installed in a separate namespace from the applications it manages. By minimizing inter-namespace access, the risk of privilege escalation and unauthorized access is significantly reduced.

```
kubectl create namespace argocd
```

Network Policies. Network policies form the core of Kubernetes network security, and their correct configuration can prevent unauthorized communications. Implementing network policies that restrict both ingress and egress traffic ensures only trusted sources can access Argo CD services.

```
kubectl apply -f - <<EOF
apiVersion: networking.k8s.io/v1
kind: NetworkPolicy
metadata:
  name: argocd-restrict-traffic
  namespace: argocd
spec:
  podSelector:
    matchLabels:
      app.kubernetes.io/part-of: argocd
  policyTypes:
  - Ingress
  - Egress
  ingress:
  - from:
    - ipBlock:
        cidr: 10.0.0.0/16
      namespaceSelector:
        matchLabels:
          name: trusted-namespace
```

```
    ports:
    - protocol: TCP
      port: 443
  egress:
  - to:
    - ipBlock:
        cidr: 10.0.0.0/16
    ports:
    - protocol: TCP
      port: 443
EOF
```

TLS/SSL Encryption. Ensuring encrypted communication between clients and servers is compulsory. Argo CD API servers must be configured with TLS to protect data in transit from interception and tampering. Argo CD comes with the ability to deploy its own self-signed certificates; however, for production environments, it's recommended to use certificates from a trusted Certificate Authority (CA).

```
kubectl patch secret argocd-secret \
  -n argocd \
  -p '{"data": {"tls.crt": "<base64-encoded-certificate>", "tls.key": "<base64-encoded-key>"}}'
```

Use of Network Segmentation. Segmenting different parts of the network is vital when examining security postures. Segmenting Argo CD's management traffic from application data traffic ensures that even if a part of the network gets compromised, the management plane remains secure, limiting lateral movement within the infrastructure.

Authentication and Authorization. Argo CD supports OAuth2 for authentication, which integrates well with SSO providers. It's essential to configure feasible authentication mechanisms to ensure only authenticated users can access the Argo CD UI and API. Moreover, tightly controlled role-based access control (RBAC) policies in Argo CD enforce minimal operator permissions, reducing potential damage in case of user credentials breach.

```
apiVersion: v1
kind: ConfigMap
metadata:
  name: argocd-cm
  namespace: argocd
data:
  configManagementPlugins: |
    - name: Example
      generate:
        command: ["/app/config", "generate"]
```

```
oidc.config: |
  name: Azure
  issuer: https://login.microsoftonline.com/{tenant}.onmicrosoft.com/v2.0
  clientID: <application_id>
  clientSecret: $oidc.azure.clientSecret
```

Audit Logs. Activating audit logs in Argo CD is a recommended practice to maintain visibility over the actions performed by users. This allows tracing of any unauthorized or dubious activity within the system, serving as a deterrent to malicious actions and aiding forensic analysis after an event.

```
apiVersion: v1
kind: ConfigMap
metadata:
  name: argocd-cm
  namespace: argocd
data:
  application.instanceLabelKey: argocd.argoproj.io/instance
  audit.log.enable: "true"
```

Securing Git Repositories. Since Argo CD is inherently tied to Git repositories, securing these repositories with proper access controls is critical. This involves configuring Git with the least privilege, typically allowing only read access to Argo CD while committing changes only done via secured and auditable channels. Additionally, integration of Git secrets management tools helps handle sensitive configurations.

Implementing multi-factor authentication (MFA) for version control systems further strengthens repository security, by requiring additional credentials beyond passwords.

Applying Security Patches. Regular updates and patch management to the underlying system are necessary for both the Kubernetes cluster and Argo CD. Up-to-date patch levels defend against vulnerabilities discovered in the software over time.

Image Security. Evaluate and standardize on trusted base container images for application deployments. The images should be signed, and integrity verified at all stages of the deployment cycle. Argo CD setups should additionally utilize Kubernetes admission controllers or tools like Open Policy Agent (OPA) to enforce policies regarding container image security.

Backup and Recovery. Ensure that a robust backup strategy is in place for everything related to Argo CD configuration. Regular snapshots should be taken not only of the Argo CD state but also of associated persistent storage volumes. This becomes crucial in terms of effective recovery from disruptive incidents.

Secret Management. Use secure stores, such as HashiCorp Vault or AWS Secrets Manager, while handling secrets. Integrating these components with Kubernetes ensures secrets remain encrypted both at rest and in transit, avoiding exposure in version control systems.

Resource Limits and Quotas. Define resource limits and quotas within each Argo CD namespace to prevent resource exhaustion, which could lead to Denial-of-Service (DoS) attacks. Resource management is essential for maintaining a balanced operational environment.

With the above strategies seamlessly implemented, Argo CD installations can maintain robust security standards, minimizing risks associated with unauthorized access, data breaches, or potential misconfigurations. These tactics not only fortify the deployment but also foster trust within the development pipeline, ensuring that security is an enabler rather than a hindrance in the deployment lifecycle.

9.2 Implementing Role-Based Access Control

Role-Based Access Control (RBAC) is a critical security mechanism used to manage access and permissions within Argo CD environments. By implementing RBAC, administrators can enforce consistent access policies, ensuring users have only the privileges necessary to perform their assigned functions. This section provides a detailed overview of RBAC within Argo CD, discussing configurations and strategies to maintain access control over resources efficiently.

Argo CD's RBAC system is built on top of the deeply ingrained Kubernetes RBAC model, extending its functionality to manage access specifically for Argo CD resources, applications, projects, and related elements. The primary objectives of RBAC implementation are to enforce the principle of least privilege and to mitigate the risk inherent in human error or malicious actions by defining clear, role-based policies.

Understanding Argo CD RBAC Components. The core components of Argo CD RBAC include roles, role bindings, policies, and subjects:

- **Roles:** Define a set of permissions within Argo CD, which could range from read access to managing entire workloads.

- **Role Bindings:** Associates roles with specific users or groups, effectively mapping the permissions to who can apply them.

- **Policies:** Articulated succinctly through policy rules, they delineate permissions granted by a role.

- **Subjects:** Entities, usually users or groups, that are granted permissions through role bindings.

Configuring Roles and Policies. Argo CD's configuration management involves defining roles and their associated policies in a ConfigMap. The following example illustrates a basic role configuration:

```
apiVersion: v1
kind: ConfigMap
metadata:
  name: argocd-rbac-cm
  namespace: argocd
data:
  policy.csv: |
    p, role:guest, applications, get, */*, allow
    p, role:developer, applications, create, */*, allow
    p, role:developer, applications, delete, */*, deny
    p, role:admin, *, *, */*, allow

  policy.default: role:guest
```

Creating and Binding Roles. Here, policies define roles such as guest, developer, and admin, with differing levels of access corresponding to action/resource pairs. Each policy is a line in the policy.csv data section, and the default role specifies fallback access for unauthenticated subjects.

Roles can be bound to users or groups using the following constructs:

```
apiVersion: v1
kind: ConfigMap
metadata:
  name: argocd-rbac-cm
  namespace: argocd
```

9.2. IMPLEMENTING ROLE-BASED ACCESS CONTROL

```
data:
  policy.csv: |
    g, alice, role:developer
    g, bob@example.com, role:guest
```

Here, alice is bound with a developer role, allowing her to create but not delete applications. Meanwhile, bob@example.com is bound as a guest, limiting his abilities primarily to viewing applications.

Issue of Namespace Scoping. RBAC needs to be considered with respect to namespace scoping. Roles can be created either cluster-wide or namespace specific. In many scenarios, particularly those incorporating multi-tenancy, it is beneficial to restrict roles to specific namespaces to prevent cross-tenant resource access.

Enforcing Least Privilege. Adhering to the principle of least privilege through RBAC means users obtain only those permissions required to perform their functions. Over-provisioning access can result in lateral movement during compromise and inadvertently expose resources to threats.

Dynamic Role Adjustments. Argo CD facilitates dynamic role assignments via CLI or the web interface to reflect organizational changes in real-time, such as team restructuring or job role changes within development operations.

Validating RBAC Policies. Validate configurations to ensure they meet organizational security policies. Misconfigurations in RBAC could inadvertently grant users more access than intended or, conversely, impede operational efficiency.

```
argocd-rbac-tool check --role=role:developer --action=create --kind=applications --deny
```

Integration with External Identity Providers. Argo CD supports integration with external identity providers (IdPs) for authenticating users leveraging OAuth2, SAML, or LDAP protocols. The connection to external IdPs allows organizations to manage users within their central directory services, benefitting from established authentication methodologies and user repositories.

Integration not only simplifies user management but also bolsters security by externalizing authentication mechanisms to IdPs which likely employ robust security measures, including Multi-Factor Authentication (MFA).

Example with OAuth2 (GitHub Integration). Integrating Argo CD with GitHub OAuth2 provides a practical implementation for managing user identities via GitHub's central repository of users.

```
apiVersion: v1
kind: ConfigMap
metadata:
  name: argocd-cm
  namespace: argocd
data:
  url: https://github.com
  oidc.config: |
    name: GitHub
    issuer: https://github.com/login/oauth
    clientID: <your-client-id>
    clientSecret: $oidc.github.clientSecret
    requestedScopes: ["user", "repo"]
```

Audit and Compliance Reporting. RBAC unravel mechanisms for auditing and compliance; through logging every access attempt, administrators have a comprehensive view into the system utilization — sudden spikes in role usage, unusual patterns of access, or denied attempts serve as vital indicators of potential security incidents.

Challenges and Considerations. Implementing RBAC is not devoid of challenges. Administrators must pay heed to the following considerations to avoid pitfalls:

- **Complexity:** As the system scales, managing numerous roles and policies could grow complex, potentially making it difficult to manage and audit effectively.

- **Change Management:** Role reassignments must be conducted in accordance with precise operational procedures, ensuring no workflow disruptions.

- **Scope Creep:** Periodic role reviews are necessary to mitigate scope creep, where users might accrue excessive permissions over time due to accumulated role assignments.

Implementing RBAC effectively within Argo CD translates into decentralized access management that provides stringent security checks while accommodating operational flexibility. It propagates a self-sustaining environment where security is inherently a part of the operational workflow, minimizing risks without imposing operational inefficiencies. Armed with a comprehensive understanding of RBAC within Argo CD, administrators can fortify their deployment infrastructure, thereby mitigating unauthorized access and ensuring confidentiality, integrity, and availability of resources.

9.3 Handling Secrets and Sensitive Data

The management of secrets and sensitive data within Argo CD is a fundamental aspect of securing deployments. Proper handling of secrets involves not only storing them securely but also ensuring their confidentiality, integrity, and availability in modern cloud-native environments. This segment will explore the techniques and strategies employed to manage secrets within Argo CD deployments, ensuring that these critical pieces of information remain protected against unauthorized access or unintended exposure.

Understanding Secrets in Kubernetes and Argo CD. In Kubernetes, secrets are objects that contain sensitive information such as passwords, OAuth tokens, or SSH keys. They are base64-encoded during storage in etcd but are not automatically encrypted. As Argo CD operates within Kubernetes, the management of secrets leverages Kubernetes constructs but requires additional considerations specific to GitOps practices within Argo CD.

Challenges in Secret Management. Traditional methods of secret handling, such as embedding credentials within application configurations or version control systems, pose significant security risks. Unauthorized access or leaks could lead to compromised systems, data breaches, or unauthorized data manipulation.

Encryption at Rest and in Transit. An initial line of defense involves ensuring that secrets are encrypted at rest and in transit. Kubernetes version 1.13 and later supports etcd encryption, which encrypts secrets stored in the etcd database.

```
apiVersion: apiserver.config.k8s.io/v1
kind: EncryptionConfiguration
resources:
  - resources:
```

```
      - secrets
    providers:
      - aescbc:
          keys:
            - name: key1
              secret: <base64-encoded-aes-key>
      - identity: {}
```

This configuration ensures that any secret stored in etcd is encrypted, thereby mitigating the risk of data being compromised on disk by unauthorized users.

Additionally, using TLS for all communications within the cluster, including inter-component and user-to-cluster interactions, ensures that secrets remain protected in transit.

Use of External Secret Management Solutions. Deployments often benefit from integrating with external secret management solutions such as HashiCorp Vault, AWS Secrets Manager, or Azure Key Vault, providing more sophisticated mechanisms for secret management. These tools typically offer robust features, including secret versioning, access logs, and fine-grained access controls, extending well beyond what Kubernetes natively offers.

Example of Integration with HashiCorp Vault.

```
apiVersion: argoproj.io/v1alpha1
kind: AppProject
metadata:
  name: my-project
spec:
  ...
  syncPolicy:
    automated:
      prune: true
      selfHeal: true
  sourceRepos:
    - '*'
  destinations:
    - namespace: '*'
      server: 'https://kubernetes.default.svc'
  vaultSecrets:
    allowedPaths:
      - 'secret/data/my-application/*'
```

This project configuration allows Argo CD to retrieve secrets from HashiCorp Vault, providing seamless secret injection into applications without exposing sensitive data.

9.3. HANDLING SECRETS AND SENSITIVE DATA

Implementing Sealed Secrets. An alternative approach involves using tools like Sealed Secrets by Bitnami, which encrypts secret manifests and stores them within Git repositories. This approach aligns closely with GitOps practices by allowing secrets to be managed in the same way as application configurations while remaining secure.

```
kubeseal --controller-name=sealed-secrets --controller-namespace=kube-system <
    mysecret.json> > mysealedsecret.json
kubectl apply -f mysealedsecret.json
```

This workflow encrypts the secret manifest and creates a SealedSecret resource, which the Sealed Secrets controller can decrypt and deploy into Kubernetes as a native Secret.

RBAC and Policy Enforcement for Secret Access. Argo CD's RBAC can be configured to control which users can access and modify secret-containing applications, thereby reducing the risk of unauthorized access.

```
apiVersion: v1
kind: ConfigMap
metadata:
  name: argocd-rbac-cm
  namespace: argocd
data:
  policy.csv: |
    p, role:devops, secrets, *, */*, allow
    p, role:developer, *, *, */*, deny
    g, john@example.com, role:devops
```

In this policy configuration, only users assigned the devops role are permitted to access and manage secrets, whereas developers are denied such access, maintaining the principle of least privilege.

Auditing and Monitoring Secret Access. Monitoring access to secrets adds an additional layer of security by enabling the detection of potential unauthorized access patterns. Enabling audit logging within Kubernetes and Argo CD facilitates the tracking of secret-related operations, providing forensic insight to investigate incidents.

Automated Secret Rotation. Automating the rotation of secrets minimizes the risk of credential misuse and maintains compliance with security policies. Tools like external secret stores often support automated rotation features, which ensure that secrets are regularly and automatically renewed without manual intervention.

Use of Environment Variables for Secrets. Although injecting secrets into containers via environment variables is a common practice, it is not without risks. Environment variables can sometimes inadvertently be exposed through logs or process listing. Therefore, it is generally better to mount secrets as volumes within pods, accessing them when necessary and avoiding persistent storage.

An Illustrative Approach: Mounting Secrets as Volumes.

```
apiVersion: v1
kind: Pod
metadata:
  name: mypod
spec:
  containers:
    - name: myapp
      image: myapp:latest
      volumeMounts:
        - name: secret-volume
          mountPath: "/etc/secret"
  volumes:
    - name: secret-volume
      secret:
        secretName: mysecret
```

By mounting the secret as a volume, applications can access the required sensitive data without risking exposure to the broader environment.

Considerations for Hybrid and Multi-Cloud Environments. In hybrid and multi-cloud infrastructures, the consistent management of secrets across diverse platforms often requires the adoption of multi-cloud secret management solutions or platforms that can integrate securely with multiple cloud providers.

Conclusion Without Deliberate Finality. Effectively handling secrets and sensitive data within Argo CD installations requires a multifaceted approach that leverages built-in Kubernetes capabilities and external secret management tools. This approach must consider operational transparency, governance and compliance requirements, and organizational security policies. By implementing comprehensive strategies and solutions tailored to specific deployment needs, organizations can ensure that sensitive data remains protected, minimizing the risk of exposure and bolstering the overall security posture of their Kubernetes and Argo CD-driven environments.

9.4 Ensuring Compliance with Standards

Compliance with industry standards is an essential facet of any organization's operational strategy, particularly when deploying applications using platforms like Argo CD. Compliance not only supports legal and regulatory requirements but also ensures a commitment to security best practices, reinforcing organizational credibility and operational integrity. This section explores the methodologies for ensuring compliance with standards when deploying applications via Argo CD, highlighting integral components such as policy enforcement, auditing, and continuous compliance monitoring.

The Importance of Compliance in Modern Deployments. In today's regulated environments, adherence to standards such as the General Data Protection Regulation (GDPR), Health Insurance Portability and Accountability Act (HIPAA), Sarbanes-Oxley (SOX), and Payment Card Industry Data Security Standard (PCI-DSS) is crucial. These standards outline requisite security controls, access management protocols, data protection techniques, and audit requirements that must be adhered to in order to safeguard sensitive information and ensure trustworthiness.

Mapping Compliance Requirements to Argo CD. For organizations using Argo CD, achieving compliance necessitates aligning its operations and configurations with the requisite industry standards. This involves:

- **Policy Definition:** Establishing clear governance policies that dictate acceptable practices and configurations.

- **Access Control:** Implementing Role-Based Access Control (RBAC) and ensuring least privilege principles.

- **Data Protection:** Ensuring encrypted data both at rest and in transit.

- **Audit Trails:** Maintaining comprehensive monitoring and logging capabilities to trace user and system actions.

- **Incident Response Strategies:** Having documented procedures for addressing potential security incidents or compliance violations.

Policy Definition and Enforcement. Central to compliance is the definition and enforcement of organizational policies. In Argo CD, policies can be automated and enforced through policy-as-code systems: tools like Open Policy Agent (OPA) and its Gatekeeper extension allow for the establishment of Kubernetes policies.

Implementing OPA with Gatekeeper example:

```
apiVersion: templates.gatekeeper.sh/v1beta1
kind: ConstraintTemplate
metadata:
  name: k8srequiredlabels
spec:
  crd:
    spec:
      names:
        kind: K8sRequiredLabels
  targets:
    - target: admission.k8s.gatekeeper.sh
      rego: |
        package k8srequiredlabels
        constraint[{"msg": msg}] {
          missing_label := input.review.object.metadata.labels.required
          msg := sprintf("The label '%v' is required.", [missing_label])
          not { has_label[mising_label] }
        }
```

Such policies enforce required configurations across deployments, ensuring compliance is baked into every stage of development and deployment, not added later as an afterthought.

Auditing and Log Management. To meet compliance needs, organizations must maintain robust logging and audit trail capabilities. Kubernetes provides logging abilities, but these can be insufficient when operating at scale or for detailed compliance reporting. Tools such as Fluentd can be deployed alongside Argo CD to aggregate logs from across the system, which then are sent to centralized logging platforms or security information and event management (SIEM) systems for analysis and reporting.

Example Fluentd configuration for capturing Argo CD logs:

```
apiVersion: v1
kind: ConfigMap
metadata:
```

9.4. ENSURING COMPLIANCE WITH STANDARDS

```
  name: fluentd-config
  namespace: logging
data:
  fluent.conf: |
    <source>
      @type tail
      path /var/log/argocd/*.log
      pos_file /var/log/fluentd-argocd.pos
      format none
      tag argocd.*
    </source>

    <match **>
      @type stdout
    </match>
```

Such configurations enable compliance teams to reconstruct system events, investigate anomalies, and demonstrate to auditors that compliance requirements are being met.

Securing Data in Transit and at Rest. Compliance often involves stringent data protection mandates, including encryption requirements. Following the practices of securing communication with TLS, ensuring etcd encryption for Kubernetes secrets, and using external vaults or secret managers is indispensable.

Encryption should be multi-layered, ensuring that redundant security measures mitigate any single point of failure. For instance, data-at-rest encryption uses filesystem encryption alongside storage volume encryption. For data-in-transit, it leverages VPNs or secure tunneling in conjunction with application-layer encryption.

Continuous Compliance Monitoring. Continuous compliance is achieved through ongoing monitoring and evaluation of current configurations against established policies. By utilizing cloud-native compliance tools like Aqua Security or Falco, organizations can implement continuous checks and reporting.

Example deployment of Falco for runtime security:

```
apiVersion: apps/v1
kind: DaemonSet
metadata:
  name: falco
  namespace: kube-system
spec:
  selector:
    matchLabels:
      app: falco
  template:
```

```
metadata:
  labels:
    app: falco
spec:
  containers:
  - name: falco
    image: falcosecurity/falco:latest
```

Falco monitors container, host, and application behavior, comparing these against a set of rules and recording activities that deviate from norms — a central part of compliance monitoring.

Incident Response and Compliance Reporting. Effective incident response programs are pivotal for compliance, involving well-documented protocols that guide teams during security incidents. These include identification, containment, eradication, recovery, and lessons learned stages.

Compliance reporting also captures essential metrics and evidence that auditors require. Reports should be generated on a routine basis and upon request, detailing the compliance status of the organization concerning its use of Argo CD and Kubernetes.

Training and Awareness. Compliance transcends technology into the realm of culture. Regular training and awareness programs help ensure that all personnel understand their roles and responsibilities in maintaining compliance. This involves instructions on best security practices, updates on regulatory changes, and drills on incident response procedures.

Compliance with standards in Argo CD deployments is not merely a check-box exercise but an integral facet of deploying secure, trusted, and verifiable systems on which businesses, partners, and customers can rely. By properly aligning Argo CD practices with recognized compliance measures, organizations not only protect data and manage risks but also fortify their governance frameworks, driving business excellence in regulated sectors.

9.5 Monitoring and Auditing Argo CD Activities

Monitoring and auditing activities within Argo CD are essential processes ensuring operational oversight, security integrity, and compliance with organizational policies. The dynamic nature of cloud-native environments, combined with the high stakes of application deployments, necessitates a robust framework for tracking and auditing activities. This section delves into methodologies, tools, and best practices for effectively monitoring and auditing Argo CD activities, ensuring organizations maintain maximum visibility and control over their deployment pipelines.

Importance of Monitoring and Auditing. Monitoring focuses on observing system performance, health, and behaviors in real-time, allowing for immediate response to issues such as performance degradations or unexpected downtime. Auditing, on the other hand, involves logging historical data about actions taken and events occurring within the system, providing a trail of evidence for compliance and forensic analysis following incidents.

Both processes are crucial for detecting unauthorized access, system misconfigurations, or breaches: factors that could compromise data integrity, availability, or confidentiality.

Monitoring Argo CD Activities. Monitoring in the context of Argo CD involves collecting metrics and logs that provide insights into the operational state of the tool and the applications it manages. A successful monitoring strategy includes:

- **Metrics Collection:** Involves gathering quantitative measurements over time. These metrics, which can be exported to monitoring dashboards, provide insights into system load, resource utilization, application performance, and more.

- **Alerting Systems:** Automated alerts based on defined thresholds inform operators of abnormal conditions, facilitating quick remediation.

- **Visual Dashboards:** Tools like Grafana can be used to visualize collected data, making trends and potential issues evident at a glance.

Using Prometheus for Metrics. Prometheus, a leading open-source monitoring system, integrates seamlessly with Argo CD and Kubernetes to collect and store metrics. It uses exporters and service discovery to gather metrics, which are then queried for monitoring purposes.

To integrate Prometheus with Argo CD, one can set up a Prometheus server in the Kubernetes cluster:

```
apiVersion: monitoring.coreos.com/v1
kind: ServiceMonitor
metadata:
  name: argocd
  namespace: monitoring
spec:
  selector:
    matchLabels:
      app.kubernetes.io/part-of: argocd
  endpoints:
  - port: 8080
```

This ServiceMonitor configuration tells Prometheus to scrape metrics from Argo CD pods, focusing on internal metrics exposed by Argo CD.

Visualizing Metrics with Grafana. Grafana acts as a front-end to visualize metrics collected by Prometheus. By configuring data sources and creating dashboards, administrators can gain insights into system operation.

Creating an Argo CD dashboard in Grafana involves:

```
{
  "panels": [
    {
      "title": "Application Sync Status",
      "type": "gauge",
      "targets": [
        {
          "expr": "argocd_app_info",
          "legendFormat": "{{app}}"
        }
      ]
    }
  ]
}
```

This JSON exemplifies a query panel configuration in Grafana that displays the synchronization status of Argo CD applications visually, ensuring that operators quickly understand the synchronization state across different applications.

Auditing Argo CD Activities. Auditing is focused on creating a reliable, immutable record of actions performed within Argo CD environments. This activity log is critical for both regulatory compliance and security investigations.

Enabling Argo CD Audit Logs. Argo CD comes with built-in auditing capabilities, logging critical changes and events, such as application sync operations, user logins, and configuration updates.

```
apiVersion: v1
kind: ConfigMap
metadata:
  name: argocd-cm
  namespace: argocd
data:
  audit.log.enable: "true"
  audit.log.level: "info"
```

This configuration snippet illustrates how to enable and set audit log verbosity to capture all activities within Argo CD, providing actionable intelligence for security operations teams.

Integrating Logs with Centralized Logging Systems. Forwarding these logs to a centralized logging system like Elasticsearch or Splunk ensures long-term retention and advanced querying capabilities.

Using Fluentd to ship logs:

```
apiVersion: v1
kind: ConfigMap
metadata:
  name: fluentd-config
  namespace: logging
data:
  fluent.conf: |
    <source>
      @type tail
      path /var/log/argocd/audit.log
      pos_file /var/log/argocd/audit-log.pos
      format json
      tag argocd.audit
    </source>

    <match argocd.audit>
      @type elasticsearch
      host es-cluster
      port 9200
```

```
logstash_format true
</match>
```

This logging pipeline moves Argo CD audit logs into an Elasticsearch cluster, enabling data analytics, anomaly detection, and audit trails.

Security Information and Event Management (SIEM). Incorporating a SIEM system can enhance capabilities by combining log analysis with threat intelligence. It provides correlation rules, user activity monitoring, and real-time alerts that indicate potential security incidents.

Compliance Reporting and Audit Readiness. Many regulations necessitate periodic audits, requiring detailed records of system activities. Pre-configured dashboards and reports within SIEMs and log management tools facilitate demonstrating compliance with standards such as PCI-DSS, making audit preparation less burdensome.

Challenges in Monitoring and Auditing. Several challenges are associated with monitoring and auditing in distributed systems:

- **Data Volume:** The sheer volume of logs and metrics can overwhelm monitoring systems if not adequately managed. Predefining what constitutes critical information helps mitigate data overload.

- **False Positives:** Misconfigured alerts or thresholds can lead to alert fatigue. Regular review and tuning of alert policies are essential to maintain efficacy.

- **Integration Complexity:** Different systems may have incompatible data schemas, complicating integration efforts. Utilizing standard interfaces or adapters can help harmonize data flows.

Training and Preparedness. Finally, organizational readiness plays a critical role. Training technical staff on interpreting metrics and analyzing log data ensures they are well-prepared to handle incidents. Likewise, having refined incident response playbooks tailored to detected anomalies accelerates response times and minimizes operational impact.

Monitoring and auditing in Argo CD environments build a framework dedicated to operational transparency, proactive threat detection, and compliance adherence. Implemented effectively, this framework fosters higher confidence levels from stakeholders, contributes to improved security postures, and bolsters the resilience of the deployment pipeline. It's an investment in operational excellence, fortifying the processes that enable the seamless and secure delivery of software applications.

9.6 Network Security and Argo CD

Network security is crucial in safeguarding Argo CD deployments and their interactions. Proper network security practices protect against unauthorized access, data interception, and integrity breaches during data transmission. This section explains the principles and practices for securing network communications between Argo CD components and Kubernetes clusters, emphasizing the application of security best practices to ensure a robust deployment environment.

Understanding Network Security in Cloud-Native Architectures. With the shift to cloud-native architectures, applications are often spread across complex, distributed environments. These architectures utilize microservices, which necessitate constant communication within and across network boundaries. This ubiquity of networking demands stringent security controls to prevent data loss, unauthorized access, and service disruptions.

Core Components Affecting Network Security:

1. **Ingress Controllers:** Manage external access to services within a Kubernetes cluster, translating external requests to appropriate services.

2. **Service Meshes:** Provide microservice-to-microservice communication, offering security controls like mTLS (Mutual Transport Layer Security).

3. **Network Policies:** Govern the traffic flow between pods and services based on defined rules.

Network Security Considerations for Argo CD.

- **Access Control:** Implement strict access controls at the network level to ensure that only authorized systems and users can access Argo CD.

- **Encryption in Transit:** Utilize Transport Layer Security (TLS) to encrypt communications between Argo CD, Git repositories, and Kubernetes.

- **Ingress and Egress Control:** Argo CD should be restricted in its ability to communicate beyond what is necessary for its function, preventing data exfiltration and unwanted intrusions.

Ingress Controllers. These manage external requests and are configured with TLS to secure data in transit. For Argo CD, setting up an ingress controller can involve using NGINX or any other supported controller to manage HTTP and HTTPS traffic securely.

Example configuring NGINX Ingress for Argo CD:

```
apiVersion: networking.k8s.io/v1
kind: Ingress
metadata:
  name: argocd-server
  namespace: argocd
  annotations:
    nginx.ingress.kubernetes.io/ssl-redirect: "true"
    nginx.ingress.kubernetes.io/backend-protocol: "HTTPS"
spec:
  rules:
    - host: argocd.example.com
      http:
        paths:
          - path: /
            pathType: Prefix
            backend:
              service:
                name: argocd-server
                port:
                  number: 443
  tls:
    - hosts:
        - argocd.example.com
      secretName: argocd-secret
```

The configuration specifies that all ingress traffic is redirected to HTTPS, ensuring secure communications.

Service Mesh Integration. Leveraging a service mesh such as Istio offers significant advantages for secure inter-service communications by providing automatic mTLS between services. For Argo CD, a service mesh can enhance security without changing the application logic.

```
istioctl install --set profile=default
kubectl label namespace argocd istio-injection=enabled
```

This command installs Istio and configures Argo CD for automatic sidecar injection, enabling secure service communication.

Kubernetes Network Policies. These define how pods within a cluster can communicate with each other and other network endpoints. Network policies are crucial for limiting unnecessary data flows, mitigating the risk of spread during compromises.

Example of a restrictive network policy:

```
apiVersion: networking.k8s.io/v1
kind: NetworkPolicy
metadata:
  name: argocd-deny-ingress
  namespace: argocd
spec:
  podSelector: {}
  policyTypes:
  - Ingress
  - Egress
  ingress:
  - from:
    - podSelector:
        matchLabels:
          access: front-end
  egress:
  - to:
    - ipBlock:
        cidr: 10.0.0.0/8
```

This policy allows ingress only from pods labeled with 'front-end' access, and egress is solely permitted to designated IP blocks, reducing the attack surface.

Zero Trust Networking. Implementing zero trust principles requires that all communications, whether internal or external, are authenticated and authorized. This model dismantles implicit trust within the network perimeter, favoring stringent verification measures.

Secure Git Connections. Argo CD's fundamental reliance on Git necessitates securing Git communication. Employing SSH for Git interactions offers encrypted tunnels, ensuring the confidentiality and integrity of code and configuration data.

Example of SSH key credential injection in Argo CD:

```
apiVersion: v1
kind: Secret
metadata:
  name: ssh-credentials
  namespace: argocd
data:
  ssh-privatekey: <base64-encoded-private-key>
type: kubernetes.io/ssh-auth
```

By using SSH keys this way, Argo CD can securely pull configurations from private repositories.

API Server Security. Argo CD's API server handles critical operations and is a target for malicious actors. Immutable logging, rate limiting, and ensuring that the API server is not publicly exposed are fundamental protections.

Configuration for logging and enforcing RBAC controls:

```
apiVersion: v1
kind: ConfigMap
metadata:
  name: argocd-cm
  namespace: argocd
data:
  server: |
    loglevel: "info"
  rbac: |
    enabled: "true"
```

These configurations position the API server for secure operations with clear logs aiding in incident response.

DDoS Protection and Scalability. Protect Argo CD services from Distributed Denial of Service (DDoS) attacks by employing cloud provider services like AWS Shield or GCP's Cloud Armor, which offer scalable protection against high-volume attacks.

Incident Response and Monitoring. Integrated monitoring tools like Prometheus can track network performance and alert operators of suspicious activity, allowing prompt intervention. Complementary to this, maintaining updated documentation on incident response procedures ensures that teams are ready to deal with breaches effectively.

Challenges of Network Security in Argo CD Deployments.

Network security in cloud-native environments has its challenges, such as:

- **Complexity:** The dynamic nature of containers and microservices increases the complexity of applying traditional security methodologies.

- **Resource Requirements:** Implementing comprehensive network security measures can be resource-intensive, necessitating dynamic scaling solutions.

- **False Sense of Security:** Misconfigured security features can provide a false sense of security, underscoring the importance of routine audits and tests.

Security Training and Awareness. By continually training staff on network security principles and staying updated with evolving threats, organizations can reinforce a security-first culture that mitigates risks associated with human factors.

Achieving nuanced network security in Argo CD deployments involves a combination of encryption, access control, policy enforcement, and technological integrations like service meshes and zero-trust architectures. Through a convergence of these methods supported by monitoring and auditing, organizations can safeguard deployments, ensuring data remains protected and services stay resilient in the face of emergent threats. These measures instill confidence, aligning system performance with strategic objectives in secure, agile delivery environments.

9.7 Integrating Security Tools in CI/CD Pipelines

The integration of security tools into Continuous Integration/Continuous Deployment (CI/CD) pipelines is a pivotal practice in DevSecOps, ensuring that security is not an afterthought but an integral part of the development and deployment lifecycle. By embedding security tools across the CI/CD workflow, organizations can detect and remediate vulnerabilities faster, enhance compliance with security policies, and deliver more secure applications. This section explores strategies and best practices for integrating security tools into CI/CD pipelines using Argo CD as a central orchestrator.

The Role of CI/CD in DevSecOps. CI/CD pipelines automate the software development lifecycle, facilitating rapid feedback and iteration. In DevSecOps, embedding security within these pipelines aligns with the shift-left ideology, pushing security evaluations to earlier stages and encouraging continuous security improvement rather than bolted-on measures nearing a software release.

Security Tools for CI/CD Integration. A range of security tools is available to address different aspects of security, from code analysis to infrastructure validation:

- **Static Application Security Testing (SAST):** Automates the examination of source code for vulnerabilities before code is integrated.

- **Dynamic Application Security Testing (DAST):** Analyzes running applications for security issues, simulating real-world attacks.

- **Software Composition Analysis (SCA):** Evaluates third-party components for known vulnerabilities and license compliance.

- **Infrastructure as Code (IaC) Security:** Tools like Checkov and Terraform Validate inspect IaC templates for configuration weaknesses.

- **Container Security:** Focuses on the assessment of containers and their dependencies for vulnerabilities.

Integrating SAST Tools. SAST tools identify vulnerabilities early, before integration, allowing developers to address issues directly in the source code. Tools like SonarQube or Snyk can be included in CI/CD pipelines to provide immediate feedback.

SonarQube integration example:

```
stages:
  - 'build'
```

9.7. INTEGRATING SECURITY TOOLS IN CI/CD PIPELINES

```
  - 'test'
  - 'deploy'

build:
  script:
    - mvn clean install
  stage: build

sonarqube-check:
  image: $MAVEN_IMAGE
  stage: test
  script:
    - mvn sonar:sonar \
      -Dsonar.projectKey=$PROJECT_KEY \
      -Dsonar.host.url=$SONAR_HOST_URL \
      -Dsonar.login=$SONAR_LOGIN
  allow_failure: true
```

This GitLab CI configuration runs SonarQube for code quality and security checks, delivering reports on vulnerabilities within the source code.

DAST Tool Integration. Dynamic tools like OWASP ZAP can automate the security testing of running applications. These tools simulate attacks against the application as it executes within a staging or production-like environment.

Example OWASP ZAP configuration in Jenkins:

```
pipeline {
    agent any
    stages {
        stage('Build') {
            steps {
                sh 'mvn clean package'
            }
        }
        stage('Deploy') {
            steps {
                sh './deploy.sh'
            }
        }
        stage('Test with ZAP') {
            steps {
                sh 'zap.sh -daemon -quickurl http://staging.myapp.com'
            }
        }
    }
}
```

This Jenkins pipeline executes OWASP ZAP to test a deployed application for runtime vulnerabilities, enhancing dynamic security analysis.

SCA Integration. Integrating tools like Dependabot and WhiteSource helps in identifying vulnerabilities in third-party libraries used by applications. This is crucial for managing dependency risks, ensuring libraries are current and secure.

Dependabot example configuration for GitHub:

```
version: 2
updates:
  - package-ecosystem: "npm"
    directory: "/"
    schedule:
      interval: "weekly"
```

Dependabot automates pull requests to update vulnerable dependencies weekly, integrating seamlessly into the GitHub repository workflow.

IaC Security. Tools like Checkov scan IaC configurations to validate security best practices. By checking Terraform or Kubernetes manifests, they help prevent misconfigurations before deployment.

Checkov integration in a CI system:

```
stages:
  - lint

tf-lint:
  stage: lint
  image: bridgecrew/checkov:latest
  script:
    - checkov -d .
```

Using Checkov in the CI pipeline identifies potential misconfigurations, improving infrastructure security measures from the outset.

Container Security in CI/CD. As containers become ubiquitous, securing them is paramount. Tools such as Aqua or Clair assess container images for known vulnerabilities during the build phase.

Integrating Aqua Trivy Example:

```
stages:
  - scan

trivy-scan:
  image:
    name: aquasec/trivy:latest
  stage: scan
  script:
    - trivy image myapp:latest
```

9.7. INTEGRATING SECURITY TOOLS IN CI/CD PIPELINES

This stage in a CI pipeline automatically scans Docker images for vulnerabilities using Trivy, producing reports to guide image remediation.

Continuous Monitoring and Feedback. Integrate monitoring solutions like Prometheus and Grafana into the CI/CD pipeline to monitor the security of deployed applications continuously. Alert configurations in Grafana can specify security threshold breaches, providing operators with real-time feedback.

Example Grafana Alert for Security Monitoring:

```
{
  "dashboard": {
    "id": 1,
    "title": "Security Monitoring",
    "panels": [
      {
        "title": "Vulnerabilities Detected",
        "metrics": [
          {
            "target": "vulnerabilities.count"
          }
        ],
        "alert": {
          "conditions": [
            {
              "type": "query",
              "evaluator": "gt",
              "threshold": 5
            }
          ]
        }
      }
    ]
  }
}
```

Alerts are set to trigger when vulnerabilities surpass a certain threshold, enabling immediate response to emergent security issues.

Automating Compliance and Governance. Establish automated checks for policy compliance using tools like OPA (Open Policy Agent), which applies security policies dynamically during the CI stage.

Example OPA Gatekeeper policy:

```
apiVersion: templates.gatekeeper.sh/v1beta1
kind: ConstraintTemplate
metadata:
  name: k8ssecurecontext
```

```
spec:
  crd:
    spec:
      names:
        kind: K8sSecureContext
  targets:
  - target: admission.k8s.gatekeeper.sh
    rego: |
      package kubernetes.admission
      deny[reason] {
        input.request.kind.kind == "Pod"
        input.request.kind.namespace == "default"
        reason := "Pods cannot be deployed to the default namespace"
      }
```

This policy enforces Kubernetes namespace security as an automated compliance check, ensuring deployments meet governance criteria.

Challenges and Best Practices.

- **Tools Overload:** An abundance of security tools can cause tool fatigue, making it difficult to maintain pipelines. Prioritize tools that offer comprehensive feature sets and integrate well with existing ecosystems.

- **Performance Impacts:** Some security tools can lengthen build times. Optimize by parallelizing scans and leveraging caching to minimize delays.

- **Education and Training:** It's essential to continually educate the development team on security implications and the correct interpretation of tool outputs to drive meaningful action.

Integrating security tools within CI/CD pipelines through Argo CD and allied technologies erects a robust line of defense, inserting security by design into every phase of development and deployment. Through careful selection and configuration, these security integrations enhance not only the resilience of application environments but also facilitate compliance, ultimately reducing the organization's exposure to security threats while fostering a proactive security culture.

Chapter 10

Troubleshooting and Monitoring Argo CD Deployments

This chapter focuses on identifying and resolving common issues encountered in Argo CD deployments. It provides techniques for debugging failed deployments and managing logs to gain operational insights. Key strategies for monitoring deployment health are discussed to ensure application stability. The chapter also highlights the use of Argo CD's built-in tools for troubleshooting and proactive alerting systems to address potential issues promptly. Through real-world examples, readers gain practical knowledge to effectively overcome deployment challenges and maintain robust operations.

10.1 Identifying Common Issues in Argo CD

Identifying common issues within Argo CD deployments necessitates a comprehensive understanding of the various components that constitute the Argo CD ecosystem. Argo CD is a declarative, GitOps-based continuous delivery tool designed to accommodate operational workflows in Kubernetes environments. Despite its streamlined approach to application lifecycle management through Git as the source of truth, users may encounter several operational challenges. This section delves into these prevalent issues with an aim to elucidate potential causative factors and foster ingrained practices for mitigation.

Central to navigating Argo CD issues is the predisposition to recognize where interferences often emerge: synchronization, configuration, access control, and system resource limits. Before delving into the minutiae, it is crucial to comprehend the architecture and processing paths commonly influencing how issues surface.

In Argo CD, the application resource represents a Kubernetes custom resource defining upstream Git repositories, their contents, and desired configurations. The Argo CD controller performs continuous reconciliation between the desired state articulated in the source repository and the live state on the Kubernetes cluster. This closed-loop control mechanism is where most common issues gestate.

1. Synchronization Errors

One of the foremost issues users may encounter revolves around synchronization failures. Synchronization in Argo CD is the process of aligning the live Kubernetes state with the desired state as specified in the Git repository. Synchronization errors typically arise due to inconsistencies in the state representations or misconfigurations.

```
apiVersion: argoproj.io/v1alpha1
kind: Application
metadata:
  name: my-application
spec:
  source:
    repoURL: 'git@github.com:example/repo.git'
    path: <path-to-manifest>
  destination:
    server: 'https://kubernetes.default.svc'
```

10.1. IDENTIFYING COMMON ISSUES IN ARGO CD

```
namespace: <namespace>
```

The YAML manifest above exemplifies a simple Argo CD Application configuration. Critical checkpoints to verify in resolving synchronization issues include:

- *repoURL*: Ensure the Git repository URL is correct, accessible, and authorized for the Argo CD environment.
- *path*: Confirm the specified path exists within the repo and points correctly to the intended manifests.
- *server*: Validate connection endpoints against intended clusters, especially in multi-cluster environments.
- Ensure manifests are correctly formatted and syntactically valid to prevent reconciliation interruptions.

Additionally, checking the health status of applications via the Argo CD UI or CLI can reveal insights into why deviations exist.

2. Network and Connectivity Constraints

Network latency and connectivity limitations can severely impair Argo CD operations, particularly when infrastructure spans multiple distributed cloud environments. These constraints manifest significantly during repository fetches and updates.

Common troubleshooting steps include:

- Verify network access from Argo CD components to the Git server, often involving checklists for egress firewall rules.
- Examine connectivity from Argo CD to Kubernetes APIs, checking ingress rules particularly under network policies.
- Deploy network diagnostic tools within the cluster to track latency or packet loss dynamics.

3. Configuration Drift

Configuration drift refers to the condition where the live state in the Kubernetes cluster diverges from the desired state in the Git repository over time. This can be a subtle yet significant issue if not promptly addressed, as it erodes reliability in deployment consistency.

Effective practices to manage configuration drift entail:

- Regular snapshots of live manifests and comparison against Git-based desired states.

- Automated scripts that frequently poll and document state changes to alert when discrepancies emerge.

- Utilize Argo CD's auto-sync feature to enforce more immediate reconciliations, though cautiously as it necessitates disciplined version control and testing practices.

4. Role-Based Access Control (RBAC) Quandaries

Secure access control is paramount, with Argo CD relying on Kubernetes-native RBAC schema to regulate permissions. Misconfiguration of roles and access policies frequently leads to authorization errors.

When encountering RBAC issues:

- Validate and align ClusterRole and ClusterRoleBindings with Argo CD's service accounts.

- Adhere to the principle of least privilege, ensuring service accounts have precisely the permissions necessary for their operational mandates.

- Regular audits of RBAC bindings and role permissions can elicit clarity and foresight into potential access problems.

```
kind: ClusterRole
apiVersion: rbac.authorization.k8s.io/v1
metadata:
  name: argo-cd-role
rules:
- apiGroups: ["", "extensions", "apps"]
  resources: ["pods", "deployments"]
  verbs: ["get", "list", "watch", "create", "update", "patch", "delete"]
```

This sample ClusterRole grants the necessary permissions for Argo CD's operation context, but any deviations might hinder essential workflows or elevate risks.

5. System Resource Constraints

Operating within Kubernetes implies an intimate involvement with resource limitations, both at application and system levels. Resource constraints may inadvertently contribute to the failure modes seen in Argo CD deployments, particularly under stressed conditions or growth surges.

Identifying symptoms such as high CPU or memory usage, lagging response times, or pod evictions entails:

- Implement monitoring solutions like Prometheus or Grafana to visualize load profiles and highlight usage peaks.

- Allocate resource requests and limits judiciously in Deployment configurations to cushion against systemic pressures.

- Periodically scale Argo CD replicas upwards to distribute burdens across more instances, if deemed necessary.

```
apiVersion: apps/v1
kind: Deployment
metadata:
  name: argo-cd-server
spec:
  replicas: 2
  template:
    spec:
      containers:
      - name: argo-cd-server
        image: argoproj/argocd
        resources:
          requests:
            memory: "256Mi"
            cpu: "250m"
          limits:
            memory: "512Mi"
            cpu: "500m"
```

6. Git and Versioning Conflicts

Lastly, Git and versioning conflicts represent another cornerstone issue, emanating from divergences in branch baselines or inadvertent merge errors. Integrity in code and manifest management fundamentally underpins Argo CD's fluency.

A disciplined GitOps regimen aids in ameliorating these through:

- Consistent synchronization of feature branches and pull requests before merging into the principal deployment branch.

- Version tagging for each release or deployment, facilitating rollback strategies during disruptive episodes.

- Employ Argo CD's diffing capabilities to preemptively scan and apprehend variances before breakpoints.

The aforementioned technical challenges reflect frequently observed pain points in Argo CD environments, each likely to exhibit nuances unique to specific infrastructures and use cases. Understanding these challenges equips operators with the foresight required to prevent, diagnose, and resolve these issues efficiently.

10.2 Debugging Failed Deployments

Debugging failed deployments in Argo CD is an intricate process requiring meticulous attention to various aspects of the application's lifecycle and system configurations. Understanding how to effectively troubleshoot these failures is crucial for maintaining the operational resilience and performance standards of Kubernetes-based deployments. This section outlines a systematic approach to diagnosing and resolving issues in failed deployments within Argo CD, drawing on practical techniques and tools to aid in this endeavor.

A failed deployment can result from myriad root causes, ranging from syntactic errors in manifests to operational constraints like resource scarcity and network failures. The first step in debugging is the identification and categorization of the failure, which provides focus and guides consequent actions.

1. Identifying Types of Deployment Failures

The foremost step in debugging involves categorizing the nature of failure. Different types require distinct troubleshooting pathways:

- *Manifest Errors*: These arise due to syntactic or semantic inaccuracies within Kubernetes manifests.

10.2. DEBUGGING FAILED DEPLOYMENTS

- *Resource Constraints*: Failures due to insufficient compute resources or resource requests and limits misconfigurations.
- *Network Issues*: These occur when there are connectivity problems between the Argo CD components, Kubernetes API server, or external services.
- *Permissions Errors*: Characterized by RBAC misconfigurations, leading to authorization denials.
- *Runtime Exceptions*: Pertaining to container runtime anomalies, such as crash loops or failed readiness probes.

2. Analyzing Application State

Once the failure type is hypothesized, inspecting the application's state provides critical clues. Argo CD provides detailed logs and history views within both its GUI and CLI, offering insights into transaction paths.

To query Application status using CLI:

```
argocd app get <application-name>
```

This command displays vital information such as sync status, health status, comparison result, and operation state. Review these outputs for deviation clues compared to desired states.

Interpret an example CLI output:

```
Name:          my-app
Project:       default
Server:        https://kubernetes.default.svc
Sync Status:   OutOfSync from HEAD (613a0f1)
Phase:         Failed
Message:       ImagePullBackOff
History:
  ID  Revision   Message
  2   613a0f1    Sync Failed: Could not pull image
```

In this output, the 'ImagePullBackOff' status suggests network or image repository authentication issues that require verification.

3. Diagnosing Manifest and Syntax Errors

Manifest errors are generally among the simplest to correct, but identifying the specific error requires careful scrutiny. Common issues from malformed YAML or incorrect Kubernetes API object schema can halt deployment.

Consider this invalid Deployment manifest snippet:

```yaml
apiVersion: apps/v1
kind: Deployment
metadata:
  name: demo-deployment
spec:
  replicas: two
  template:
    metadata:
      labels:
        app: nginx
    spec:
      containers:
      - name: nginx
        image: nginx:latest
```

In the above YAML, the 'replicas' field should be an integer, not a string. Correcting syntax follows immediate validation.

Utilizing linting tools like 'kubectl' or manifest validators (such as 'kubeval') can be advantageous:

```
kubectl apply --validate -f <manifest-file>.yaml
```

4. Resource Management and Quota Issues

Deployments may fail when they exhaust the allocated compute or memory resources. To ascertain resource exhaustion, reviewing pod descriptions and events is pivotal:

```
kubectl describe pod <pod-name>
```

Analysis against the 'status' and the reasons provided under events can indicate resource allocation failures:

```
Events:
  Type     Reason             Age    From                  Message
  ----     ------             ----   ----                  -------
  Warning  FailedScheduling   34s    default-scheduler     ResourceExhausted
  Normal   SuccessfulCreate   1s     replicaset-controller Created pod: demo-deployment-xxxx
```

To resolve, adjust manifest specifications to incorporate realistic 'requests' and 'limits':

```
resources:
```

10.2. DEBUGGING FAILED DEPLOYMENTS

```
requests:
  memory: "512Mi"
  cpu: "500m"
limits:
  memory: "1Gi"
  cpu: "1"
```

Moreover, evaluate the cluster resource quota (using kubectl get resourcequota) to ensure it aligns with expectations.

5. Network Troubleshooting

Network configurations play a critical role. Failed deployments caused by connectivity issues manifest as 'timeout', 'connection refused', or 'host unreachable' errors.

Conduct a kubectl exec into relevant pods to utilize diagnostic tools like 'ping', 'curl', or 'nslookup':

```
kubectl exec -it <pod-name> -- /bin/sh
curl -v -s <destination-url>
```

For image pull errors, validate registry access by inspecting Docker credentials:

```
kubectl get secret <secret-name> -o jsonpath="{.dockerconfigjson}"
```

Changing the image pull policy to 'IfNotPresent' aids where image caching might merit a re-evaluation.

6. Debugging RBAC and Permissions

Authorization failures due to RBAC misalignment compel a review of role definitions and bindings. Utilize the kubectl auth can-i command to perform checks for specific operations under specific contexts.

```
kubectl auth can-i create deployments --namespace=<namespace>
```

Ensure role and binding resources are correctly defined:

```
kind: Role
apiVersion: rbac.authorization.k8s.io/v1
metadata:
  namespace: default
  name: deployment-manager
rules:
- apiGroups: ["apps"]
  resources: ["deployments"]
  verbs: ["create", "update"]
```

A thorough understanding of RBAC hierarchies within both Argo CD and Kubernetes contexts mitigates potential access issues.

7. Runtime and Application-Level Diagnostics

Runtime issues, including application errors or script failures within containers, need insights from logs generated by the respective pods:

```
kubectl logs <pod-name>
```

Access to logs and analyze runtime error messages or debug statements elucidates internal application paths leading to failures.

For recurring runtime application errors, configuration of the Liveness and Readiness probes in deployments should anticipate fault-tolerance through graceful retries or fallbacks.

```
livenessProbe:
  httpGet:
    path: /healthz
    port: 8080
  initialDelaySeconds: 15
  periodSeconds: 20
readinessProbe:
  httpGet:
    path: /ready
    port: 8080
  initialDelaySeconds: 5
  periodSeconds: 10
```

Debugging failed deployments in Argo CD is a multifaceted task that requires diligence across various dimensions of application and cluster architecture. A methodical approach, combined with a tactical application of observability tools, enables identification of root causes and informs corrective actions that drive towards successful deployment resolutions.

10.3 Effective Log Management

Effective log management is essential for robust Argo CD operations, serving as the front line in monitoring application behavior, diagnosing issues, and ensuring compliance with operational standards. Logs provide the critical historical record and real-time insight necessary to understand the sequence of events within Argo CD deployments, mak-

10.3. EFFECTIVE LOG MANAGEMENT

ing them indispensable for troubleshooting and performance optimization. This section explores strategies, techniques, and tools to optimize log management in Argo CD environments, emphasizing clarity, organization, and data-driven insights.

Argo CD logs include several elements from application-level transactions, controller actions, network communications, and Kubernetes API interactions. Managing this potent combination of log data requires sophisticated strategies to capture, store, analyze, and respond to log messages effectively.

- **Understanding Log Types and Sources**

  Argo CD logs can be categorized based on their origin and function:

    - *Application Logs*: Generated by the applications managed within the Argo CD environment, these logs typically offer data on business logic execution and internal states.
    - *Controller Logs*: Emitted by Argo CD controllers, these logs provide insights into synchronization operations, reconciliation processes, and state transitions.
    - *Pod Logs*: Related to Kubernetes Pods, covering lifecycle events, configuration status, and resource usage warnings.
    - *Network and System Logs*: Reflect network interactions and underlying node operations, useful for connectivity diagnostics and performance monitoring.

  Capturing logs requires defining sources and understanding where intermixed log data enriches versus confounds insights.

- **Choosing a Log Aggregation Strategy**

  The goal of log aggregation is to unify disparate logs into a coherent system, enabling sophisticated querying, consistent access patterns, and scalable storage. Common strategies include:

    - *Centralized Logging*: Unifying all logs into a single data warehouse, often employing services like the ELK Stack (Elasticsearch, Logstash, Kibana) or cloud-based solutions like Google Cloud Logging.

```
output {
  elasticsearch {
    hosts => ["http://localhost:9200"]
    index => "argo-cd-logs-%{+YYYY.MM.dd}"
  }
}
```

Logstash configuration file example for indexing Argo CD logs into Elasticsearch.

– *Distributed Logging*: Maintains logs with contextual local transcripts, exploring decentralized models for redundancy and autonomy, exemplified through Fluentd with file or object storage drivers.

```
<match pods.**>
  @type file
  path /var/log/td-agent/pods
  format json
</match>
```

Fluentd configuration for writing pod logs to local files in JSON format.

The choice between centralized and distributed approaches should consider scaling requirements, access latency, and resilience to data loss.

- **Structuring Log Data for Clarity**

Structuring log outputs significantly impacts clarity and downstream processing. Effective log design includes:

– *Using Structured Formats*: Adopting JSON or similar formats promotes ease of parsing, filtering, and enriching data.

```
{
  "timestamp": "2023-01-01T12:00:00Z",
  "level": "INFO",
  "message": "Deployment event",
  "context": {
    "deployment": "demo-app",
    "status": "Succeeded"
  }
}
```

– *Consistency in Log Statements*: Define consistent formats and fields across components, ensuring they harbor standardized labels for timestamps, levels, and identifiers.

10.3. EFFECTIVE LOG MANAGEMENT

- *Log Level Definition*: Classifying correctly under INFO, WARN, ERROR, or CRITICAL provides immediate visual cues and aids in importance-based filtering.

Proper structuring forms the backbone enabling regular expressions for searchability while retaining rich, context-driven insight potential.

- **Implementing Log Retention and Rotation Policies**

  Effective log management hinges not only on collection but also on appropriate retention. Excessive accumulation places strains on storage and retrieval processes.

  - *Defining Retention Periods*: Log retention should be informed both by relevance for ongoing operations and regulatory requirements. Typically, operational logs may be stored for 1 to 6 months, whereas audit logs should enjoy extended perspicuity.
  - *Rotating Logs*: Employing log rotation prevents depletion of storage resources. Tools like "logrotate" in Linux automate this process based on size thresholds or time intervals.

  ```
  /var/log/argo-cd/*.log {
      daily
      rotate 30
      compress
      missingok
      notifempty
  }
  ```

  A sample "logrotate" configuration for daily rotation and compression, retaining the last 30 log files.

- **Configuring Effective Alerting and Notification Systems**

  Alerting mechanisms ensure prompt awareness and response to unusual patterns or failure events captured within log datasets. Implementing systems that percolate notifications requires:

  - *Defining Thresholds and Triggers*: Use anomaly detection or analytic thresholds to decide what constitutes actionable information. This can include patterns of repeated errors in controller logs or sustained downticks in performance matrices.

- *Integrating with Communication Channels*: Leverage chat applications (e.g., Slack, Microsoft Teams), ticket systems (e.g., JIRA), or direct email notifications for routing alerts to relevant stakeholders.

  ```
  alertManagerConfig:
    receivers:
      - name: default-receiver
        slack_configs:
          channel: "#alerts-channel"
          send_resolved: true
  ```

  Configured Prometheus Alertmanager integrating alerts within a Slack channel.

- **Harnessing Analyzing Tools for Insight Extraction**

  Analysis goes beyond mere collection to the elucidation of trends, anomaly detection, and lessons learned from previous disruptions.

  - *Employing Visualization Tools*: Platforms like Grafana and Kibana transform log entries into dynamic dashboards, facilitating visual analysis of metrics and timelines.
  - *Using Machine Learning for Anomaly Detection*: Leveraging ML models aids in detecting subtle deviations from expected log patterns that traditional rule-based thresholds might miss.
  - *Conducting Root Cause Analysis (RCA)*: Thoroughly investigating to correlate log entries as causative for singular or cross-system issues solidifies understanding and prevention of recurrences.

  The close coupling of logs with analytic platforms elevates their value beyond transient records, positioning them as pivotal tools in operational strategy and continuous improvement cycles.

Effective log management in Argo CD is not merely about capturing vast swathes of data but involves a nuanced, organized approach to processing and leveraging this resource for predictive and corrective measures. Harnessing logs with purpose and methodology supports application stability, enhances user satisfaction, and accelerates the lifecycle of identification to recovery during system perturbations.

10.4 Monitoring Deployment Health

Monitoring the health of deployments managed by Argo CD is a critical aspect of maintaining application stability and performance in Kubernetes environments. This process involves overseeing the various components that comprise deployments, scrutinizing their operational states, and ensuring that any issues are promptly detected and addressed. This section discusses advanced methodologies, tools, and strategic considerations instrumental in effectively monitoring deployment health within Argo CD ecosystems.

Just as important as establishing reliable deployments is ensuring their sustained correctness and efficiency within their operational lifespan. Monitoring, hence, becomes an unbroken continuum of observation and analysis.

1. Establishing Key Metrics and Indicators

Effective monitoring begins with identifying key metrics and indicators crucial to assessing deployment health. Such metrics should address aspects of performance, availability, and resource utilization, providing a comprehensive picture of current health status and potential areas of concern.

Key metrics include:

- *Pod Availability and Status*: Monitoring the status of pods to detect if they enter undesirable states, such as 'Pending', 'CrashLoopBackOff', or 'Error'.

- *Resource Utilization*: Gauging CPU and memory usage by deployment components, ensuring they remain below defined thresholds to prevent exhaustion.
  ```
  kubectl top pod <pod-name>
  ```
  Command to retrieve resource utilization metrics for a specific pod.

- *Error Rates and Latencies*: Tracking the rate of failed requests and latency in microservice-based architectures, providing early warnings of bottlenecks or degraded performance.

- *Replica Set Status*: Monitoring the number of available versus desired replicas, ensuring alignment with defined deployment specifications.

2. Leveraging Advanced Observability Tools

Modern observability tools are equipped with robust feature sets designed to streamline monitoring workflows for Argo CD deployments. Popular tools and frameworks include:

- *Prometheus*: A powerful open-source monitoring solution that collects and stores metrics, enabling real-time alerting and querying.

  Configuring Prometheus to scrape Kubernetes metrics:

  ```
  scrape_configs:
    - job_name: 'kubernetes-nodes'
      kubernetes_sd_configs:
        - role: node
      relabel_configs:
        - action: labelmap
          regex: __meta_kubernetes_node_label_(.+)
  ```

- *Grafana*: Used in conjunction with Prometheus, Grafana offers a visualization layer for metric data, allowing the creation of dynamic dashboards that illustrate real-time operations.

  Example of configuring a Grafana dashboard to visualize CPU usage:

  ```
  {
    "title": "CPU Usage",
    "type": "graph",
    "targets": [
      {
        "expr": "rate(container_cpu_usage_seconds_total[5m])"
      }
    ]
  }
  ```

- *Kiali*: Provides observability for Istio service meshes, offering insights into traffic flow, service dependencies, and operational insights critical for microservices.

- *Thanos and Cortex*: Enhance Prometheus capabilities by offering long-term storage options and multi-cluster metrics aggregation.

10.4. MONITORING DEPLOYMENT HEALTH

Employing these tools provides multidimensional perspectives on deployment health, contributing to strategic decision-making and continuous improvement efforts.

3. Implementing Efficient Alerting Mechanisms

Alerts serve to notify operators of deviations from normal states, acting as a frontline defense in maintaining deployment health.

Key points in implementing alerting mechanisms include:

- *Defining Alert Rules*: Set thresholds on key metrics such as response times, resource limits, or imposed latencies that, once exceeded, trigger alerts.

  Example rule in Prometheus for alerting on high CPU usage:
  ```
  alert: HighCPUUsage
  expr: sum(rate(container_cpu_usage_seconds_total[5m])) by (instance) > 0.9
  for: 5m
  labels:
    severity: critical
  ```

- *Integrating Notification Systems*: Link alerting frameworks with communication channels like PagerDuty, Opsgenie, or custom applications for response coordination.

- *Providing Contextual Information*: Ensure alerts carry detailed context, such as potential causes or linked resources, to aid rapid diagnosis.

By structuring alerting systems around comprehensive intelligence, operators can quickly move from notification to preemptive action.

4. Conducting Continuous Configuration Audits

Routine audits of configuration are pivotal in maintaining deployment health. Audits identify discrepancies in live configurations from the desired state and necessitate adopting an automated, regular process.

Techniques include:

- *Periodic Reconciliation*: Use automated tools to continuously reconcile Kubernetes objects against desired states archived in Git repositories.

- *Running Configuration Checks*: Instantiate scheduled checks using utilities such as 'kubectl diff' to display divergences and discrepancies.

```
kubectl diff -f <manifest-file>.yaml
```

- *Configuration as Code (CaC)*: Embed configuration management within software development lifecycles, ensuring traceability and repeatability.

By integrating these audits into regular operations, discrepancies can be addressed proactively, preventing configuration drift and resultant deployment fragility.

5. Enhancing Response Strategies and Feedback Loops

Effective monitoring is not a terminal state; rather, it fuels a cycle of continuous improvement, enabling enhancements in subsequent deployments. Central to this concept is the establishment of robust feedback loops.

Components of effective feedback loops include:

- *Post-Incident Reviews*: Conduct retrospectives post-failure or performance degradation events to identify the root cause and validation of alert effectiveness.

- *Process Refinement*: Leverage insights gained from monitoring to refine deployment pipelines, escalate mitigation pathways, and experiment with optimizations.

- *Training and Knowledge Sharing*: Create opportunities for skill enhancement based on monitoring insights, cultivating expert knowledge and collective intelligence within teams.

Consequently, monitoring informs strategic technological advances while simultaneously equipping operators with the acumen necessary for heightened situational awareness.

6. Leveraging Predictive Analytics

Integrating predictive analytics into monitoring frameworks empowers operators to forecast potential disruptions and enact preventative measures. This encompasses identifying patterns that might prelude failures, resource saturations, or security anomalies.

Techniques and tools include:

- *Machine Learning Integration*: Utilize ML algorithms to analyze historical log data, identifying precursor patterns synonymous with problematic occurrences.
- *Time-Series Analysis*: Apply models like ARIMA (Autoregressive Integrated Moving Average) to foresee trends in metric fluctuations or anomalies beyond expected deviations.
- *Capacity Planning*: Use predictive models to anticipate scaling requirements, ensuring adequate resource provisioning ahead of demand spikes.

Predictive analytics thus equips organizations with a forward-looking stance, allowing for more informed resource allocation and risk aversion.

Through strategic amalgamation of robust monitoring practices, thoughtful configuration audits, intelligent alert mechanisms, and agile response systems, the health of Argo CD deployments can be effectively overseen and continuously enhanced. This reflective approach reduces downtime, ensures optimum resource utilization, and aligns deployments with overarching organizational objectives.

10.5 Using Argo CD's Built-in Tools

In utilizing Argo CD for continuous delivery and deployment in Kubernetes environments, one of the considerable advantages rests in its assortment of built-in tools and features specifically designed to facilitate application management, provide insights into deployment status, and simplify troubleshooting challenges. These tools are critical in ensuring that deployments align with their Git-based desired states and facilitate straightforward operations even amidst complex architectures. This section delves into the functionalities of Argo CD's core tools and processes, providing an in-depth analysis of their application and utility.

Central to Argo CD's GitOps paradigm is the notion of continuously monitoring and reconciling the declared state of applications, and its built-in tools are structured to support this perpetual synchronization.

1. The Argo CD CLI The Command Line Interface (CLI) is a powerful utility in Argo CD, offering a direct interaction lane for managing applications. It brings the comprehensive power of Argo CD directly into the terminal, proving invaluable for scripting, automation, and remote management.

Key CLI functionalities include:

- *Application Management*: CLI commands facilitate the creation, modification, and deletion of applications, offering a text-based alternative to the UI.

```
argocd app create myapp --repo https://github.com/example/repo --path /app-path --dest-server https://kubernetes.default.svc --dest-namespace default
```

In this command, a new application named 'myapp' is created using a specified Git repository.

- *Sync and Rollbacks*: Directive commands allow for manual synchronizations or rolling back to previous application versions, ensuring deployments can rectify deviations or issues quickly.

```
argocd app sync myapp
argocd app rollback myapp 1
```

'sync' initiates reconciliation, and 'rollback' reverts to an earlier application version.

- *Monitoring and Log Access*: Users can publicize application health and sync status, and extract logs to decipher operational intricacies.

```
argocd app logs myapp
```

These utilities make the CLI indispensable for developers and operators keen on maintaining a concise yet powerful control mechanism over their Kubernetes applications.

10.5. USING ARGO CD'S BUILT-IN TOOLS

2. The Argo CD Web UI The Web UI is the visual ledger of Argo CD, offering an intuitive and detailed graphical interface for overseeing application states. It provides insights into the real-time deployment status, syncing operations, and health of applications.

Prominent UI features include:

- *Visual Diff and Sync*: The UI allows users to visualize differences between live and desired states, facilitating informed synchronizations.

- *Dashboard Overview*: Comprehensive views of all managed applications, with status summaries encompassing health, synchronization, and configuration states.

- *Detailed Application Trees*: Display hierarchical relationships between services, deployments, pods, and other Kubernetes entities as they relate to a singular application.

The UI caters to operators requiring detailed visualizations and often complements the command-driven flexibility of the CLI.

3. Application Controller and Auto-Sync Capabilities The Argo CD application controller is the engine driving self-healing deployments through continual synchronization processes. It polls for discrepancies between live and Git-based states and acts to correct them when detected.

Auto-sync features are paramount in enforcing desired state management without necessitating manual oversight. In its configuration:

```
spec:
  syncPolicy:
    automated:
      prune: true
      selfHeal: true
```

- *Prune Feature*: Enables the removal of extra resources not defined in Git when enabled, therefore keeping deployment environments succinct.

- *Self-Heal Capability*: On detecting drift or manual modifications in the cluster, Argo CD reverts changes to ensure alignment with the repository.

Together, these tools reinforce the core principles of GitOps-driven CI/CD, offering reliability and consistency even in dynamic environments.

4. SSO and RBAC Features Security management within Argo CD is fortified by Single Sign-On (SSO) integrations and Role-Based Access Control (RBAC), ensuring secure, auditable access to deployments and minimized risk from unauthorized changes.

Configuration entails:

- *SSO Integrations*: Depending on organizational ecosystems, Argo CD supports integrations through OpenID Connect, OAuth2, and other identity providers.

```
server:
  oidcConfig:
    name: Okta
    issuer: https://dev-xxxxxx.okta.com
    clientId: MyClientId
    clientSecret: MyClientSecret
```

- *RBAC Customization*: Utilizing policies that strictly define user actions in decision matrices, thereby mapping roles to specific project scopes or components.

```
policy.default: role:readonly
policy.csv: |
  p, role:admin, applications, create, /project/myproject, allow
  p, role:developer, applications, sync, /project/myproject, allow
```

These features synergistically contribute to fortified operational controls where minimal access is afforded, striving for compliance with enterprise governance frameworks.

5. Repository Management and Configuration Templates
Argo CD's support for managing multiple repositories concurrently allows large-scale parallel management of environments. Additionally,

10.5. USING ARGO CD'S BUILT-IN TOOLS

it strengthens templating efforts through toolsets like Kustomize and Helm.

- *Kustomize*: Merges base configurations with overlay files, streamlining environment-specific variances.

```
apiVersion: kustomize.config.k8s.io/v1beta1
kind: Kustomization
resources:
  - base
patches:
  - path: replicas.yaml
```

- *Helm Charts*: Utilize Argo CD's capabilities to deploy and manage Helm charts, further simplifying the integration of templated Kubernetes applications.

```
source:
  chart: example-chart
  repoURL: https://charts.example.com/
```

Through templating, Argo CD amplifies efficiency and minimizes errors, allowing agile modifications while persisting consistency across deployments.

6. Declarative GitOps Workflows   Argo CD excels in declarative application management through its dependency on Git repositories, optimizing resource configurations alongside ideal state definitions. This paradigm enforces a systematic and transparent workflow intrinsically binding code and operations.

This concept is reflected in:

- *Policy Definitions*: Capture application manifests inline with environments, ensuring complete version histories and audit trails.

- *Branching Strategies*: Utilize strategies in Git to merge, test, and deploy iteratively, relying on features like pull request-based reviews to insert checkpoints in development lifecycles.

These workflows facilitate progressive infrastructures and foster collaborative, accountable development cultures.

Argo CD's built-in tools serve as a cohesive force within Kubernetes continuous delivery, proffering streamlined capabilities to handle complex scalability requirements while offering tangible endeavors towards operational assurances and productivity advances in DevOps and GitOps practices. Integrating these tools with operational routines poises Argo CD as an indomitable entrant in modern application management landscapes.

10.6 Proactive Alerts and Notifications

The implementation of proactive alerts and notifications within Argo CD ecosystems is pivotal for maintaining continuous awareness of the operational state and health of deployments. This proactive approach ensures that issues are identified and addressed before they escalate into critical problems, thereby minimizing disruptions and enabling efficient resource management. By integrating effective alerting mechanisms, teams can respond swiftly to any deviations from expected behavior, thereby maintaining the integrity and performance of applications within Kubernetes environments.

Proactive alerting involves a well-thought-out system that allows for timely detection and notification of potential issues, providing operators with actionable insights to preemptively resolve problems. This section examines the design of effective alerting systems, the integration of alerting tools with existing workflows, and the strategies to optimize alert sensitivity and specificity.

1. Designing Effective Alerting Systems

The design of a robust alerting system necessitates a comprehensive understanding of what constitutes a 'trigger' across various operational contexts. Effective alerts should accurately capture conditions that reflect meaningful deviations from desired states.

Key considerations include:

- *Thresholds and Conditions*: Carefully define thresholds for vari-

10.6. PROACTIVE ALERTS AND NOTIFICATIONS

ous metrics that align with operational goals. These include CPU and memory limits, error rates, and response times.

```
alert: HighMemoryUsage
expr: sum(container_memory_usage_bytes) by (pod_name) > 0.8 * sum(
    kube_pod_container_resource_limits_memory_bytes)
for: 5m
labels:
  severity: warning
annotations:
  summary: High memory usage detected on pod!!!
```

- *Alert Categorization*: Classify alerts by severity such as WARNING, CRITICAL, or INFO to ensure appropriate prioritization and response.

- *Avoiding Alert Fatigue*: Adopt strategies to minimize excessive alerting, which can lead to critical messages being overlooked. This includes setting appropriate thresholds and utilizing multi-stage escalation policies.

Alerts should be carefully designed to maximize coverage while minimizing false positives, thereby enhancing the operational focus and responsiveness of the engineering team.

2. Integration with Monitoring and Notification Tools

Seamlessly integrating alerts with existing monitoring solutions and notification systems is crucial for ensuring that alerts are both visible and actionable.

- *Prometheus and Alertmanager*: Prometheus, with its robust metric collection capabilities, is often coupled with Alertmanager to facilitate sophisticated alerting workflows.

  Prometheus configuration with Alertmanager:

  ```
  global:
    resolve_timeout: 5m

  route:
    receiver: email-alerts
    group_by: ['alertname']

  receivers:
  - name: 'email-alerts'
    email_configs:
    - to: 'admin@example.com'
  ```

```
           from: 'alertmanager@example.com'
           smarthost: 'smtp.example.com:587'
           auth_username: 'alertmanager@example.com'
           auth_password: 'password'
```

- *Integration with ChatOps Tools*: Tools like Slack and Microsoft Teams can be configured to receive notifications, facilitating collaborative responses to incidents.

  Example Slack configuration for Alertmanager:

```
receivers:
  - name: 'slack-alerts'
    slack_configs:
      - api_url: '<my_slack_webhook_url>'
        channel: '#alerts-channel'
        send_resolved: true
```

- *A ticketing system integration*: JIRA or PagerDuty can be employed to create incident tickets upon alert firing, providing structure to incident management processes.

This integration ensures that alerts permeate relevant communication channels, reaching the people best equipped to address them without delay.

3. Optimize Alert Sensitivity and Specificity

Calibrating alerts to achieve an ideal balance between sensitivity and specificity is paramount. The challenge lies in configuring alerts to capture genuine issues with minimal noise.

Strategies include:

- *Dynamic Thresholds*: Utilize machine learning models or adaptive threshold systems to establish thresholds that adjust based on historical data patterns.

- *Correlation and Aggregation*: Employ techniques to correlate events across multiple data sources, reducing false positives by combining related alert conditions into singular alerts.

```
groups:
  - name: example-rules
    rules:
      - alert: AggregatedErrorRate
```

10.6. PROACTIVE ALERTS AND NOTIFICATIONS

```
expr: sum(rate(http_requests_total{status=~"5.."}[5m])) by (service)
    > 0.05
for: 10m
labels:
   severity: critical
annotations:
   description: "Error rate is over 5\% for service {{ $labels.service }}"
```

- *Retention Analysis*: Periodically review alert history to recalibrate thresholds, ensuring they adapt to evolving operational norms.

These approaches aim to enhance the quality of information provided by alerts, refining them to offer substantial insight into conditions enticing immediate and impactful interventions.

4. Creating Feedback Loops

Incorporating feedback loops into alerting systems constitutes a proactive approach that fosters continuous improvement and learning from operational experiences.

- *Incident Reviews*: Conduct thorough analysis following each alert-driven incident to determine root causes and verify the efficacy of the alert setup.

- *Iterative Improvements*: Adapt alert configurations based on insights gained from post-mortem reviews, improving system resilience and alert accuracy.

- *Stakeholder Engagement*: Establish channels for frontline users to provide feedback on alerting systems, lending insights from direct operational interactions.

These loops transform alert systems into dynamic entities, responsive to the nuances of specific deployments and organizational changes.

5. Use Case Scenarios for Proactive Alerting

A sophisticated alerting system is adaptable, deployable across various contexts within an organization's ecosystem.

Examples include:

- *Performance Degradation Monitoring*: Alerts configured to detect regression in application response times, prompting immediate investigations to uncover bottlenecks or resource issues.

- *Security Incident Alerting*: Dedicate channels within alert systems to recognize unusual patterns consistent with security breaches, such as unexpected traffic surges or access attempts.

```
alert: SuspiciousLoginAttempt
expr: increase(http_requests_total{path="/login-failed"}[30m]) > 20
labels:
  severity: critical
annotations:
  summary: "Excessive failed login attempts detected, potential breach risk."
```

- *Infrastructure Health Monitoring*: Focus on system-level metrics like pod restarts or node health, maintaining infrastructure integrity vital for application stability.

By deploying alerting in defined use cases, organizations can tailor systems to fit operational requirements, securing both application and infrastructure reliability.

Proactive alerts and notifications in Argo CD present a cornerstone for optimizing operational response and maintaining seamless application delivery. When carefully crafted and intelligently integrated within the existing organizational fabric, these mechanisms afford decisive advantages, ensuring timely emulation of issues and efficacious resolutions while ultimately preserving vestiges of business continuity and stakeholder satisfaction.

10.7 Case Studies: Overcoming Deployment Challenges

Exploring real-world case studies illuminates the practical applications and intricate problem-solving required to overcome deployment challenges within Argo CD ecosystems. By examining these scenarios, valuable insights can be garnered into the methodologies and strategies necessary to navigate issues faced during continuous deployment

10.7. CASE STUDIES: OVERCOMING DEPLOYMENT CHALLENGES

and integration, expanding upon the theoretical underpinnings and enhancing operational practices.

These case studies delve into the nuances of deployment challenges, exploring the corrective actions taken to address these challenges, and providing actionable insights that can be applied to similar situations. Each case study offers a contextual examination of unique challenges accompanied by the strategic interventions that led to their resolution.

1. Case Study: Handling Resource Exhaustion in High-Load Environments

A prominent organization utilizing Argo CD for large-scale microservices deployment encountered significant challenges related to resource exhaustion during high-traffic events. Specifically, CPU and memory spikes resulted in impaired application performance and cascading failures across interdependent services.

Challenge Description: During events with increased user activity, resource requests and limits configured in Kubernetes manifests did not accurately reflect real-world usage patterns. This misalignment triggered frequent pod evictions and node resource saturation.

Analysis and Solution:

- *Dynamic Resource Allocation*: Leveraging horizontal pod autoscaling (HPA), the organization introduced dynamic scaling to adjust resource allocation in response to traffic demands. Thorough testing led to the fine-tuning of scale thresholds to match load forecasts.

  ```
  apiVersion: autoscaling/v1
  kind: HorizontalPodAutoscaler
  metadata:
    name: web-app-hpa
  spec:
    scaleTargetRef:
      apiVersion: apps/v1
      kind: Deployment
      name: web-app
    minReplicas: 3
    maxReplicas: 10
    targetCPUUtilizationPercentage: 60
  ```

- *Resource Quotas and Limits Review*: A revision of resource quotas led to an increase in allocation ceilings, while limits were recalibrated to reduce risk of overprovisioning.

```
apiVersion: v1
kind: ResourceQuota
metadata:
  name: compute-resources
spec:
  hard:
    requests.cpu: "5"
    requests.memory: "10Gi"
```

- *Enhanced Observability and Alerts*: View transitions to proactive monitoring facilitated early detection of latency issues or resource thresholds breaches, coursing appropriate scaling actions.

The successful adaptations minimized disruptions, enhanced reliability, and underscored the importance of elasticity in resource-constrained environments.

2. Case Study: Overcoming Configuration Drift through Automated Reconciliation

A tech firm suffered a series of deployment inconsistencies due to manual interventions leading to configuration drift across their multi-cluster architecture induced by drift between cluster states and desired Git configurations.

Challenge Description: Irregularities arose from inconsistent application states, causing unpredictable deployment outcomes and complicating state management attempts across clusters.

Analysis and Solution:

- *Automated Synchronization*: Enabling automated sync policies within Argo CD ensured continuous state checks and remediations. The self-healing feature automatically reverted configurations diverging from declared repository states.

```
syncPolicy:
  automated:
    prune: true
    selfHeal: true
```

- *Implementation of Git Best Practices*: Strengthening GitOps accountability through improved commit hygiene and enforcing re-

10.7. CASE STUDIES: OVERCOMING DEPLOYMENT CHALLENGES

view processes prior to merges.

- *Version Control in Check*: Utilizing tags and branch protection rules broadened confidence in rollbacks during erroneous deployments, fostering enhanced coordination between development and operations teams.

Together, these strategies fortified deployment assurance, standardized configurations across clusters, and remedied variability pitfalls inherent to manual workflows.

3. Case Study: Tackling Service Dependency Failures

A multinational organization managing a complex web of microservices via Argo CD faced disruptions in service availability derived from tightly coupled dependencies.

Challenge Description: Introduced updates seemingly caused unexpected cascading failures, owing to inherent unavailability or miscommunication between evolving service endpoints.

Analysis and Solution:

- *Dependency Mapping and Monitoring*: Visualization of service architectures through tools like Kiali and construction of dependency matrices clarified inter-service dependencies and informed prospective communication pathways.

- *Failure Injection Testing*: Implementing Chaos Engineering paradigms verified system robustness, actively testing service fallbacks and circuit breaking—culminating in infrastructure more tolerant to dependency failures.

```
apiVersion: networking.istio.io/v1beta1
kind: VirtualService
metadata:
  name: myapp
spec:
  hosts:
    - myapp.local
  http:
    - route:
        - destination:
            host: myapp
      fault:
        abort:
          percentage:
            value: 10
```

- *Adoption of Service Mesh Technologies*: Incorporating Istio facilitated granular traffic management and service-to-service authentication, curbing service dependency issues, and refining communication controls.

Transformative adjustments and parallel testing paradigms paved the way for strategy-driven enhancements, supervising service dependencies with great precision.

4. Case Study: Ensuring Compliance through Policy Enforcements

An organization within a highly regulated industry grappled with compliance adherence where Argo CD-managed deployments demanded conformance to strict security and operational benchmarks.

Challenge Description: Unyielding regulatory conditions necessitated comprehensive auditing and evaluation of security policies across all deployment layers.

Analysis and Solution:

- *Policy-Driven Security Improvements*: Integrating Open Policy Agent (OPA) enabled seamless enforcements for compliance benchmarks. Policies composed with Rego ensured auto-trigger adaptations.

```
package kubernetes.admission

allow {
  input.review.object.kind == "Pod"
  input.review.object.spec.containers[_].securityContext.runAsUser == 1001
}
```

- *Deployment Policy Audits*: Conducted regular audits via automated scripts to ensure all deployments conformed to defined security and operational guidelines.

- *Enhance Logging Mechanisms*: Constructed sophisticated logging infrastructures to monitor and trace adherence metrics, consequently boosting compliance observability.

These efforts mitigated regulatory challenges and confirmed every deployment stuck predetermined compliance pathways.

5. Case Study: Scaling Across Multi-Region Deployments

Handling multi-region deployments at scale, a global e-commerce provider confronted intricacies tied to network latencies and data synchronization across geographically disparate Kubernetes clusters managed by Argo CD.

Challenge Description: Insight disparities as well as sync delays prevented coherent alignment of applications synchronizing across diverse regions.

Analysis and Solution:

- *Geographical Load Balancing*: Applied load balancers with regional affinity to moderate user traffic and channel requests to the nearest cluster, optimizing latency metrics.

- *Synchronization and Replication Tactics*: Embracement of consistent hashing algorithms reduced discrepancies in database state synchronization, particularly over great distances, sustaining data consistency and availability.

- *Cluster Federations*: Undertook Kubernetes federation initiatives to coherently manage distributed infrastructure across regions while retaining observability and declarative control.

This systematic confluence of technologies scaled operations effectively, distributing loads and harmonizing data potentials to ultimately augment cross-region coherence.

These case studies collectively illustrate how organizations deploy problem-solving acumen within Argo CD to realize deployment consistency amidst intrinsic challenges. The adaptive tactics demonstrated reinforce the value of strategic alignments and underscore Argo CD's versatility within multifaceted deployments, fueling innovation and sustaining resilience.

www.ingramcontent.com/pod-product-compliance
Lightning Source LLC
Chambersburg PA
CBHW052140220526
45471CB00004B/1456